AN ANALYSIS OF THE SHORT STORIES OF JUAN CARLOS ONETTI

Fictions of Desire

AN ANALYSIS OF THE SHORT STORIES OF JUAN CARLOS ONETTI

Fictions of Desire

Mark I. Millington

The Edwin Mellen Press
Lewiston/Queenston/Lampeter

Library of Congress Cataloging-in-Publication Data

Millington, Mark.
    An analysis of the short stories of Juan Carlos Onetti : fictions
of desire / Mark I. Millington.
        p.   cm. -- (Studies in Latin American literature and culture ; v. 1)
    Includes bibliographical references and index.
    ISBN 0-7734-9340-9
    1. Onetti, Juan Carlos, 1909-   --Criticism and interpretation.
2. Sex in literature. 3. Psychoanalysis and literature.   I. Title.
PQ8519.O59Z773   1993
863--dc20   93-29918
                                                                  CIP

This is volume 1 in the continuing series
Studies in Latin American Literature and Culture
Volume 1 ISBN 0-7734-9340-9
SLALC Series ISBN 0-7734-9343-3

A CIP catalog record for this book
is available from the British Library.

The Edwin Mellen Press   The Edwin Mellen Press
        Box 450   Box 67
Lewiston, New York   Queenston, Ontario
    USA 14092   CANADA L0S 1L0

Edwin Mellen Press, Ltd.
Lampeter, Dyfed, Wales
UNITED KINGDOM SA48 7DY

Printed in the United States of America

ⁱᶜᶜᴼ\2\73X

CONTENTS

Acknowledgements   vii

Abbreviations and Editions   ix

1   "Unto the Breach...": Theorizing Reading   1

2   First Fictions/First Desires   11

3   Snapshots from beyond Masculine Desire:
"El álbum" and "El infierno tan temido"   43

4   Gossip and the Other in "Historia del caballero de
la rosa y de la virgen encinta que vino de Liliput"   67

5   Negotiating the Text: "La cara de la desgracia"   81

6   Masculinity and the Fight for Ignorance:
"Jacob y el otro"   97

7   Objects and Objections: "Tan triste como ella"   115

8   Her Story/Our Story: The Textuality of
"La novia robada"   137

9   A Case of Lethal Paternity: *La muerte y la niña*   155

10   Ambivalence and Desire in *Cuando entonces*   183

11   "Once More...": The Limits of Repetition   197

Bibliography   207

Index   213

ACKNOWLEDGEMENTS

I should like to thank Bernard McGuirk for his constant intellectual support and encouragement during the period in which this book took shape. In addition, I am grateful to Marlies Chrzanowski (a name for Onetti cognoscenti) who always knew the answers about WP5.1.

I should also like to acknowledge permission to reprint material from *Dispositio* XV:40 (1990) (with thanks to the Department of Romance Languages at the University of Michigan), *Neophilologus* LXXV:2 (1991), *Antípodas* III (1991), and *The Bulletin of Hispanic Studies* LXIX (1992).

ABBREVIATIONS AND EDITIONS

In the discussion which follows I have abbreviated the titles of some of the texts. The abbreviations are as follows:

"Avenida"	–	"Avenida de Mayo-Diagonal-Avenida de Mayo"
"Obstáculo"	–	"El obstáculo"
"Baldi"	–	"El posible Baldi"
"Sueño"	–	"Un sueño realizado"
"Bienvenido"	–	"Bienvenido Bob"
"Nueve"	–	"Nueve de Julio"
"Regreso"	–	"Regreso al sur"
"Esbjerg"	–	"Esbjerg en la costa"
"Casa"	–	"La casa en la arena"
"Historia"	–	"Historia del Caballero de la Rosa y de la virgen encinta que vino de Liliput"
"El infierno"	–	"El infierno tan temido"
"Cara"	–	"La cara de la desgracia"
"Jacob"	–	"Jacob y el otro"
"Tan triste"	–	"Tan triste como ella"
"Novia"	–	"La novia robada"
"Matías"	–	"Matías el telegrafista"
Réquiem	–	*Réquiem por Faulkner y otros artículos*

The location of these and all other texts analyzed in this study is specified in the bibliography. Wherever possible, page references are to the *Obras completas*; otherwise, they are to the *Cuentos completos* or to other, individual sources.

AN ANALYSIS OF THE SHORT STORIES OF JUAN CARLOS ONETTI

Fictions of Desire

CHAPTER 1

"UNTO THE BREACH...": THEORIZING READING

> We must begin *wherever we are* and the thought of the trace, which cannot not take the scent into account, has already taught us that it was impossible to justify a point of departure absolutely. *Wherever we are*: in a text where we already believe ourselves to be.
> – Jacques Derrida

> ... the interpretive gesture with its assumption of superiority over a mute object is always based upon a prior rebellion against the object's power. It is the aggression and the desire in that rebellion which constitute the most authentic encounter with the object's power, where we experience not only the object's force but equally our own powerful drive to understand, to possess, that which moves us so intensely.
> – Jane Gallop

This is not the first book that I have written about Onetti, and it may or may not be the last. But it represents at least partial continuity with the first insofar as it takes up and develops a preoccupation with reading and with one of the emergent strands of my *Reading Onetti*. This is part of the "wherever I am" in my beginning to read Onetti's short fiction.[1]   *Reading Onetti* was

---

[1] Where *Reading Onetti* looked at the most widely studied area of Onetti's work – the novels and the three major novellas, *El pozo*, *Los adioses*, and *Para una tumba sin nombre* – , this study concentrates on the short stories and the less well-known novellas, *La muerte y la niña* and *Cuando*

methodologically rather hybrid, and one of its strands, which emerged rather towards the end of its formulation, was psychoanalysis. Now, this book is not a psychoanalytical study of Onetti in any systematic way, but it draws on some psychoanalytical concepts explicitly and it relies to some extent on a psychoanalytical mode of thinking. However, in my view, the thinking in the analysis owes as much to feminist theory as to psychoanalysis: the line of thought and the critical reflexes are deeply conditioned by both areas of theory. I would insist particularly on the way that feminist theory has helped me to grasp the dynamics of gender in Onetti. Feminism has stimulated many of the fundamental questions that I ask of Onetti's short stories, and it has prompted me to bring into view their reliance on certain aspects of dominant masculine attitudes and practices.

Having said that, however, I want now to concentrate on the psychoanalytical concepts which I have employed and to explain their relation to my reading practice. Psychoanalysis seems a particularly helpful tool in analyzing Onetti because of his attention to the minute detail of the experience and responses of the human subject. On the one hand, psychoanalysis can provide a defined discourse of concepts to clarify and articulate the elements in the stories. But on the other, it is a discourse from outside and to which Onetti makes no reference, and so it can also be used to confront and question the processes at work in these representations of decentred, lacking subjects. The analyses that follow do not draw on psychoanalysis systematically, however, since the ambiguous assumption of authority in that discourse is precisely what I want to problematize in my reading. Any appeal to a system of knowledge feeds a desire for identity and

---

entonces. This latter area of his output has been the object of much less systematic study. One should not overlook the fact that the classification of Onetti's fiction into genres has provoked different reactions since some of the stories and novellas are quite lengthy. However, as far as my analysis is concerned, such generic divisions are not germane. The subject of genre in Onetti has been partially studied in Klahn.

fixity, and while those are by no means avoidable, neither are constant questioning and reassessment impossible.

I am not going to employ psychoanalytical concepts as a way of making sense of characters' psychology, and still less of Onetti's. My aim is to trace the structures and dynamic of the thought processes in Onetti's work – the articulation of the stories as fictional constructs. In aiming to do this, I am particularly wary of the role of psychoanalysis in literary analysis, given the different analytical environment in which it originated. The relation between text and critic is somewhat different from that between analyst and analysand in therapy. To begin with, the critic has taken the initiative to choose the text, presumably for some purpose, whereas it is the analysand who generally approaches the analyst in therapy. In the nature of the critic and the text, their "dialogue" is relatively limited as compared to that between analysand and analyst, and the questions and obstacles proposed by the text to the critic can be negotiated only from the latter's position. The text is not mute, but it cannot participate in analysis with quite the same degree of independence as the analysand, though there are analogies to be drawn in the way the text resists, projects on to, cooperates with and surprises the critic. In sum, I would not claim to be carrying out a psychoanalytical reading partly because of the limited *explicit* use that I make of its concepts, partly because the richness and complexity of psychoanalysis cannot fully be exploited in literary study, and partly because I would resist the strength of psychoanalysis and its capacity to appropriate its objects of analysis into itself. At best I would claim a provisional relation to psychoanalysis.

It will be helpful to look at the main psychoanalytical concepts referred to later in order to create a base for the following analyses.[2] The Imaginary and the Symbolic are terms which recur consistently. They should be understood as

---

[2] The main sources of the psychoanalytical concepts used here are: Lacan 1977, 1979, and 1982. Major works on Lacan and psychoanalysis which have furthered my understanding are: Ragland-Sullivan 1986, Benvenuto and Kennedy 1986, and Rose.

interactive in the constitution and being of the human subject: they have distinct functions and operations which are in tension but mutually implicated. The Imaginary is made up of images and fantasies, and it is the area of object choice and interaction in relationships, hence in Onetti it is particularly significant in the male characters' relation to identity and to female characters. The subject's Imaginary projections would fix and merge identity, but its projections distort and deceive, producing misrecognition and hence the potential for further projection. The Imaginary evolves out of the mirror stage of full identification in the infant's life, but it continues into the adult's experience of relations with others. There is a drive in the Imaginary towards the impossible recapture of the infant's mirror-stage unity or fusion with its specular form, but the impossibility arises because, in its quest for fusion and unity, the Imaginary is in conflict with the Symbolic, with its insistence on difference. Hence, the Imaginary seeks to avoid the Symbolic, whose constraining laws and norms disrupt its narcissistic goals. It needs to be stressed that the Imaginary has nothing to do with the unreal, for it is part of the real experience of the subject and of its complex network of drives and demands. So there is no question of choosing to "give up" the Imaginary (any more than there is of giving up the Symbolic), but what is important analytically is to understand the subject's propensity for the mirroring projections of the Imaginary. Hence, this area of psychoanalytical thinking is helpful in articulating something of the drive of male characters in Onetti to seek an escape or relocation which implies the search for a (re)new(ed) identity and a plenitude of being.

The Symbolic is the sphere of culture and language. Language introduces a third term into the dyadic relation of the infant with its mirror image, and it comes to define as well as modify that relation. It is associated with the Law and the Father which make demands of and place restrictions on the emerging subject. The Symbolic is the area of the function of symbols, of linguistic and cultural forms, and through these it is a vehicle for the subject to represent and thus to constitute itself. The Symbolic and the Law insist on the principle of separation and differentiation, where in the Imaginary the subject's ego remains caught in identification with the Mother and the unconscious. The subject formed through the intervention of the Father's Law derives from the loss of original union, it is a construct constituted to cover up the wound of separation from the Mother. In my analysis I associate the Symbolic and the Law with Santa María (or its urban equivalent), and, underpinning this, it is important to note that story-telling is located within the town, that is, within the order of language and cultural forms. The meaning of the outside, of the effort towards Imaginary evasion, is formulated symbolically from inside Santa María: this other, this outside, is seen in the fictions from within the Symbolic. Not that this creates any security in "truth", for the Imaginary also deflects the operation of the Symbolic, so that the narrating "yo" or "nosotros" in Santa María will also be implicated in the Imaginary. By logical extension, staying outside Santa María, in the other world, is beyond the mediation of linguistic formulation, hence the characters most in touch with the outside do not narrate themselves but are mediated by those within the town.[3] The repeated returns to Santa María of characters who have tried to get away, or the difficulties in the path of getting away from it, are indicative of the subject's condition. There is no achieved regression to a mirror-like merging in Onetti, and for that reason the stories often end with a return to the town or with death. In psychoanalytical terms, the subject's social functioning and psychic survival require repression and the coming to terms with the conditions of shared life – without this, reality, society and compromise are lost.

In sum, the Symbolic, or the Other, infers a familial history, and a social order of symbols, rules and language, of myths and conventions. The Symbolic is the principle of intersubjectivity and cause of all subjectivity: the demands made by the Symbolic are constitutive of the subject's unconscious (that which is not

---

[3] Analogous comments on the positioning of the story-teller on the "inside" are made in Benjamin.

allowed into social life) insofar as the Symbolic is radically eccentric to the narcissistic, specular relation of the self to the other. In my analysis, the Symbolic/Other is linked to Santa María (or an equivalent urban environment) which is governed by a patriarchal law. This does not preclude the subject's reflexive awareness of the Symbolic or the possibility of gaining some distance on it, and these points are especially important in my analysis. One might sum up the complex reality of representation in this way: Real objects and events as well as Symbolic language and cultural codes are transformed and made personal by Imaginary, mirroring processes, and then returned to the world in the universalizing Symbolic system of language which named the Real in the first place. Acceptance of compromise with the Symbolic does not imply utter subservience to it, although in adulthood subjects tend to reform their identities to conform with the Symbolic. This complex of individuation and conformity will be very important in my analyses, which, like all analysis, is positioned on the side of the Symbolic, of signifiers, symbols and cultural meanings rather than on that of the Imaginary of signifieds, signs and personal memories. As Lacan puts it in talking of the reality of the subject:

> The psychoanalytic experience has rediscovered in man the imperative of the Word as the law that has formed him in its image. It manipulates the poetic function of language to give to his desire its symbolic mediation. May that experience enable you to understand at last that it is in the gift of speech that all the reality of its effect resides; for it is by way of this gift that all reality has come to man and it is by his continued act that he maintains it. (Lacan 1977, 106)

Another term of crucial importance in my analysis is desire. This is the drive which impels much of the subject's movement. Desire is the residue arising from the subject's unfulfilled demand; in psychoanalytical terms, no matter how much is given to the subject in response to its demands and no matter how much needs seem to be satisfied, there is a remainder or excess. The demand for love goes beyond the objects which might satisfy need, and desire arises out of the unease over the subject's lack or incompleteness. In psychoanalysis, it is in this excess of demand that desire is constituted, as Lacan puts it:

> Desire begins to take shape in the margin in which demand becomes
> separated from need: this margin being that which is opened up by demand, the
> appeal of which can be unconditional only in regard to the Other, under the form
> of the possible defect, which need may introduce into it, of having no universal
> satisfaction (what is called "anxiety"). (Lacan 1977, 311)

The objects of desire are to achieve recognition and to be a unity: the desire is to be replied to and verified as what one fantasizes oneself to be. This aspect is particularly revealing in relation to Onetti's characters (especially the male ones), since they repeatedly experience the drive of what one might call desire, which energizes them and disrupts settled patterns of identity and compromise. Frequently, this is articulated via location in respect of Santa María or the Symbolic environment: to be elsewhere or other may be desired, but it does not necessarily bring recognition or unity for the characters.

Desire seeks to replace lost (repressed) objects, so past images play an important role in current object choice: in Onetti, the role of girls and women in making up for male loss is central to their representation. The "absence of relation" with girls or women, the repeated lack of coincidence, is a reflection of the fact that the objects of desire can never replace the lost objects of the pre-Oedipal phase. It is the loss of the primordial object(s) and the relation of the subject to that loss which become the structure of desire. Desire is inevitably bound up with the Law, in that desire comes about because of the Law's role within the subject: the subject's dependence on language and the price paid for access to the Symbolic create structural lacks which desire tries to overcome. One could argue that it is fundamentally the exploration of this "lack in being" which Onetti keeps returning to. It is predominantly his male characters who live this lack and endeavour to eliminate it or to elide its impact. In this way, desire is crucial in the subject in insisting on its recalcitrance simply to be in the Symbolic: desire brings into view and puts pressure on the critical relation between dispersal and constraint in the interaction of the elements of subjectivity.

In relation to specifically masculine desire in Onetti, it is essential to appreciate the role of female characters. Within patriarchal social systems, and emphatically in Onetti, women (or girls) are constructed as an absolute category (simultaneously excluded and idealized), a category which often serves to underpin hegemonic masculinities (Connell 183-86). Hegemonic masculinities tend to place women as the basis of their fantasy or constitute their fantasy through women. Women therefore become symptomatic of man's condition: they are the place on which lack is projected and disavowed. In Onetti's short fiction, it is pertinent to ask where the female characters ever occupy a central position, and the answer is hardly at all. A prime example of that is in "Cara", where a girl is the means whereby a male character attempts to disavow his lack. Even where female characters do appear to be key sources of information or experience (in "Esbjerg", "El infierno" and "Novia") they are mainly objects of male attention. Indeed, it is hard to see them as external to or questioning of patriarchal discourse anywhere in Onetti, though Gracia in "El infierno" does seem to gain some critical potential before she is effectively exiled by Santa María. By contrast, both "Convalecencia" and "Tan triste" have a woman character's consciousness as their vehicle, but ultimately both are subordinated to the acts and desires of male characters. Hence in Onetti, female characters very rarely move beyond actions defined solely in relation to male power and desire, which virtually monopolize his fiction.[4]

Two further psychoanalytical concepts inform my understanding of reading in relation to Onetti's short fiction: transference and the Real.[5] Transference is inevitable in literary analysis just as it is in psychoanalysis, indeed it has been referred to as "the whole engine of analysis" (Gallop 28). In order to try and disrupt the mirroring of the reader's desire in the text, I endeavour in my readings to turn back on analysis at critical moments, to disrupt any smooth sense of

---

[4] For a broader and more detailed treatment of women characters in Onetti see Millington (1987).

[5] The relation between psychoanalysis and reading is explored most fruitfully in Felman (1987), and in Gallop (1985).

transparent contact. That effort could be articulated as the attempt to identify at least something of what reading "leaves out", as Shoshana Felman explains:

> The question of a reading's "truth" must be at least complicated and rethought through another question, which Freud, indeed, has raised, and taught us to articulate: what does such "truth" (or any "truth") leave out? What is it *made to miss*? What does it have as its function to overlook? What, precisely, is its residue, the remainder it does not account for? (Felman 1977, 117)

To locate all that transference excludes is, by definition, beyond self-reflexivity, whatever theory is employed to boost it. But the structural awareness of the text's escape from the critic's presumption-to-know is productive and highlights the fact that there is not just a text and a reading, but rather that there is a dialectics of engagement. The elusive returns of the text, evading the critic's transference, are as crucial to locate as the blindspots of the text. Both text and critic are caught up in networks of language and meaning that go beyond conscious control, and any mere "making sense" of the text is a way of compensating for that, for the lack in subjectivity, of the subject in language (Rose 46-47).

Out of the dialectic process of reading and revising reading, of advance and obstruction, of knowledge and illusion, comes my awareness of the textuality of Onetti. His short fiction, like all literary texts, interweaves Symbolic and Imaginary elements: without the Symbolic there would be no texts in communicable form, and without the Imaginary there would be no innovation or invention. But what needs to be insisted upon is that Onetti's short fiction also exists in the Real, as something concrete outside the Symbolic and Imaginary. The fictions have an object status which the critic's Imaginary and Symbolic can work on in an effort to account for or "make sense" of them, but without ever exhausting them. The short stories are ultimately irreducible. It is this which takes them beyond any definitive control via the identificatory logic of the Imaginary, or via the codifying and naming of the Symbolic. It is that quality which I refer to when I talk in my analyses of the textuality of Onetti's fiction.

In the light of the transferential tendency of reading and the elusive though irreducible Real of the texts, I will often try in my analyses to resist the texts' apparent logic, to break with the movement of their Symbolic and Imaginary formulations. I do this in the hope of finding something of their underlying presuppositions or of moving into any breach in their meaning which the texts themselves do not seem to know. This strategy might be defined as a refusal simply to fill the position of the implied reader, but, as always, that position will have to have been assumed in order to break away from it. So I will often aim at a double vision of the texts, which will be apparent in the structure of my analyses, with their frequent, initial acceptance of the text as a given, stable object leading to a reengagement with and problematizing of any such Imaginary object. What results from this process might be described as a critical movement in and out of (un-)knowability. Reading is "not-all" in this understanding: it is a continual negotiation for control, a process of temporary and partial stabilizations, a series of mirrorings always on the verge of being deflected down new paths.

CHAPTER 2
FIRST FICTIONS/FIRST DESIRES

Before 1950 Onetti is known to have written and published at least fifteen short stories starting with "Avenida" (1933) and ending with "Casa" (1949).[1] Most of these are not of the highest quality, though at least four of them are important and will therefore be the object of analysis at the end of this chapter. Quite a number of the early stories are rather laboured, being cluttered with concrete description and having a rather tenuous narrative thread. Their somewhat mechanical and self-conscious presentation stands in contrast to the much more fluid and heterogeneous writing after 1950 when Onetti seemed to find a genuinely mature voice. However, even in the early stories there is a high degree of consistency particularly in terms of the repetition of certain structures, which are varied slightly from story to story. The focal points of the early stories are dreams, locations, age and identity, and Onetti maintained this tight thematics over sixteen years (if not his entire writing career). I will begin my analysis of the early stories by looking in general at this thematic nucleus, before focusing on the four stories which seem to me to be the most successful.

---

[1] In Onetti 1986b, Prego and Petit include two detective stories which were published under pseudonyms in 1939 and 1940 in *Marcha*. Onetti has acknowledged that these were written by him, and has suggested that there may be others in the magazine. See Omar Prego's prologue (13-14). The two stories are: "El fin trágico de Alfredo Plumet" (1939), 163-70, and "Un cuento policial. Crimen perfecto" (1940), 171-76.

Double structures are ubiquitous in early Onetti. The stories constantly posit a world divided between a here and there, between a known and an other world, between reality and dream, with desire as the driving force within the fictions (both the characters' and Onetti's). That desire is never satisfied this side of death: there is a truly Lacanian sense of desire as unending drive with its roots in subjectivity and sexuality. But the relations between the here and there, reality and dream, are various in their specifics. The relation may be one of either/or ("Convalecencia", "Regreso" and "Obstáculo"), or of rapid alternation ("Avenida", "Baldi"), or of one world lost and definitively replaced by another ("Bienvenido" and "Nueve"). This dualism of the known and the desired other is fundamental in Onetti, and it has many of the problems of such dualisms in being based on a polarization that seems to invite deconstruction.

In addition to the dual(istic) structures, there is a strong reliance in the early fiction on urban settings, which are sometimes explicitly designated as Buenos Aires. Whether Buenos Aires or not, the urban environment is projected as a profound problem that certain characters wish to evade, although the stories do not explore the nature of the problem in very specific terms. So in "Convalecencia" and "Excursión", the stress is on getting away from or being outside what is apparently a repressive, deadening urban location. In "Avenida", "Baldi" and "Esbjerg", the particular problem of confinement is Buenos Aires, and it therefore recalls the River Plate's literary tradition of exploring the problematic of the new urban environment, frequently with an immigrant inflection.

This environment is counterbalanced by myriad other locations, most purely mental or imaginary (even if remembered), some relatively concrete. In "Avenida", there are multiple, imagined and exotic alternatives to the streets of Buenos Aires. Some transport the male character, Suaid, to Alaska, one to a beach in Miami, one to the Yukon, and one involves the machine-gunning of people on the streets around him. These Imaginary evasions of Buenos Aires are not grounded in any explanation, for all that is presented is a quasi-stream of consciousness with abrupt juxtapositions of fragments of the Buenos Aires streets and Imaginary alternatives, somewhat like the pulsing on and off of the lights at the end on the story (26). What is shared by the fantasies is the casting of the masculine self into heroic contexts where physical action or combat are involved, which is strikingly at variance with the banality of Suaid's walking along city streets. In this contrast there are implicit conclusions to be drawn about the male character's lack, for which the fantasies would be a supplement. But there is also an implicit conclusion to be drawn from the circularity of Suaid's itinerary which is indicated by the story's title: for all his fantasies he constantly returns to his point of departure.

In "Baldi" there are similar projections out of a concrete reality and into quasi-heroic contexts: the Wild West in the United States or South African gold mines. The situation in which these alternatives are elaborated is also more explicit than in "Avenida": the male character, Baldi, relates/invents the stories he tells in order to impress a woman with his impetuous bravado after she has suggested that she finds him different from other men, even at a first encounter (46-47). There is, therefore, an underlying gender element here. But the masculine fantasies turn sour on Baldi as he insists on the more and more adventurous and bloodthirsty possible self of the stories which forces him to confront the dullness of the real self (51). This contrast is then elaborated into a judgement on Baldi by the narrator, who talks of the shortcomings of conformity:

> Porque el doctor Baldi no fue capaz de saltar un día sobre la cubierta de una barcaza, pesada de bolsas o maderas. Porque no se había animado a aceptar que la vida es otra cosa, que la vida es lo que no puede hacerse en compañía de mujeres fieles ni hombres sensatos. Porque había cerrado los ojos y estaba entregado como todos. Empleados, señores, jefes de las oficinas. (51-52)

In the case of this conformist, Baldi, even his impetuous lying/story-telling are in vain as his name suggests, since it cannot save him from the truth of his own identity, indeed it does not even distract him briefly from that truth (as it can later Onetti protagonists). While both Baldi and Suaid appear to include a strong adolescent element in their fantasies, what is adult about them is that they are both left with their familiar selves at the end of their stories: the Imaginary other is not sustained.[2]

In "Esbjerg", the alternative location is partly based on memory and is centred on a woman's experience. The projection out of Buenos Aires is much less fantastical than with Suaid's and Baldi's though it is still idealized. In this case, Kirsten's yearning to reach rural Denmark, though just as remote as Suaid's Alaska or Baldi's Wild West, is one long, unchanging desire that consumes her and eventually her husband too, indirectly. Despite that, however, it is just as remote from fulfilment.

A similar consistency of desire is presented in "Excursión", but this story is again rather vague about the problem of the urban context. The lone male character who leaves the city in disgust goes to the countryside (albeit with a return ticket) in search of fulfilment. The heart of the story is an imagined rural idyll, which seems to be positive insofar as the city is negative, and suggests an underlying exclusive binary:

> Huir de la ciudad, meterse en una casita cualquiera, perdida en los costados de la cuchilla que se azulaba en la distancia. Solo. Hacerse la comida con sus manos, cuidar los árboles... Se veía, medio cuerpo desnudo, altas las botas, tostado el rostro dentro de la barba... Absoluta soledad de su alma, fantástica libertad de todo su ser, purificado y virgen como si comenzara a divisar el mundo. Paz; no paz de tregua, sino total y definitiva. (86-87)

The problematic notion of running away to return to some virgin purity is not put into question, as if realities could simply be abandoned and alternative ones taken up. This lack of doubt is profoundly symptomatic of the strength of the unease in the urban environment in this and the other stories in that anxiety overrules rationality: there is an affective logic which is implicitly eloquent about the characters' starting-point. The rural idyll of "Excursión" switches into a scene of idealized domesticity with two young boys and a singing woman, hinting at a potential familial quartet involving the protagonist. This is a disconcerting moment in Onetti: in a writer with little overt interest in the family, this moment

---

[2] See Diez 1979.

uncharacteristically suggests a potential resolution in domestic plenitude. However, it does not constitute the story's ending, which reverts to the continued walking of the protagonist through the countryside in metaphorical suggestion of the insistence of his desire and the lack of fulfilment of it.

"Obstáculo" apparently reverses this repeated structure of evasion of the city into an exotic or rural other. In this case, the source of entrapment is a reform school and the objective of release is Buenos Aires. In fact, this structure of confinement and release is the same as in the other stories, it is merely the terms which are different. And here too, interestingly, the desired other is still vague, since el Negro's view of Buenos Aires is a fragmented mix of childish memories and reports from friends and newspapers. In short, his objective is hardly clear and concrete, but (not uncharacteristically) the projection of an impressionable adolescent.

A motif which is repeated in these early stories and which recurs almost throughout Onetti's fiction is that of the beach and/or of the chalet ("casita") on the beach. This sort of location is strongly associated with the desire for alternative experience with the promise of potential fulfilment. This location is explored in "La larga historia" and in "Casa" and is already in place in "Convalecencia".[3] In this story, the well-being of the woman in convalescence is directly related to being on the beach away from the city: on the beach she is free and well. The summons back to the city at the end of the story also marks the return of illness. Her convalescence is from an unspecified illness, which recurs as the beach is lost beneath the incoming, dirty tide and she has to leave:

> La arena, los colores amigos, la dicha, todo estaba hundido bajo un agua sucia y espumante. Recuerdo haber tenido la sensación de que mi rostro envejecía rápidamente, mientras, sordo y cauteloso, el dolor de la enfermedad volvía a morderme en el cuerpo. (58)

The freedom and fulfilment associated with the beach play on connotations of summer holidays, but nothing in the story suggests a responsible attempt to cope

---

[3] The rural fulfilment sought in "Excursión" also includes the finding of a "casita" (86).

with the difficulty posed by urban life. The escape to the beach therefore seems futile when, once more, the character has to return to the city. Again there is no analysis of what the city threatens and no attempt to set up a critical dialogue for growth. The structure is posed in either/or terms, which are just as Imaginary as the characters' own view of their situation.

The interplay of here and there with desire as the impetus connecting them is constantly related to the theme of identity. That is clear in "Avenida" and "Baldi" where the protagonists look to transform themselves into Imaginary others. But it is also the case in different guises in "Bienvenido" and "Nueve". In these stories, the different locations are, as it were, two phases of life: youth and middle age. In both there is a single movement out of plenitude and into loss, focused on via an idealized view back from middle age. The ageing brings a change to the central male characters in both stories. In "Nueve", the crucial watershed is the date in the title when Grandi takes his erstwhile young girlfriend to have an abortion. His guilt over his responsibility for what happens to her – her defilement and loss of purity – is compounded by the judgmental attitude towards him of the young Alcides, who appears to Grandi to mock and condemn him merely for being twice his age and so "definitivamente terminado" (118). The two phases of life are set up as mutually exclusive, and Grandi has passed out of one into the other. Here, there is no return journey to youth and no willed or Imaginary escape from condemnation for Grandi, the more so as it appears that he kills Alcides at the end of the story (118), so that the young man cannot himself age. By contrast in "Bienvenido", the fact that the young Bob grows old himself is something which mitigates his severe judgment of the middle-aged narrator: he is forced to share defeat.

The question of identity is also present in the early sequence of stories in relation to the female characters. But here it has a certain negative aspect. In "Mascarada", a young woman makes the transition from innocence to prostitution. That process is mapped in detail in the story and is notably underscored by her

physical movement out of the secrecy of darkness and into a zone of intense light
in full public view (1288). The move into the public zone of noise and light is
also the move from invisibility to visibility. To be a success as a prostitute she has
to attract someone's gaze and sustain it: she must be seen and taken for what she
wants to be (1289-90); as soon as the face she adopts for her new role is seen and
understood, she has achieved the switch of identity and has become a "public
figure". Here, the gender freight is plain to see: where the early male protagonists
seek new identities ("Avenida", "Baldi" and "Excursión"), or have identity crises
("Bienvenido" and "Nueve"), in "Mascarada", the issue for the woman is to be
identified by a man in terms of her use value to him. Hence, the fat man at the
end of the story takes possession of María Eugenia with his look and his hand
(1290-91). That same dubious switch of identity occurs in "Regreso". Here, the
young Perla leaves home and literally disappears: she is no longer visible to the
"respectable" eyes of *tío* Horacio. The world of prostitution into which it is
implied that she goes is a demarcated zone south of Rivadavia in Buenos Aires.
The spatial distribution into the known and unknown with connotations of the
acceptable and unacceptable, is already familiar in Onetti. Significantly, *tío*
Horacio has no trouble "seeing" his son Walter who moves freely north and south
of Rivadavia and who sees Perla "on the other side". At the end of the story, Perla
returns to the south, her new identity as prostitute drawing her back to that zone,
out of the view of the young Oscar who is the focalizing agent.

     Not all of the women characters are linked to prostitution, and indeed some
are the agents of attempted evasion in these stories. In "Esbjerg", "Convalecencia"
and "Sueño", the women characters are all crucial to the fundamental preoccupation
with leaving the city in search of fulfilment. But in none of them does the woman
character have that element of autonomy which the male characters seem to
possess. In "Esbjerg", the dream of escape is Kirsten's, but the effort to realize it
is her husband's. In "Convalecencia", the woman who finds relief away from the

city obeys a man's summons back to it.[4] And in "Sueño", the realization of the woman's dream is achieved, but only by her surrendering its staging to two men. So in each case the female character is dependent on male power. That is particularly striking in "Esbjerg" and "Sueño" where the knowledge or experience of the other is a woman's but is conveyed to the reader only indirectly by a largely uncomprehending male narrator. Though they are often apparently privileged in their access to the other, very rarely in Onetti's short fiction do female characters achieve the power or status of consciousness that is given to male characters. This state of affairs is linked to the fact that the focus of consciousness is virtually always within desire, within the unfulfilling constrictions of circumstance. There are no examples in the early fiction of a sustained point of view within the other world. There is no sustaining of evasion – the glimpses of "the other side" are all conditioned by brevity and by their status as desiring projections from the side of non-fulfilment.   So, for example, the consciousness of an other world in "Convalecencia" is significant only insofar as the woman loses it, and the man in "Excursión" cannot settle into an idyllic life but continues his walking and searching at the end of the story. El Negro in "Obstáculo" simply finds a way to escape to Buenos Aires with no guarantee of what he will find or of his not being recaptured and returned to the reform school like his friends before him. The fulfilment of the dream in "Sueño" seems incompatible with continued life: the woman dies at the end of its realization. All these openings to the other and their closing are profoundly symptomatic of the underlying rhythm of Onetti's fiction, whether short story, novella or novel.

There is then a degree of consistency in certain of the thematic threads of the early fiction. But in the structure of my analysis, this has been registered in order to be able to concentrate on other things. The repetition of certain ideas and

---

[4] Interestingly, this story first appeared under the pseudonym of a woman writer, H.C. Ramos, in a short story competition in the magazine *Marcha* in 1940. Having won a share in the prize, Onetti wrote a brief presentation of the story stressing that it was a contribution to the formation of a female literature in Uruguay. See Onetti 1986b, 253-58.

structures in Onetti is something to which I shall return in my final chapter, but repetition and consistency will not form the core of my analyses since I want to engage the stories in a questioning way, and not simply accept the sort of reading position that they seem to encourage. Hence, I want to look at the stories with an acute awareness of what reading itself does in its encounter with the texts, and that is the basis of my interest in the issues of gender and textuality. Those issues are the consistencies of my reading. The engagement with the stories in this way seems to me to dictate individual analyses. And that will be my method from now on, beginning with readings of what I consider to be the four most important of the stories written before 1950: "Sueño", "Bienvenido", "Esbjerg" and "Casa".

*

"Un sueño realizado"

The three main characters of "Sueño" share the fact that they are in an unusual place – they are all visitors to a provincial town. This shared re-location seems to run counter to the general grain of the story, which focuses on the differences between them. They are carefully constructed as complementary in relation to what they understand and experience of the woman's dream and its meaning: the interplay of positions and ignorance/knowledge is at the heart of the story.

The narrator, Langman, is an impoverished theatrical producer, a practical man with no imaginative or artistic ambitions. Hence, Blanes' tediously repeated and disparaging joke about his self-inflicted ruin in putting on *Hamlet*, a play about which Langman knows absolutely nothing (1206). As narrator, his (initial) utter incomprehension of the woman is crucial: he is unable to understand her as a woman and cannot grasp what she is talking about. What he does appreciate is her capacity to make him uneasy:

> Pero había, sí, algo en la sonrisa de la mujer que me ponía nervioso, y me era imposible sostener los ojos en sus pequeños dientes irregulares exhibidos como los de un niño que duerme y respira con la boca abierta. (1207)

In reacting to this potentially disturbing presence, Langman first tries to patronize her, assuming his own power as impresario and casting her as a neophyte writer (1208-09). He then attempts to control her presence by absorbing what she says about her dream into the known theatrical discourse (1209-10). Even he is forced to acknowledge that he fails on both counts. Hence his other defensive ploy, sustained for much of the story, which is to see her as a "bicho raro" (1209), and, more significantly and repeatedly, as "loca", which gives him relief: "Comprendí, ya sin dudas, que estaba loca y me sentí más cómodo" (1208). To describe her as mad seems to put her beyond the reach of rational categories, and it "others" her completely. The gap in comprehension between them is only bridged when they can talk about money. The woman may be nonplussed by Langman's banalities, but she knows what to do: she offers him money for the production of her dream and he instantly understands. He stops labelling her when money speaks (1210). From this point, Langman basically stops worrying about trying to understand her and concentrates on the practical business of earning his fee (1212-13), though he still has difficulty in looking at her (1211, 1214) and still thinks that she is mentally ill. In fact, Langman looks after the *reality* of the performance, in which he takes no part: he is strictly an observer in the wings when it comes to the dream itself.

However, when the performance is about to start, there is a suggestion that Langman may be responding to the underlying point of the disturbance created by the woman, in fact, seeing beyond his own practical reality:

> Pero fue entonces que, sin que yo me diera cuenta de lo que pasaba por completo, empecé a saber cosas y qué era aquello en que estábamos metidos, aunque nunca pude decirlo, tal como se sabe el alma de una persona y no sirven las palabras para explicarlo. (1217)

Even Langman seems to appreciate that the performance evolves very well for all the ordinariness of what the actors have to do. But this switch seems to be reversed at the end of the performance and he breaks the mood by talking to the two extras. Langman reverts to being the producer, clearing up the stage and tipping the driver of the car. For all the earlier "understanding", Blanes now berates him for missing the point and for failing to realize that the woman is dead. Again Langman claims to understand what has happened, but this second assertion is questionable and will need to be analyzed in more detail later.

The woman is almost exclusively focalized by Langman, which necessarily restricts the view of her. But the overtness of his incomprehension and Blanes' ironic view of him help to indicate that there is much more to her than he can say. Langman tries hard to "other" the woman by seeing her as ill or mad, but he is clearly defensive and unreliable in doing that. The uncertainty about the woman's sanity is compounded by Blanes who, on the one hand, denies that she is mad (1215), but then says that she is mad (1216). This contradiction is significant not only for the complexity of the representation of the woman, but also for its suggestion of the instability of Blanes' character. The woman's otherness to male categories (and it is that for which "loca" is shorthand) is at least registered in this way: she appears as a boundary, or a disruption, and the very ending will underline that. However, for all the wavering of male comprehension in "Sueño", it is the woman's role which provokes the narrative – it is built on her desire.

Uncertainty in Langman is also provoked by the woman's constant smile, which he takes to confirm her oddness, and yet this might be counterbalanced with her evidently firm grasp of organization: she is lucid and practical in setting up the performance. That practicality is first in evidence when Langman is struggling to understand what she wants. She observes him, sees his inadequacy and then takes charge:

> Ella me miró y tenía en la cara algo parecido a lo que había en la de Blanes cuando se veía en la necesidad de pedirme dinero y me hablaba de *Hamlet*: un poco de lástima y todo el resto de burla y antipatía. (1210)

Her ironic view bolsters the reader's wariness about Langman. Her lucidity is also clear in the simplicity of her description of her dream both to Langman (1213) and to Blanes (1216). She is prepared to admit that the dream does not conform to a rational view of the world, but she underlines the importance of its affective logic.

The elusiveness and complexity of the woman are also apparent in her appearance. She is middle-aged but has very youthful features. She has grey hair and wears old-fashioned clothes, but they are the clothes of an adolescent (1207). Similarly, her breasts are "senos agudos de muchacha" (1207). This mixture of age and youth is crucial and memorable for Langman:

> La mujer tendría alrededor de cincuenta años, y lo que no podía olvidarse en ella, lo que siento ahora cuando la recuerdo caminar hasta mí en el comedor del hotel, era aquel aire de jovencita de otro siglo que hubiera quedado dormida y despertara ahora un poco despeinada, apenas envejecida pero a punto de alcanzar su edad en cualquier momento, de golpe, y quebrarse allí en silencio, desmoronarse roída por el trabajo sigiloso de los días. (1207)

This same point concerning her age about to be fully realized with the onset of decay is repeated shortly after and underlies the performance at the end of the story, where the race to beat time before age unravels her appears to be won. This point about the woman is one of unusual subtlety for Langman, and may betray the story in wanting to have an unperceptive narrator who also has important insights. In the dream at the end, the woman acts firstly *like* a girl, which is the first step in overcoming the age/youth dualism: "... vi cómo ella salía de la puerta de la casucha, moviendo el cuerpo como una muchacha..." (1217). By the end of the performance of the dream, she *is* a girl: "... divisé a la muchacha del cordón de la acera que bostezaba..." (1218). Just as the dream and reality seem to fuse, so do the different elements in the woman: the underlying point seems to be that death cheats time and its ability to destroy her. And this bolsters her otherness too: the hinting at madness, the dream realized and the recapturing of youth all seem to take her beyond the categories of the known, rational world in which she is located. In the woman's case, the desire for fulfilment, as so rarely in Onetti, seems to be achieved.

Blanes is an intermediary character between Langman and the woman. He is rather wild and disruptive with Langman, deliberately not cooperating and getting drunk. The relationship with Langman is not easy, but he does share with him not only the theatre but also a grasp of the importance of money: when

Langman offers him money to perform the woman's dream, Blanes acquiesces quickly. But Blanes also understands the woman from their very first meeting (1213). And they seem able to discuss the performance in a direct and personal way, since Blanes can interpret precisely what she means. There even comes a point when Langman thinks that he has caught the woman's madness so much is he in tune with what she wants. But his understanding is partial as he admits later. The electrician tells him that he has seen Blanes and the woman going to a hotel where couples go to have sex, and Langman is furious, thinking that Blanes has been taking advantage of an unbalanced woman. But Blanes explains that he wanted to know what her dream was all about, since he is not content (as Langman apparently is) merely to pocket her money. Hence, he seeks an explanation of the dream, but, as Langman stresses, Blanes never does understand in any rational sense (1216), any more than the woman does. It is not surprising, therefore, that of the male characters it is Blanes who comes nearest to sharing the affective meaning of the dream with the woman. Not only is he the actor closest to her in the performance, but he is also the one to realize that she has died (1219). He is furious that Langman is oblivious to this, as it were taking the woman's part in outrage against the producer. At the end, Blanes' almost habitual drunkenness is linked to madness as he storms about the stage angrily, and that link confirms his propensity to otherness, his openness to the different experience that the woman represents.

If Blanes is not aligned exactly with the woman or with Langman but has elements to connect him with both, there is a basic geography that all three share. All three are displaced from their usual locations, suggesting that this is a moment of potential reorientation. Both Langman and Blanes have stayed in the provincial town after the rest of their theatre company has returned to Buenos Aires; and the former clearly states his intention of going back to the city, which is indicative of how restricted is his potential to be open to the other. The woman is also from outside the town, only coming there, as Langman is told by the electrician, during the summer, implicitly as a break from normal life. Given this common relocation, it is striking that the woman's dream is sited within a big city (she insists on that to Langman and Blanes [1213]). Now, the structure of the dream does not suggest that it is a projection on to the city as a place of escape (as is the case in "Obstáculo"), nor that it is a projection out of the city as a place of confinement (as is the case in "Avenida" or "Excursión"). However, the location of the dream's realization *is* outside the city, so there is still an implicit polarization here: the dream is not realized in the city. This is a more subtle use of location than in Onetti's other early fiction, though "Sueño" does share some of the same geographical logic.

Within the shared relocation of the characters in "Sueño", they occupy different relative positions, as we have seen. The familiarity of Langman and Blanes is offset by the tension between them: Langman's disapproval of Blanes' drinking and ill-discipline is balanced by the latter's contempt for the other's lack of artistic understanding. That discrepancy between them allows for Blanes' greater proximity to the woman. But given that Langman is the one who least understands the woman, it is striking that he is the story's narrator. On the one hand, his lack of understanding risks missing the point of the woman's dream altogether. On the other, Blanes' strong ironical view of Langman's intelligence undermines his position as reliable source of information. Both features, therefore, leave the reader questioning the narrator's competence, and that questioning reveals something important, which is that the acts of observing and narrating are firmly located on this side of the dream and with the male. There is no direct narrating by the woman to the reader: she merely describes to Langman what she wants in the performance or tells Blanes about the roots of the dream. In that sense, "Sueño" has two male mediators, Langman and (briefly) Blanes (1216). This gender arrangement in narrating will become very characteristic in Onetti: in his fiction, it is girls and women who tend to be projected as having direct access to the other world of dream and fulfilment (for which male characters long), but, when they do have such access, it is usually male characters who narrate or who are the main centres of consciousness "on this side", in the Symbolic.

Apart from this problematic gendering of narration, the choice of Langman as narrator does sustain tension as to the ultimate direction of the story, and so delays closure, a prerequisite in narrative. When closure comes, it appears to be double. In the first place, and most obviously, the woman seems to bring dream and reality together. In the second place, Langman claims to begin to understand what is happening, thus apparently closing the gap separating him from the woman throughout. But at the start of the performance Langman also claims to understand her (1217), though this does not help him to see something as obvious as the fact that the woman has died. And just what it is he understands the second time, he cannot say:

> ... comprendí qué era aquello, qué era lo que buscaba la mujer... lo comprendí todo claramente como si fuera una de esas cosas que se aprenden para siempre desde niño y no sirven después las palabras para explicar. (1219)

He cannot name the content of his knowledge, and it comes to seem that knowledge and narration are mutually exclusive. Hence, the story seems to rest on the (slightly clichéed) notion that knowledge is outside language. By reverse extension, and more interestingly, the narrating structure built around Langman suggests the paradox that to speak is not to know.

There is a further paradox in the other aspect of closure at the end concerning the realized dream. "Sueño" seems to run against the outer limit of subjectivity, as desire pushes even beyond life and therefore beyond the capacity to live it. The very realization of the woman's dream and the preserving of her youth from decay may mean death. Now it is a moot point whether the death was part of the original dream or not since the woman does not mention death in her summaries to Langman and Blanes, hence it may be that the story's ending hints (at least in part) at a contradiction between life and fulfilled desire.[5] The desire

---

[5] See Ruffinelli and Puccini who both argue that the woman wants to die as that is the culmination of the dream.

for happiness or plenitude (and the woman does talk of being happy in the dream) may seem paradoxically to take her beyond the chance of living them. The problem here and in much later Onetti is how to try and live desire without losing the very subjectivity from which it arises.

*

"Bienvenido Bob"

"Bienvenido" is as much dependent on a structure of convergence as "Sueño". Where the earlier story brings together a dream and its realization, in this story, convergence has two potential forms, only one of which is realized. These two forms relate to the two dominant categories in "Bienvenido": youth and age.

The story projects a strong polarization of youth and age. This familiar structure in early Onetti is not related to physical locations but rather to characters and what they are seen to be. It is this polarization of identity which is, in a sense, partially overcome by the end. At one extreme there is Bob. He is young, solitary, critical, abstemious, pure and assured; in short, he epitomizes what the narrator calls a "juventud implacable" (1223).[6] Counterbalanced with the idea of youth is the narrator, a man whom Bob guesses is thirty or forty years old. This encapsulates his polarization with Bob: he is the empty negative of all that is positive in Bob.

The relation of these characters evolves in two phases separated by ten years (1226), but both are structured in terms of a power-play over identity. In the first phase (1222-26), the power-play between the two males revolves around Bob's refusal to respect or accept the narrator. Bob remorselessly disdains him, mocking his life and dismissing what he stands for. In particular, Bob stares at and scrutinizes him, which seems to be the vehicle of his initially silent condemnation, and, as a result, the narrator is keen to forget Bob's eyes (1222). Confronted with this scrutiny by Bob's integrity and youth, the narrator is defenceless, feeling

---

[6] Bob is even associated with plans for building a city on the coast (1221) with its connotation of creating an ideal outside the known urban environment.

haunted by the boy's presence even when he is not there. But he desperately wants to achieve tolerance and understanding from Bob, which would put an end to the scrutiny which reveals him to himself as he does not wish to be. Bob breeds a self-consciousness in him of his pathetic and ridiculous condition so that the narrator is left divided: hating and respecting Bob for what he does and for what he is (1222). This is especially intolerable to him as he desires to show Bob that he is wrong, that the two of them are similar. He wants to overcome the polarization that Bob imposes by proving to him that "había en mí algo más que aquello por lo que me había juzgado, algo próximo a él" (1222). This is his effort to counteract Bob's power in the relation, to deny that he himself has aged.

In the effort to prove his own view of his identity, the key for the narrator is Bob's sister, Inés. Marriage to her would overcome Bob, reversing the structure of power in their relations. To attain Inés is to possess youth and so to prove that he is like Bob. This is the narrator's desired convergence, the first one potentially in the story. But it never materializes:

> ... hasta llegué a pensar que en su cara inmóvil y fija estaba naciendo la comprensión por lo fundamental mío, por un viejo pasado de limpieza que la adorada necesidad de casarme con Inés extraía de abajo de años y sucesos para acercarme a él. (1223-24)

At its climax, the duel between the narrator and Bob centres on the possession of Inés. She is the focus of male hatred and polarization. The female character only appears in a brief, highly summarized passage (1225-25), and is no more than a marker of male desires and identities relating to the possession of youth. By implication, as much may be at stake for Bob in controlling Inés/youth and excluding the narrator as for the narrator, from whose perspective the duel is perceived.

The duel over Inés leads to Bob's being explicit in his repudiation of the older man. Before this moment his looks and physical presence alone object to the narrator. In speaking to the narrator, there is a confirmation of what might previously have been the workings of the narrator's imagination. And Bob can summarize his views in a pithy way:

> "No sé si usted tiene treinta o cuarenta años, no importa. Pero usted es un hombre hecho, es decir deshecho, como todos los hombres a su edad cuando no son extraordinarios." (1224)

Bob idealizes Inés for he claims that even he is unworthy to look at her. In response, the narrator tries to reverse their power relations by pitying Bob, but has to admit his failure. After this confrontation, he sees Inés only twice more and he knows that he has lost the duel.

Interestingly, the alignment of Bob with Inés is figured strongly in the text by his physical resemblance to her, as if the symbol were visible in Bob:

> En aquel tiempo Bob era muy parecido a Inés; podía ver algo de ella en su cara a través del salón del Club, y acaso alguna noche lo haya mirado como la miraba a ella. (1222)

This resemblance is alluded to three more times, the second including a suggestion that Bob might be a substitute for Inés:

> Si aquella noche el rostro de Inés se me mostró en las facciones de Bob, si en algún momento el fraternal parecido pudo aprovechar la trampa de un gesto para darme a Inés por Bob, fue aquella, entonces, la última vez que vi a la muchacha. (1225)

Given the complexity of the relation between Bob and the narrator, this hint at a double object of desire is intriguing, suggesting a drive counterbalancing Bob's which keeps the narrator in the duel. The narrator's own desire for Inés (for Bob) is clearly necessary to sustain anything like a duel. It is also important to note in relation to the sexual undercurrents, that although the narrator is very uneasy about Bob's scrutiny of him, there is abundant evidence in the text of his own detailed scrutiny of Bob. The narrator's gaze is fixed on Bob throughout, and that, combined with the confusion over the object of desire hints quite consistently at a homosexual undercurrent. And this is not counteracted by anything in the story's second phase.

In that second phase, a convergence does take place. Bob reappears in the narrator's life after a gap of ten years, and he is transformed: he drinks heavily, is married, works in an office (perhaps), and (significantly) has dirty hands (1221). This new figure, called Roberto, is pathetic in the narrator's eyes. The change in Roberto is that he has now lost what the narrator had already lost in the first phase. So Roberto and the narrator converge in the "defeat" of the adult, and the narrator can barely find traces of Bob in Roberto's face (1226).

However, the power-play between them goes on (at least in the narrator's mind). The narrator has finally "won" the duel, it seems, though it is a totally hollow victory. Now he can hate Roberto and take revenge for Bob's having prevented him holding on to Inés. Hence, the narrator revels in Roberto's loss of youth (1227). The emotional and sexual complexity derives now from his loving Roberto in his downfall: "Nadie amó a mujer alguna con la fuerza con que yo amo su ruindad, su definitiva manera de estar hundido en la sucia vida de los hombres" (1227). There is still ambiguity in the relation, especially as the narrator says that it is even more intense than his relation with Inés (1227). To take his revenge the narrator urges Roberto on in his flights of fantasy about impossible returns to youth, not dissimilar to those which he himself entertained about possessing Inés before. Roberto is aware of his defeat but accepts the narrator's promises about a return to youth in the future: now the narrator encourages him in his dreams, where previously Bob had his own dreams about the city on the coast. What power there now is rests squarely with the narrator.

"Bienvenido" is built on loss, but there is an implicit supplementary force in play: the narrator's desire, his mixture of hate and love in relation to identity. So he may have been defeated but he knows that defeat, and his consciousness does not allow complete conformity (any more than it does with Roberto, who still desires and imagines). However, at the end, the narrator is still implicitly projecting the polarization of youth and age and valorizing youth absolutely. So, although loss may breed awareness, caution is still needed in dealing with the narrator, in investing too readily in him as one-who-knows. In the first place, the structure that he insists on, that polarization, is the basis for his "victory" over

Roberto: he may be defeated but so is the other. In the second place, he has an implicit commitment to an essence of identity: what Bob *was*, what Roberto *is*, what the narrator *was/is*. And in the case of Inés' identity, there is a clear process of essentializing: "Ausente y perdida para siempre, podía conservarse viviente e intacta, definitivamente inconfundible, idéntica a lo esencial suyo" (1226). Inés is an idealized, unchanging marker of masculine identity. Significantly, she disappears from the text into married life in Buenos Aires (1226), and any change in her is therefore invisible or precluded. She has no independence of the narrator's or Bob's desire, and that is revealing of the mode of thought in play here. The Imaginary structuring of the story – involving the essentializing and fixing of identities in terms of polarizations as a function of a male duel over identity – seems somewhat problematic and should preclude too simple a view of the narrator and what he narrates. In other words, the force of male desire may be seen to undermine the narrator's position as sole source of knowledge.

In one formulation of Roberto's downfall, the narrator likens him to an immigrant:

> Como ese puñado de tierra natal, o esas fotografías de calles y monumentos, o las canciones que gustan traer consigo los inmigrantes, voy construyendo para él planes, creencias y mañanas distintos que tienen la luz y el sabor del país de juventud de donde él llegó hace un tiempo. (1228)

The metaphor here is that youth is a location, an-other place from which there is a one-way journey to adulthood. This idea clearly links "Bienvenido" with Onetti's other early fiction, where physical movement suggests switches in subjectivity, and it also links it with "Esbjerg" where the immigrant motif is crucial.

*

"Esbjerg en la costa"

There are at least two areas of speculation in "Esbjerg", one financial, the other involving narrative. They have ramifications which go beyond the narrator's conscious control, but both sorts of speculation rely on men even though they are triggered by a woman's dreams and memories. This points to the underlying

gender economy in the story. The woman's contact with the other has been direct
(in her childhood) and is now indirect (her memory and the photos and letters she
receives), and as in "Sueño", this contact is the basis for male speculation – in
financing and narrating.

Kirsten's function in "Esbjerg" is as a stimulus, a source of destabilization.
Her dreams and memories of Denmark are recounted to her husband, Montes, and
are then successively recounted to the narrator and by him to the reader. At each
step in the chain of narration, contact with the other becomes more remote. Born
in Denmark, Kirsten dreams of and remembers it, and, though she twice denies
wanting to return (1232), her behaviour and insistent dreaming seem to deny this.
The Denmark that she thinks of is the one she knew in childhood and it appears
idealized: for example, bicycles can be left unlocked in the street because there are
no thieves, and the country has the oldest trees in the world with a very special
smell (1232). Given the temporal gap, this Denmark seems irrecuperable, it is a
world of childhood, and that irrecuperability is underlined by the current state of
Kirsten's relatives there. Like Risso in "Infierno", Kirsten is sent photos from the
other/Denmark, and she also receives letters which tell her that all is not well with
her relatives (1233). Underlying Kirsten's experience is the paradigm of the River
Plate immigrant living through a sense of loss in a new urban environment.
Counterbalancing the port of Buenos Aires of Kirsten's current state is the port of
Esbjerg of her desire. This is signalled in the title as an idealized destination by its
linkage with the coast: this coincides with the topos of the non-urban, coastal other
in Onetti's early fiction (see "Convalecencia", "Bienvenido", "La larga historia" and
"Casa"). And this coastal motif is included despite the content of Kirsten's dreams
which insist on the rural. If Buenos Aires might be a port of departure, Esbjerg
would be a port of entry, doubly so since for Montes it is a phrase in Danish
containing the word Esbjerg that most strikes him initially and draws him into
Kirsten's dilemma (1232).

Montes is the first of the male characters to respond to Kirsten's dreams and memories: he is provoked into action by them. Without this there is no story. Like Langman and Blanes in "Sueño", Montes tries to help the woman realize her dreams. And the implicit logic may be that he does this because of his capacity to share something of the sense of what Kirsten tells him; he seems to grasp what she means even without fully understanding: "Eso que no entendía lo ablandaba, lo llenaba de lástima por la mujer... , y quería protegerla como a una nena perdida" (1232). His attempt to help involves his "dreaming up" a scheme to obtain her a return ticket to Denmark. He is the first to mention the idea of a return (1232), and he is the one who insists on it as a possibility; he is also the one to evolve the idea of how to buy the ticket:

> Así fue como llegó a pensar que podría hacer una cosa grande, una cosa que le haría bien a él mismo, que lo ayudaría a vivir y serviría para consolarlo durante años. Se le ocurrió conseguir el dinero para pagarle el viaje a Kirsten hasta Dinamarca. (1233)[7]

Hence, he risks cheating with the bets on the horse races. There are two speculations here: his imaginative speculation that might resolve Kirsten's dilemma, and his financial speculation that might realize the return journey. But the financial speculation fails and so the return journey is never realized. The debt that Montes incurs also takes away control of his story, for he has to reveal it, to hand it over, to the narrator. This means that, as the dream is blocked, so the chain of narration develops: the financial failure supplies an ending to his story of helping Kirsten and it can then be told to the narrator.

Just as Montes relates to speculation in two ways, so does the narrator, though differently. In relation to the financial, the narrator rescues Montes from total disaster. The narrator is a master of financial speculation, being the owner of the betting business in which Montes works. He is also engaged in other financial businesses: "Tengo esta oficina de remates y comisiones para estar más

---

[7] This structure of a male character's contributing to the realization of a female character's journey is highly reminiscent of *Para una tumba sin nombre*.

tranquilo... " (1231). Hence, the narrator can assume Montes' debt and impose a structure of repayment on him. But simultaneously, he takes over control of the story, at least its surface, for he understands its meaning only partially. Montes tells his story and Kirsten's story to the narrator, who is thus empowered to pass the combined stories on to the reader. And in his guise as narrator, he also participates in narrative speculation. There are various examples of this. Firstly, the narrator speculates on Montes' and Kirsten's psychology. In a passage which is unusually complex for him (after the initial pages in which he projects himself over the material rather crudely), the narrator imagines Montes announcing his hoped for triumph in obtaining the money for a ticket. The verb "deber" keys in his speculation about Montes' thought-process:

> Debe haber sido así, sin saber lo que le estaba pasando. Conseguir los dos mil pesos y decírselo a ella una noche de sábado, de sobremesa en un restaurante caro, mientras tomaban la última copa de buen vino. Decirlo y ver en la cara de ella... que Kirsten no le creía... "Ya se me va a pasar", diría ella; y Montes insistiría hasta convencerla... (1233)

In another passage, the narrator speculates on how Montes came to decide to take the financial risk and rejects Montes' own explanation that he spent a month thinking about it; his own narrative speculation contains the verbs "apostar" and "jugar", both metaphors from financial speculation: "Pero yo apostaría mucha plata a que en eso miente; jugaría a que lo hizo en un momento cualquiera, que se decidió de golpe, tuvo un ataque de confianza y empezó a robarme tranquilamente al lado de la bestia de Jacinto... " (1234). And finally, the very start and ending of the story are based on the narrator's speculations about Montes' and Kirsten's thoughts as they walk on the port, although there is no evidence that the narrator knows what either thinks.

Underpinning the capacities to dream and narrate the discourse of the story relies on a gender division. As the emphasis moves from the source of the dream to the act of narrating there is a relative shift from an implied feminine to the masculine. It is important to stress the relativity of the shift because neither extreme is absolute. So, it is Kirsten who dreams, though it is significant that she does not conform to feminine stereotypes. The narrator is brutally dismissive of her unattractiveness, referring to her "cuerpo campesino" (1229), her fatness and her bad smell. She also wears man's shoes (1229). This assimilation to masculinity may underlie her capacity to narrate her dreams and memories to Montes. She is not without a narrative capability, even if she is not apparently an object of masculine desire. The narrator, by contrast, is involved in imaginative speculation only at a fairly superficial level, but he projects himself as strongly masculine. His masculinity is exercised at the expense of Kirsten and Montes whom he dismisses as contemptible and inconsequential: he is mostly utterly indifferent to their small tragedy. Interestingly, however, in the middle section of the story (1232-34), where he does include some greater degree of sympathy for them, he is less intent on projecting his masculinity. However, at the end he reverts to a more crudely masculist voice, and disparages the others again (1234-36). Confirming this gender commitment, in the area of financial speculation, the narrator likes to show himself as in control, setting the terms of Montes' debt and knowing how to take risks.

Between Kirsten and the narrator, Montes seems to share elements with both, rather like Blanes in the comparable triangle in "Sueño". On the discourse's more active masculine side, he tries to undertake and control financial speculation, and he attempts to realize Kirsten's dream. It is also significant that Montes never plans to accompany Kirsten to Denmark: he promises to wait for her return (1233) as if rooted in the here-and-now of Buenos Aires. In the discourse's terms, these activities and his location in Buenos Aires give him certain attributes of masculinity, but that is counterbalanced by the narrator's contempt for him and by his having to cede control both of the story and of his finances: he becomes passive in the narrator's manipulating hands. The loss of control, in fact, coincides with his capacity to participate more fully than the narrator in Kirsten's dreams. And his link with Kirsten and femininity is confirmed at the end when they go together to watch the ships depart. Revealingly, the narrator says that in this way

Montes is paying his debt to Kirsten, just as he is also paying his debt to the narrator. Montes is balanced between the narrator and Kirsten: "... así paga en cuotas la deuda que tiene con ella, como está pagando la que tiene conmigo... " (1236). His debt to the latter is obvious, but the one with Kirsten derives from the fact that (according to the narrator's perspective) her work now pays for them both to live. Montes has lost the traditional male role of supporting his wife which he seemed to occupy before.

So the unspoken gender economy of "Esbjerg" seems to be that masculinity is in control of finance and of narrating, although the source of the disturbance and therefore the very material to be narrated are nearer to femininity. This may explain why so unsympathetic, even so unknowing, a narrator is in charge of the telling: this narrator adds up the debt and recounts the story. As with Langman in "Sueño", the location of narrating is in the shared and patriarchal Symbolic, which barely comprehends the dream. "Esbjerg" is a story of "an unrealized dream", and, as with Roberto in "Bienvenido", there is no return journey to the place of Imaginary projection.

Underlying all that has been said so far is an implicit contract of trust in the narrator. However, once again (and anticipating many later cases in Onetti) caution is needed in relation to him. For, in addition to his other speculations, he is a speculator of a more fundamental kind: he bets on the ordering of his gender economy as a secure way of making sense, as a reliable way of mapping events and other characters and placing them in hierarchies. Hence, he invests in his own projection of his power on the basis of the weakness within his system of values of Kirsten and Montes. But if we see that as a gender speculation with strong implications for meaning and understanding, we in turn might speculate that as a narrator he fails to convince as much as Montes fails in the financial field. That could enable a refusal to see him on his own terms and a reengagement with and questioning of the explicit content of his story. In that way, another reading would emerge: refusing simply to accept his elaboration of the material that Montes provides, "Esbjerg" would become a text revealing of the workings of the narrator's desire, a fiction about himself, gender and power.

*

"La casa en la arena"

Of key importance in "Casa" is the way Díaz Grey remembers and reworks his past. Just as the narrator in "Esbjerg" sets up a personal framing of the material of the story, so does Díaz Grey, the difference being that with Díaz Grey the reinvention of the remembered material is foregrounded explicitly in the story. What seems to be a cornerstone is the idea that direct, unequivocal knowledge (even of a character's own past) is unavailable. Hence, what is crucial is the relation between fiction and desire, and how that relation seems to enable identity. But there is no core to identity in evidence in "Casa", on the contrary, identity seems to be the very process of desire and reworking of the past. This strong metatextual layer in "Casa" precludes any positivistic fixing of sense by the reader and needs careful analysis.[8]

There are two passages dealing with Díaz Grey's relation with the past: the opening two paragraphs and a paragraph on the penultimate page (1247). The first paragraph is particularly important:

> Cuando Díaz Grey aceptó con indiferencia haber quedado solo, inició el juego de reconocerse en el único recuerdo que quiso permanecer en él, cambiante, ya sin fecha. (1237)

The condition for reworking memory is a current state of indifference to isolation, a loss of involvement in the present. That distancing allows the game of seeking identity ("reconocerse") in memory. Elements of this first sentence of the story are repeated with small variations near the end of the story where "... Díaz Grey... se entregó al juego de conocerse a sí mismo mediante este recuerdo... " (1247). Here, as elsewhere in Onetti's early fiction, there is an older self looking back at an

---

[8] See Brower who also discusses these issues.

earlier self which had an experience of a sort which is now only available in memory. But memory is changeable, subject to desire:

> Veía las imágenes del recuerdo y se veía a sí mismo al transportarlo y corregirlo para evitar que muriera, reparando los desgastes de cada despertar, sosteniéndolo con imprevistas invenciones, mientras apoyaba la cabeza en la ventana del consultorio, mientras se quitaba la túnica al anochecer, mientras se aburría sonriente en las veladas del bar del hotel. (1237)

Memory is flexible and in need of reworking to keep it alive: to correct the memory, to reinvent it, is, by implication, to subject it to the effect of present desire which works, as it were, via a double visual effect: seeing images of the past and seeing the current self. The self is thus reduced to one memory whose meaning is malleable. There is nostalgia and current loss, but a will to hold the self together by the process of falsification: reinventing the self becomes the process of the self, it has no specific, constant content:

> Su vida, él mismo, no era ya más que aquel recuerdo, el único digno de evocación y de correcciones, de que fuera falsificado, una y otra vez, su sentido. (1237)

The second paragraph starts to show how the present can resemanticize the memory by referring to the retrospective capacity to read its beginning as an anticipation of the rest:

> El médico sospechaba que, con los años, terminaría por creer que la primera parte memorable de la historia anunciaba todo lo que, con variantes diversas, pasó después; terminaría por admitir que el perfume de la mujer... contenía y cifraba todos los sucesos posteriores... (1237)

The coding of later events in her perfume is something not known during the experience itself, and this is precisely because knowledge seems to come in proportion as the experience recedes – the more the older Díaz Grey reinvents and falsifies the memory as a function of knowledge of the self in the present, the more the basic experience becomes remote and intangible. The effect of reinvention on the past also reduces everything that happens before the arrival of *el Colorado* to the events of a single day (1238), and it compresses the later events after Molly's arrival into the passing of one rainy afternoon spent indoors (1241). Such is the smoothing and condensing effect of remembering. Hence too the ending of the story as written in "Casa" is simply Díaz Grey's "final preferido" (1247), indicating that there are other versions available.

If the process of identification is central to the fictional project of "Casa", there are also certain relatively fixed parameters within it. The current desire in relation to the past is focused on a moment of desire: Díaz Grey's feeling for Molly. So the desire for past desire is crucial, as is the location of that past desire *outside* the known world. The relation with Molly flowers briefly in the special circumstances that bring them to the chalet on the beach, after all they had known each other before being there. Díaz Grey and Molly are both at cross purposes with the law in the city and that briefly renders them outsiders to normality. The chalet on the beach is the location of their otherness and is characteristic of the search for fulfilment in early Onetti. As elsewhere, however, the presence in such a location is brief and both Díaz Grey and Molly return to normality at the end. This coincides with the break in the supposed reciprocity of their emotions and is caused by the arrival of a third figure, Quinteros, who is Molly's partner and who, in breaking their dyadic relation, relocates them within the Law: the return to the city. These familiar parameters – male desire for fulfilment via the female character, the condition of the outsider, and the location on the coast – are secure only to the extent that they define Díaz Grey's desire internally, they are no guarantee of the reality of the reinvented memory in which they occur.

If "Casa" is a story of subtle fluidity in identification, it is also one which is fluid in the reading process. Just as there is no direct, unequivocal knowledge in the subject's relation to the past and to desire, so there is no simple relation to the story for the reader. The stress on the reinvention of memory underlines "Casa"'s status as one version among many: the story is a version of Díaz Grey's relation to the past. The process of invention itself is evident in "Casa"'s insistence on its own textuality. It is a story which resists translation into transparent meaning. This resistance is particularly clear in the insistence on physical action and appearance, and, in the absence of internal interpretation. The

physical produces a sort of blankness which renders explicit interpretation
precarious and laboured.

Even when there are descriptions of characters (including the central object
of desire, Molly), it is difficult to establish stable meaning or an underlying thread
of connotations.   The appearances and actions seem to be simply registered in
themselves:

> ... en el inmóvil, único atardecer lluvioso, ella elige el rincón donde colocará su
> cama, guía al *Colorado* en la tarea de vaciar el pequeño cuarto que da al Oeste.
> Cuando el dormitorio está preparado, la mujer se quita el impermeable, se calza
> unas zapatillas de playa; modifica la posición de la lámpara sobre la mesa,
> impone un nuevo estilo de vida, sirve vino en tres vasos, reparte los naipes y trata
> de explicarlo todo sin otro medio que una sonrisa, mientras se alisa el pelo
> humedecido. Juegan una mano y otra; el médico empieza a comprender la cara
> de Molly, los ojos azules e inquietos, lo que hay de dureza en la mandíbula
> ancha, en la facilidad con que puede alegrar su boca y hacerla inexpresiva de
> inmediato. (1242)

It is hard to see anything being signified here except the occurrence of a series of
simple physical movements or an appreciation of physical appearance. Even Díaz
Grey's reaction to Molly suggests only general interest: his understanding of her
face is a form with no specific content.

Another example of this sort of physical blankness concerns the burial of
the ring given to Díaz Grey by Molly. No internal interpretation of this repeated
act is hinted at and so the eight repetitions seem to suggest the carrying out of a
private ritual:

> Entonces – a veces en el final de la tarde, otras en su mitad – cava un pozo en
> la arena, tira el anillo y lo cubre; lo hace ocho veces, en los lugares que pisó *el
> Colorado*, en los que él mismo había señalado con una sola mirada. Ocho veces,
> bajo la lluvia entierra el anillo, y se aleja; camina hasta el agua, trata de equivocar
> sus ojos mirando los médanos, los árboles raquíticos, el techo de la casa, el
> automóvil en el declive. Pero vuelve siempre, en línea recta, sin vacilaciones,
> hasta el sitio exacto del enterramiento; hunde los dedos en la arena y toca el
> anillo. Tumbado cara al cielo, descansa, se hace mojar por la lluvia y se
> despreocupa; lentamente inicia el camino hasta la casa. (1246)

Interpretation can achieve little definitive here, since it quickly becomes tenuous
or banally explicit. The context of the burying of the ring is the return of
Quinteros and the break in the relation of Molly and Díaz Grey. The loss of the

relation (whose reach and mutuality are in any case never clear) may be represented by the burial of the ring that Molly has given the doctor, but that hardly accounts for the eight repetitions. However, the precision of the doctor's actions does suggest control and that may connote a structure of ritual in which the act in itself is paramount as a way of filling space and time. Loss might be attenuated through controlled action. In the end, Díaz Grey does not bury the ring at all. Instead he retains it and then ritualizes his relation to Molly through repeatedly reinventing his memory years later. Whatever sense is made of the ritual with the ring, its concrete presence is hard to dissolve into transparent meaning.

The sliding of sense across the surface of the text is even more striking in the final example where strong emotion is invoked in a context of blank physical action: this blankness is at odds with the sudden fixing on despair and a life-long commitment:

> Ella se sienta en la mesa y bebe; Díaz Grey vigila al *Colorado* sin dejar de ver los dientes de Molly, manchados por el vino, exhibidos en una mueca reiterada que no intenta nunca ser una sonrisa. Ella deja el vaso, se estremece, habla en inglés a nadie. *El Colorado* continúa haciendo guardia al fuego muerto cuando ella reclama un lápiz y escribe versos, obliga a Díaz Grey a mirarlos y guardarlos para siempre, pase lo que pase. Hay tanta desesperación en la parte de la cara de la mujer que él se anima a mirar, que Díaz Grey mueve los labios como si leyera los versos y guarda con cuidado el papel mientras ella fluctúa entre el ardor y el llanto. (1244)

The insistence on the physical in all three examples, allied with the frequent lack of continuity of action from sentence to sentence, frequently precludes or obstructs any move into the abstraction of meaning. Here, at a higher level of engagement, the reader may perceive not just the operation of desire in the character's retrospective reinventions, but in the process of textualization itself, which produces no fixed identity either of subjectivity or of meaning, but a projection and a sliding of desire in the character and in the reader in search of an always elusive object.

This sophistication in the writing of "Casa" is highly indicative of Onetti's future, mature work. The play of textuality in the space between desire and knowledge will be returned to again and again, not just as a theme but as a formal practice. Writing occurs in Onetti in the space of the known, but always in relation to the observed or remembered experience of the desire of/for the other. Even though necessarily confined within the signifying capacity of the known, of the Symbolic – they could not exist outside its language and structures of representation – , the fictions are driven by another dynamic, that of desire with its endless recreative capacity.

CHAPTER 3

SNAPSHOTS FROM BEYOND MASCULINE DESIRE:
"EL ALBUM" AND "EL INFIERNO TAN TEMIDO"

"El álbum"

> La vi desde la puerta del diario, apoyado en la pared, bajo la chapa con
> el nombre de mi abuelo, Agustín Malabia, fundador. (1273)

The opening of "El álbum" is paradigmatic. In the first place, it locates enunciation and perspective with the use of the key verb "ver": the "yo" (Jorge Malabia) sees her. She is only identified with a name (Carmen Méndez) on the penultimate page when she has left Santa María. Otherwise she is "la mujer", which is indicative of her otherness and objectification within the frame of Jorge's gaze, the frame of a certain hegemonic masculinity.[1] That objectification is emphasized in the initial sequences in which she appears, 1273-74 and 1276-77, which both begin with the words "La vi...". Both sequences are characterized by long, careful observation of the woman by Jorge in which she is apparently hardly aware of him. Even when he has followed her into a bar in the second sequence it is not clear that he can do more than speculate that she has seen him until she moves to his table. This asymmetry of looking and awareness is indicative of their (non-)relation. She does look at him eventually (1277), but the nature and motive of her look are hard to ascertain. And the asymmetry of seeing is maintained at

---

[1] On hegemonic masculinity see Connell 183-86.

the very end of the story when Jorge finds the album with photographs of her – he looks at her again and she is necessarily oblivious of his gaze. The question of his gaze is the first element keyed in by the story's opening sentence.

In the second place, Jorge and the woman are positioned by the opening sentence. He observes from the door of his father's newspaper *under* the plaque with the name of his grandfather, the newspaper's founder. This positioning might be read as symptomatic, for Jorge is trying to emerge from the world of authority in Santa María and within his bourgeois family, which are linked via the newspaper. Jorge is, therefore, on a threshold and the woman is outside, a position to which he is implicitly aspiring. He will come to *see* her as the "means" of escape from all that his father and the newspaper represent. At the start he still belongs to the world of his father and Santa María, as is clear from the fact that he has been sent by his father to the offices of the newspaper to deliver an article.

If his gaze and positioning are alluded to in the opening sentence, one other crucial element is absent and indeed is never mentioned explicitly. This third element is Jorge's demand to be seen, and specifically his attempt to construct a certain self as an object for others. In that respect there is an underlying tension in the story between his demand and what is given. The implied author and many of the characters frame him as an adolescent, with the typical (almost clichéed) preoccupations of the young male. In particular, he is hungry for sex, as are his friend Tito and the other boys at school (1278). In its banality and typicality this limits Jorge and renders him anonymous, hence his striving to stress his difference from others, to construct his *visibility*. He works hard to be seen, and his very act of narrating falls into that category. There are numerous manifestations of his desire for visibility. He wishes to differentiate himself from the other boys by disparaging them, and specifically he wants to be seen as mature and knowledgeable. That is apparent in his projection of his attitude to his sexual hunger:

> Yo estaba hambriento y mi hambre se renovaba y me era imposible imaginarme sin ella. Sin embargo, la satisfacción de esta hambre, con todas sus pensadas e

inevitables complicaciones, se convirtió muy pronto, para la mujer y para mí, en un precio que necesitábamos pagar. (1279)

On the one hand, there is an absoluteness here which confirms Jorge as completely adolescent, while, on the other, he is conspicuously seeking to establish a parity with the woman which would make him worthy of adult attention. It is the same unironized absoluteness with which he ridicules his peer Tito for compromising over his sister's marriage to the shop assistant, simultaneously seeking to differentiate himself because he has ideals:

– Y tu hermana se va a casar con el dependiente de la ferretería, no este año, claro, sino cuando tu viejo no tenga más remedio que darle una habilitación. Y vos algún día te vas a poner atrás del mostrador, no para disputarle tu hermana al dependiente, como sería justo y poético, como haría yo, sino para evitar que te roben entre los dos. (1283)[2]

The same effort at self-projection and the same values are manifest in his dismissal of Tito's view of his poem: Jorge apparently knows what real poetry is (1282-83). It is the aspiration to "maturity" and "understanding" which leads him to stress his "man to man" complicity with Maynard (1284-85), even while Maynard is in part mocking him. This epitomizes the tension surrounding Jorge, for neither Tito, Maynard nor Vázquez sees him in the way he wants. The question remains as to how the woman sees him, a vital dimension to which I shall return.

Jorge's desire to imitate adult male attitudes leads him into machismo and the objectification of women: he seems to aspire to act out a certain hegemonic masculinity. That attitude is already manifest in Vázquez at the start of the story in treating the unknown woman as a sexual object (1274), and Jorge is complicitous with it. So, later, he is arrogant and destructive about Tito's female cousin (1276), fragments the woman's body into parts for his own pleasure (1278), and stresses his being taken seriously by Maynard in the machinations to have sex with the woman: Maynard is said to "understand" his "need" (1278-79). The imitation of adult machismo is reinforced by other elements of adult posturing and

---

[2] The question of a brother's "protecting" a sister or not is reminiscent of "Bienvenido Bob".

attitudinizing, which are further ways of presenting the self to be seen. Hence he ostentatiously lights or fills his pipe (1273, 1277), makes references to "mi turbulente experiencia, mi hastiada madurez" (1284), puts on a gruff voice for Maynard (1284), wonders what pose to strike for the woman (1275), and is cynical at others' expense for the reader's benefit:

> Montado en una escalera, vestido hasta los tobillos por el guardapolvo gris hierro, gris polvo, el dependiente tenía una caja de madera en las rodillas y examinaba agujeros de tuercas para enterarse de si la rosca giraba hacia la izquierda o hacia la derecha. Cuando terminaba de olerlas, las clasificaba. (1282)

This construction of the self for others (characters and readers) as independent and mature is based on and undermined by implicit anxiety about his position in respect of his father and Santa María. It is not insignificant that he is initially placed *under* the plaque at the newspaper which represents the authority and solidity of his highly respectable family (1273). In one respect, this positioning of Jorge is a rare example in Onetti of a clear class foundation for a character. Jorge is the son of the bourgeoisie: he is still in school and is destined for university.[3] To differentiate the self from his father, Jorge treats him and his opinions with contempt: ironically, he insists on his father's pompous attitudinizing in his newspaper editorials (1273, 1275), and he links this with Santa María through a shared imbecility (1275). Jorge therefore makes use of his father and Santa María as points against which to set the self: he tries to build an ego in distinction to his father and the town. But that sort of polarization is manifestly Imaginary in that Jorge is the anxious product of privilege in Santa María and is still taking advantage of it to pursue his would-be independent life: hence he borrows his father's car and uses his own financial resources to pay the woman's hotel bill.

So Jorge is a complex interplay of the demand for a certain perception of himself, an Imaginary polarization of the self and his context, and an occasional

---

[3] See *Para una tumba sin nombre* (1959) where Jorge and Tito are at university in Buenos Aires.

capacity for irony. But his moments of self-irony are never sustained into real self-insight: his identity is, by implication, too fragile for that. And Jorge never goes so far as to ironize his view of the woman despite his knowledge as retrospective narrator of the fundamental mistake he makes about her. The point here is the discrepancy between his knowledge as subject of the enounced and as subject of the enunciation. The crucial questions are not so much *what* Jorge sees, as *how much* did he see/understand, and *how much* does he see/understand? In other words, is there a qualitative growth in him as a result of his having to confront his error about the women's stories? Or is his desire for a certain sort of perceived self still in play when he is narrating?

In fact, Jorge's demand to be seen in a certain way reaches beyond, runs in excess of, the available recognition by the other. The discrepancy leaves a remainder which is desire and which underpins his narrating practice. This discrepancy, the space of desire, is most obvious in the role played for Jorge by the woman. She acts as a would-be mirror for his narcissistic self-projection, and yet she comes to epitomize the lack of coincidence of demand and object.

The woman has certain minimal but recognizable features that link her to Onetti's treatment of women characters in general.[4] The woman emerges into Santa María by coming up from the port (1273): she has to climb the street into Santa María. Locations which are lower than and outside the town are often placed in Onetti's fiction in Imaginary polarization with it, as places of desired escape or fulfilment.[5] The woman's outsider status seems confirmed when Vázquez describes her as a little mad (1274).[6]

---

[4] See Millington 1987.

[5] See chapter 2 on the significance of locations on the coast.

[6] This outsider status is also underpinned by her constantly carrying a bag, which might be read positivistically as her being on the move, a traveller. But compare the problems of reading a similar object in the dream of the woman in "Tan triste", discussed in chapter 7.

Jorge begins to associate her with other apparently positive elements. In walking on the dock she seems to him to be lying, in fact to be waiting for nobody despite appearances (1276), and that, as becomes clear later, is not a criticism since her highly valued stories are also called "mentiras":

> "Tal vez nadie en el mundo sepa mentir así," pensaba yo...
>   Y en el centro de cada mentira estaba la mujer, cada cuento era ella misma, próxima a mí, indudable. (1280)[7]

Jorge also associates her with dream, an irrecuperable state that reality cannot compensate:

> La mujer fingía siempre estar dormida y despertaba con un pequeño sobresalto, con cambiantes nombres masculinos, deslumbrada por los restos de un sueño que ni mi presencia ni ninguna realidad podrían compensar. (1279)

The "mentira" and the dream are both given positive connotations that place the woman as other to the reality of Santa María.

Interestingly, when Jorge starts to talk of the stories which the woman tells, he insists that it is the beginning of "la verdadera historia" (1279), as if "truth" lay in the invention and not in the reality of life in the town. This is a crucial inversion for Jorge, and one which he cannot sustain. In fact, the content of the woman's stories that he recounts is fairly banal despite their remote locations – Scotland, Venice, Cairo, India and Amatlán. The one set in Scotland is very similar to romantic fiction (1280),[8] but the point is that he insists on the *effect* that the stories have on him and not on their content. He claims that they are more powerful than the sexual experience with the woman. Revealingly he says: "... nada podía compararse con el deslumbrante poder que ella me había prestado..." (1281). He construes the stories in a way that narcissistically empowers him, but that position is destroyed at the end when he discovers the photographs which show that the stories are not "mentiras" but snapshots of reality. This shatters his

---

[7] See the discussion of the "mentira" in *Para una tumba sin nombre* in chapter 7 of Millington 1985.

[8] It also shares a number of details with one of the "sueños" that Linacero recounts to Esther in *El pozo* – see Onetti 1970: 55-56.

self-identification in the relationship with the woman, and, in retrospect, there is some evidence that he continually projects his desire on to the woman. For example, he construes her thought and emotions with no corroboration:

> La seguí hasta el hotel, creyendo que ella – sin volverse, sin mirarme – sentía mi presencia media cuadra atrás, y que yo le era útil, le ayudaba a subir las calles, a vivir. (1277)

Similarly, a little later, he assumes an equal desire in the woman for their sexual relation, without showing any evidence for his belief:

> Sin embargo, la satisfacción de esta hambre, con todas sus impensadas o inevitables complicaciones, se convirtió muy pronto, para la mujer y para mí, en un precio que necesitábamos pagar. (1279)

However, his first sighting of the woman epitomizes the nature of their real (non-) relation. They coincide in time and place but with no apparent sharing of intentionality. They are together and yet separated, frozen at a distance:

> Yo sabía que no era por mí – y tal vez por nadie, ni siquiera por ella misma – que la mujer se había sosegado en la vereda, inmóvil y ocre en el centro de la tarde de domingo... Pero me mantuve sin moverme, sin dejar de mirarla, hasta que la pipa estertoró vacía exactamente en el momento en que ella tuvo que adelantar un pie y descender, continuar avanzando en dirección al hotel por el desierto de la bocacalle que nos había separado y reunido... (1274)

But this early physical posing of the nature of their relationship does not lead on to a sustained, conscious knowledge of it on Jorge's part. He feels called by her (1275), but her disappearance at the end strongly suggests that feeling is not reciprocated: she does not see him as he wishes to be seen. There appears to be no real relation between them – Jorge simply construes one and elaborates it. Indeed one might speculate that when the man appears he gives the lie to Jorge's claim that she was not waiting for anyone on the dock. However, Jorge does briefly recast their relationship at the end:

> Y así como al decirle adiós a la mujer en la tarde del viaje tempestuoso sobre el Rin me estaba separando de mi madre, me encontré con mi padre al día siguiente, a las seis de la tarde. (1284)

The idea of the woman in the role of mother is strongly suggestive of his Imaginary investment, an evasion of the Symbolic in Santa María. Hence, the loss

of the woman is a sort of Oedipal separation: the dyadic relation which Jorge
perceives with the woman is broken in classical fashion by the intervention of the
father/Maynard who tells him that she has gone and by the arrival of the man who
takes her away.

The paradox of "El álbum" lies here. It is that while valuing within the
story the woman's supposed story-telling, it is Jorge himself who is inventing by
projecting his desire on to the woman. This propensity is alluded to within the
text. In order to justify his visits to the woman in the hotel, Jorge invents a
"mentira" for the hotel manager which he repeats to his parents:

> No quise inventar otra mentira para mis padres; repetí el cuento de los
> informes a máquina, que me había encargado el viajante... (1279)

He equates his own "mentira" and "cuento", just as he does with the woman's
story-telling. The story which Jorge appears to invent for the reader is a symptom
of his desire for the visibility of a certain kind of self. His humiliation at the end
is the product of the impossibility of sustaining his fantasy of the nature of the
woman's stories and the meaning of his relation with her.

That humiliation is actually compounded by dependence on others in
finding and losing the woman. On first sighting her, Jorge knows and has invented
nothing about her when Vázquez appears from behind him out of the newspaper
offices. Jorge projects himself as in control of the situation and speculates about
how he will pass the woman in the role of dominant male:

> Encendí la pipa, esperando el momento de moverme para cruzar en diagonal la
> calle, rozar tal vez a la mujer, enterarme con certeza de su edad y meterme con
> un portazo en el automóvil... (1273)

However, it is Vázquez who has concrete information about the woman:

> – Debe estar un poco loca de la cabeza – dijo Vázquez –. Hace una
> semana que está en el hotel, el Plaza; vino sola, dicen que cargada de baúles.
> Pero toda la mañana y la tarde se las pasa con esta valijita ida y vuelta por el
> muelle, a toda hora, a las horas en que no llegan ni salen balsas ni lanchas. (1274)

And it is also Vázquez who crosses the street first and acts the part of the dominant male after putting his finger on precisely what Jorge will do with the woman later:

> "Más de uno se tiraría su lance – me tocó el hombro en despedida y cruzó diagonalmente, casi como yo proyectaba hacerlo, gris y pequeño, con el andar heredado de su amigo *Junta*, tratando de apoyar sobre el asfalto fangoso la rotundidad de un peso que no tenía. Pasó muy cerca de la mujer en la esquina del Berna, sin mover el cuello para mirarla, y entró en el negocio." (1274)

Vázquez utterly undermines Jorge's posturing in relation to the woman, and that is consistent with the sort of character he is. Not only is he a friend of *Junta* (a character in Onetti with strong marginal connotations[9]), but he is characterized as "el de la reventa" (1273), a detail which implies that he is a *middleman* in a chain of selling. He also acts as an intermediary for Jorge and sets the story in motion: it is Vázquez who provides a sort of access to the woman, by passing on the initial information that gives her some substance.[10] And there is a further middleman for Jorge in the story – Maynard, the travelling salesman, another man in a chain of selling. Being a travelling salesman, Maynard is not fixed in Santa María and so he has access to the world outside it, a world which Jorge aspires to and from which the woman also appears to have come. It is indicative that both Maynard and the woman stay at the same hotel, where Jorge's meetings with her and her story-telling take place – the hotel is the temporary location of the traveller. The mobility of Maynard makes him a source of authority since he literally knows the world (1285). He becomes an ally to Jorge, giving him access to the woman by providing the false excuse for his visits to the hotel: he helps Jorge's desire. He is also the one who knows first of her departure, just as Vázquez knew first of her arrival: Jorge is always second to know. But Maynard's consoling advice to Jorge is that he is following the right course in trying to get out of Santa María:

---

[9] See *El astillero* and *Juntacadáveres*.

[10] The salesman, Godoy, in *Para una tumba sin nombre* fulfils the same function of middleman between Jorge and Rita.

> "... no es posible que vivas como todos estos pobres tipos que compran las camisas, o se las compran las esposas, en la Moderna y eligen los trajes en el catálogo de Gath y Chaves. Esperando que les caigan mujeres y negocios, o ya no esperando nada. Tenés que disparar." (1285)

Thus Vázquez and Maynard, though they have better real knowledge of the woman than Jorge and so belittle him, both help to bolster his basic trajectory towards fiction and escape. But that is only to be expected since Jorge's "mentira"/"cuento" projects them as allies. And they are therefore less revealing than what obstructs him – the photographs.

The photographs at the end of the story do not reciprocate Jorge's look: they provide no acknowledgement, no reflection, but insist on their difference from his desire. Hence the narcissistic desire for recognition is disrupted and forced (momentarily, at least) towards seeing itself. Jorge's anger is the product of the realization that his route out of Santa María, and out of what the town sees him to be, is not an easy one. He remains inside Santa María, excluded from his projected other – he is not so different after all. In fact, he ends the story where he started it, inside Santa María looking at the woman as an outsider (in the photographs of Scotland, Cairo and so on). One might speculate that the photographs force the recognition that his desire to escape the Symbolic in Santa María is unappeased. Like so many of Onetti's male protagonists (especially in the 1940s and early 1950s) he is coming to terms with living on in the Symbolic. His story-telling is therefore still shot through with the symptoms of the desire to supersede that Symbolic: his learning is partial.

In terms of his subjectivity, Jorge is constituted in relation to a variety of others: he is located in shifting networks of object relations.[11] Hence, care is required in reading, as his narrating itself is potentially manipulating the relation with the reader – his desire to be perceived in a certain way is still in play. This is particularly important given the narrative form of "El álbum": the revelation of Jorge's "not knowing" comes suddenly at the very end, and part of the story's

---

[11] In this he is reminiscent of the narrator of "Cara".

effect derives from the shift in reading from supposing him to know to seeing that he does not know. But for much of the story he does carry the reader's conviction. The switch that takes place is relatively simple, and rather like the one that occurs in the nearly contemporaneous *Los adioses*, where the narrator is also forced to see his own mistakes about another character but also without achieving a qualitative growth in self-understanding as a result.   Hence, the sudden change in understanding at the end of "El álbum" marks it as a product of Onetti's writing in the early 1950s. It still relies on a central male character desiring to escape from the constraints of the Symbolic (as do *El pozo, Tierra de nadie, La vida breve*), while also beginning to put stress on textuality, the making of fictions, and on the instability of perception which will become characteristic in the 1950s and beyond (*Para una tumba sin nombre,* "Historia", "La novia robada"). In the later texts, the uncertainties of story-telling forestall the impetus of narrative and reduce the illusion of escape.

*

"El infierno tan temido"

The opening of "El infierno" is paradigmatic. The story begins with Risso's routine of writing his column in *El Liberal* with "la familiar felicidad" (1293). The contentment of his routine is shattered by the arrival of the first letter containing a photograph. One of the underlying tensions in the story is precisely that between routine and change. Despite the continual arrival of the photographs, Risso strives for the continuity of the familiar and the routine. That is clear with the first photograph. When he has looked at it, he gets ready to go home and talks to a colleague. He tries to minimize the impact of the photograph by denying its importance:

> La conservó durante un día entero, y en la madrugada estuvo imaginando una broma, un error, un absurdo transitorio...
>   – Bueno – dijo en voz alta – , está bien, es cierto y es así. No tiene ninguna importancia, aunque no lo viera sabría qué sucede. (1296)

The same process occurs before he opens the third letter containing a photograph:

> La tercera foto... se la trajo la mucama al final de una tarde en que él
> despertaba de un sueño en que le había sido aconsejado defenderse del pavor y
> la demencia conservando toda futura fotografía en la cartera y hacerla anecdótica,
> impersonal, inofensiva, mediante un centenar de distraídas miradas diarias. (1297-
> 98)

These reactions reproduce in miniature his response to meeting and marrying
Gracia. His routine and unfulfilling visits to a brothel are superseded by his
relation with Gracia, though he tries to limit the impact of change:

> Se casaron, y Risso creyó que bastaba con seguir viviendo como siempre,
> pero dedicándole a ella, sin pensarlo, sin pensar casi en ella, la furia de su
> cuerpo... (1295)

Not surprisingly, Risso's first reaction to the departure of Gracia is to cling to the
familiar pattern of life (1300). It is this inertia which will prove to be one of his
major difficulties in the challenge of the relation with Gracia.

Risso's location and his job are both indications of why he reacts to Gracia
as he does. Risso is firmly part of Santa María (in contrast to Gracia he never
leaves it in the course of the story), and he works for *El Liberal*, which appears
in Onetti's other fiction ("El álbum", for example) as the epitome of the town's
establishment. The relation with Gracia hardly fits with this foundation for the
character. It represents a partial opening to something neglected in Risso – there
is an emotional logic here in which his frustration as a widower seems to coincide
with Gracia's enthusiasm. It is significant that the coinciding of the two strikes
Risso while he is in the brothel on the coast – he is outside the town in a place
associated with the desire for fulfilment in Onetti:

> Lo cual estaba bien, debe haber pensado él, era deseable y necesario,
> coincidía con el resultado de la multiplicación de los meses de viudez de Risso
> por la suma de innumerables madrugadas idénticas de sábado en que había estado
> repitiendo con acierto actitudes corteses de espera y familiaridad en el prostíbulo
> de la costa. Un brillo, el de los ojos del afiche, se vinculaba con la frustrada
> destreza con que él volvía a hacerle el nudo a la siempre flamante y triste corbata
> de luto frente al espejo ovalado y móvil del dormitorio del prostíbulo. (1295)

For all the coincidence here, their emotional asymmetry is also apparent: his lack
in being, and her youthful energy. The relation itself is also asymmetrical. Risso
devotes physical frenzy to her, if unconsciously, but, as becomes clear, Gracia very

consciously observes him in order to see who he is (1297). The unconscious process in Risso is particularly emphasized: he is not in control of an experience that seems to be imposed on him from within:

> En realidad, nunca había tenido antes una mujer y creía fabricar lo que ahora le estaban imponiendo. Pero no era ella quien lo imponía, Gracia César, hechura de Risso, segregada de él para completarlo, como el aire al pulmón, como el invierno al trigo. (1297)

And yet they both seem to believe in their coinciding in love; they hold similarly absolute convictions:

> [Gracia] hacía planes y los cumplía, estaba segura de la infinitud del universo del amor, segura de que cada noche les ofrecería un asombro distinto y recién creado.
> – Todo – insistía Risso – , absolutamente todo puede sucedernos, y vamos a estar siempre contentos y queriéndonos. (1297)

It is Risso who withdraws from the relationship after Gracia's relation with another man (1301). His reason is not clearly stated though "traición" is mentioned later (1304), suggesting wounded pride. But the effect is clear: Risso splits the relation and closes out the possibilities offered by Gracia.

The arrival of the first photograph is a sort of repetition of Gracia's arrival in the first place, since it and the rest of the photographs disturb Risso's cloistered life. His return to routine and self-protection are exposed as inadequate. In the first place, the photographs create an emotional turmoil in Risso. Despite his attempts to diminish their impact and routinize them, he suffers acute confusion. He is shocked and baffled by them (1293) and experiences a sort of emotional hell in which he feels trapped (1302). He has no resources to cope with an experience with which he is utterly unfamiliar:

> Cuando llegó la segunda fotografía... , Risso temió, sobre todo, no ser capaz de soportar un sentimiento desconocido que no era ni odio ni dolor, que moriría con él sin nombre, que se emparentaba con la injusticia y la fatalidad, con el primer miedo del primer hombre sobre la tierra... (1295)

The complexity of the emotional turmoil is beyond his capacity:

> En la noche correspondiente a la segunda fotografía pensó que podía comprender la totalidad de la infamia y aun aceptarla. Pero supo que estaban más allá de su alcance la deliberación, la persistencia, el organizado frenesí con que

se cumplía la venganza. Midió su desproporción, se sintió indigno de tanto odio, de tanto amor, de tanta voluntad de hacer sufrir. (1296)

Gracia comes not only to embody a complex emotional terrain, but also to thrust him relentlessly into it: she forces him towards the beginnings of consciousness. There is no escape for him because she destabilizes his entire set of relations.

This emotional quagmire elicits no single response. At first, Risso is inclined to inertia, to wish all would go on as if nothing had occurred. He has recourse to self-pity, and feels unable to move to protect his vulnerability. In his view of himself as a victim he posits two alternatives: if ignorance and inertia cannot be achieved to end the pressure, then only death can release him:

Sólo podía salvarse de la muerte y de la idea de la muerte forzándose a la quietud y a la ignorancia... sólo podía esperar el agotamiento de la furia ajena. Sin permitirse palabras ni pensamientos, se vio forzado a empezar a entender; a confundir a la Gracia que buscaba y elegía hombres y actitudes para las fotos, con la muchacha que había planeado, muchos meses atrás, vestidos, conversaciones, maquillajes, caricias a su hija para conquistar a un viudo aplicado al desconsuelo... (1302-03)

This final sentence is crucial in my reading of the story, for it suggests the beginning of dialectical growth to overcome inertia. It suggests the start of thinking together the two Gracias (the Gracia whom Risso married and the Gracia who sends him the photographs), as if they could ever have been different. For in their relation, and particularly in his memory of it after their separation, Risso has idealized Gracia. He remembers what he saw as their love and longs for its return: it was something special, a "madness" without future or half-measures (1300). But the moment has passed, and Risso tends to idealize Gracia as a lost object. He desires the Gracia/grace of the total relation he thinks he knew, hence (in characteristic Onetti thinking) she is projected in the past as a "muchacha":

Pensaba en la muchacha que se paseaba del brazo de dos amigas en las tardes de la rambla, vestida con los amplios y taraceados vestidos de tela endurecida que inventaba e imponía el recuerdo... (1303)

It appears that this Imaginary projection cannot help Risso to move forward, hence the promise of the dialectical process of bringing the Gracia of the past and the Gracia of the photographs together into a new, sustainable relation:

> Había empezado a creer que la muchacha que le había escrito largas y
> exageradas cartas en las breves separaciones veraniegas del noviazgo era la misma
> que procuraba su desesperación y su aniquilamiento enviándole las fotografías.
> (1303)

The initial, self-protective idea that there are two Gracias may need to be overtaken
by the view that Gracia acts throughout towards Risso with love:

> Por qué no, llegó a pensar, por qué no aceptar que las fotografías, su
> trabajosa preparación, su puntual envío, se originaban en el mismo amor, en la
> misma capacidad de nostalgia, en la misma congénita lealtad. (1303)

This is an indication of the struggle over consciousness in Risso, a struggle out of
inertia, routine and Santa María and into something less clearly defined and
reassuring. This would require a new, more complex and non-polarizing view of
women: a move beyond the representation of Gracia as either a virginal girl (before
their marriage), or a whore (after the relation in Rosario), which are both
archetypes in Onetti.

In this context, the last moments of Risso are significant and highly
ambiguous. During what is possibly his last night, an important change overcomes
him – understanding seems to occur at last:[12]

> Volteado en su cama, Risso creyó que empezaba a comprender, que, como una
> enfermedad, como un bienestar, la comprensión ocurría en él, liberada de la
> voluntad y de la inteligencia. (1305)

There is already an ambiguity here in the play of negative ("enfermedad") and
positive ("bienestar") connotations. And interestingly, Risso is not in control of the
process, just as he was not in control of his previous emotional turmoil. His new
state is reemphasized as the dawn arrives, and the idea of renewal is reflected in
the change in the weather:

> Sintió después el movimiento de un aire nuevo, acaso respirado en la niñez, que
> iba llenando la habitación y se extendía con pereza inexperta por las calles y los
> desprevenidos edificios... (1305)

---

[12] This sort of "understanding" with no specified content occurs elsewhere in Onetti, with
Langman in "Sueño", for example.

On waking the next day, he feels a sort of untroubled serenity "un paternal cariño hacia los hombres" (1305), which seems distinct from the previous confusion. But the content of his "understanding" and "renewal" is not specified. He tries to avoid knowing what it is that he understands:

> La comprensión sucedía en él, y él no estaba interesado en saber qué era lo que comprendía... Veía la muerte y la amistad con la muerte, el ensoberbecido desprecio por las reglas que todos los hombres habían consentido acatar, el auténtico asombro de la libertad. (1305)

The mystification and ambiguity here reside in whether the understanding means a passive acceptance of death or a resolution to start anew, and that is sustained by the two suggested outcomes. Firstly, Risso resolves to find Gracia's address and to call or go to her, which consolidates the idea of a new start and a reconciliation with what she is (1305). But then the story ends with Lanza's report of Risso's suicide (1306). One might speculate that Lanza is not wholly reliable since he clearly expresses the dismissive and uncomprehending view of Gracia taken by Santa María. He works on the conservative *El Liberal* and has previously dismissed Gracia as "loca" [1304], to which he gives a negative inflection, but which might be seen as indicating Gracia's otherness to Santa María. Hence, the ending has certain ambiguities – the "renewed" Risso is hard to reconcile with Lanza's report of his suicide, and this duality suggests that the story does not move beyond the tensions with which Risso has grappled throughout. The potential for dialectic is not advanced.

The possibility of Risso's taking a step beyond his confusion is concentrated in the photographs and Gracia, both being sources of disturbance or irritation to Risso's passive state within the conventionalism of Santa María. The photographs come to be quite numerous and (as with those in "El álbum") significantly come from multiple other places: Bahía, Asunción, Lima, Santiago, Buenos Aires and Montevideo. Their literal content is very vague, and we only learn fragmentedly of elements in the first three. Gracia appears in them with a variety of men, their nature is explicitly sexual, and, given the poor lighting in them and the references to "el odio" and "la sordidez" (1294), they are seen as degrading by Risso. In fact, their content is more easily guessed from their devastating impact on him.

The implicit content of the photographs is more crucial and is alluded to several times. They seem to be messages (1302), and, despite their complex emotional impact, the message is basically one of love (1296, 1299), with the aim of stimulating dialogue (1298), that is, a response or movement in Risso. And, whatever his initial revulsion, the photographs do move him towards a new understanding in which there is possible continuity between the Gracia of the photographs and the Gracia whom he thought he married. That continuity may precisely be love.

Gracia's initial placement in the story is of some interest: she is unconventional, an actress working in the cooperative called El Sótano (1294). Both of these features are significant. One of the characteristic marginal activities of the young escaping from Santa María (it occurs in *Para una tumba sin nombre*, and "La novia robada") is to live in a phalanstery down on the coast: a collective life in a marginal place. The theatrical collective and its association with a low location (El Sótano) clearly echo the structure of the phalanstery. In addition, Gracia is pictured in her introduction to the story looking at Santa María from a poster: a larger-than-life image gazes at the town. Moreover, her young face covers the "paredes hechas vetustas por el final del otoño" (1294), which again polarizes her with Santa María: her youth against its age. Interestingly, her poster has been defaced (with "bigotes" and rips) as if the town were damaging her. But her look is interpreted by the narrator to be naive, and he deflates her youthful absolutism (1294).

Despite the iconic character of her features (which link her with many another woman character in Onetti), Gracia seems to be a rare case in Onetti of a woman character who has independent consciousness,[13] and who enters a

---

[13] There are also hints of this in the woman character in "Tan triste".

relationship with a man, rather than being merely a function of the male condition. Hence, Risso is seen as fulfilling a role in her life – after two fruitless engagements he may be "un puente, una salida, un principio" (1295) to or for experience.

Gracia's consciousness is a significant element in producing the reader's understanding of Risso and his shortcomings, and again that is unusual in Onetti. She reads his character, she sees his loneliness and bitterness, but knows that he is not defeated (1297). She senses that he needs a way out, a "desquite", without his realizing that he does, and this implies that her understanding is superior to his. It is as if she were saving him from himself through her love. That is part of her youthful ideals (she is twenty to Risso's forty) and her belief in life's capacity to surprise (1297), so distinct from Risso's desire for routine.

There is a suggestion that the marriage with Risso (and marriage is very rare in Onetti) does conventionalize her: the girl becomes a woman. Running parallel with this, after the marriage, the theatre company becomes subsidized by Santa María's "municipio" (1297), and it is renamed the "Teatro Municipal de Santa María" (1299). As if reacting against this conventionality, Gracia's "infidelity" to Risso occurs when she has accompanied the theatre to El Rosario: she has gone outside Santa María again, as at the beginning. The "infidelity" is consistent with being outside the "law" (marital or otherwise) of Santa María. And it is significant that her perspective on what she does is quite different from Risso's. As far as she is concerned, nothing can alter their relation:

> Nada de lo que ellos hicieran o pensaran podría debilitar la locura, el amor sin salida ni alteraciones. Todas las posibilidades humanas podían ser utilizadas y todo estaba condenado a servir de alimento. (1300)

The positive reference to "locura" suggests a valuation incompatible with Santa María (and with Lanza's view of her). So when Gracia has sex with another man in El Rosario, she thinks of Risso while it is happening (1301), and feels that it is utterly irrelevant to them (1301). Hence, to tell Risso about it is not an act of guilty conscience but a way of caressing him, of adding experience to their relation

– it is a new invention in their creativity (1301). Her reaction to Risso's severing of their relation is critical – he has not understood:

> ... volvía a reprocharle no haberle pegado, haberla apartado para siempre con un insulto desvaído, una sonrisa inteligente, un comentario que la mezclaba a ella con todas las demás mujeres. (1299)

Her difference (which the story has been at pains to emphasize) is simply not grasped by Risso at that stage; he treats her according to a set of rules she cannot respect. By implication she is seen as a prostitute. Hence she leaves Santa María since her place in it with Risso has evaporated, and, like other disappearances in Onetti (for example, Rita in *Para una tumba sin nombre*), she becomes untraceable by or incomprehensible to Santa María: she leaves contradictory addresses in the town. The photographs which she sends are, therefore, messages from Santa María's other and find no real comprehension in it. In addition, the photographs are a stimulus to the plot of "El infierno": not untypically of Onetti, a woman character is the source of the narrative movement.

At the level of story organization there are some problematic elements deriving from Gracia's disappearance. Given the location of story-telling within Santa María, her relocation outside it means the loss of her viewpoint: all that remains are its traces in the infiltrating photographs. This tends to underscore the fact that the fundamental framing of the story is from within the town's perspective, and that in turn suggests an unsettling element: for all Gracia's consciousness being registered in the story, it is registered within the frame of masculine discourse, and, in effect, Gracia seems to cast herself in the role of helping Risso, a role which Onetti's male characters often simply thrust on women characters. It is not so much that the story explores Gracia's consciousness as that she is represented as what Risso is lacking or what he still might grasp. This is still a male-centred discourse. And her exit from Santa María reinstates the sort of Imaginary polarization which seems to freeze that discourse into a metaphysics of failure. In addition, and confirming the masculism of the discourse, the content of the photographs – the suggestion of Gracia's sordid sexual exploits – represents her sexuality as that of the "voracious female" potentially destroying the "innocent man". This indicates an underlying masculine anxiety, for which "el infierno tan temido" is the metaphor. Hence, there is quite a deep ambivalence underlying the representation of Gracia: a feeling of need and love in the male character coupled with a profound fear and insecurity about the consequences of an independent woman character's power and sexuality.

The contradictory threads in the controlling masculine discourse highlight the question of mediation. It is a curious fact that all the photographs whose arrivals the reader is informed about in any detail reach Risso indirectly: each time there is an intermediary. The first letter with a photograph goes by mistake to Risso's colleague on *El Liberal*, Partidarios (the political correspondent) (1293), who hands it to Risso. The second letter goes to Policiales (the crime reporter) (1295). The third letter is handed to Risso by the maid at his lodgings (1297-98). The next photograph whose arrival is mentioned establishes a new pattern: it is sent not to Risso but to another colleague, Lanza (1304), who simply reports on the contents of the photograph, and so acts as another sort of intermediary. Similarly, subsequent photographs are not sent to him: one goes to his mother-in-law from his first marriage who shows it to him (1304), and the last photograph goes to his young daughter at her school (1306). This is a consistent pattern of mediation and suggests Risso's remoteness from Gracia and what is not Santa María. In that, "El infierno" is repeating a pattern familiar in other texts of Onetti in which Santa María's other is mediated by a privileged third party, for example, Vázquez and Maynard in "El álbum", and Godoy in *Para una tumba sin nombre* (all salesmen of a sort).

The mediation within the story also underlines the mediation of "El infierno"'s presentation. The narrating voice is the "nosotros" which becomes familiar in Onetti from the early 1950s. On its first appearance, the "nosotros" speaks as if on the same narrative level as Risso and Gracia:

> Cuando Risso se casó con Gracia César, nos unimos todos en el silencio, suprimimos los vaticinios pesimistas. (1294)

There is a sort of equality established here, as if the "nosotros" were also inhabitants of Santa María, even though their opinion about the marriage suggests that they know more than Risso and Gracia. Very soon, however, the "nosotros" switches status to become much more authoritative. Without alluding to any speculation, the narrator proceeds to inform the reader about Gracia's imaginings and private thoughts, about Risso's reactions to the photographs when alone and about Gracia's tricks to lure men to participate in the photographs. This is manifestly inconsistent, though not, as sometimes in Onetti, foregrounded as a problem. The switch is significant not merely because of the imposition of a masculist discourse that is associated with Santa María, but also because of the underlying framework for understanding Risso and Gracia which contrasts the past perfection of their love with the split precipitated by her relation with another man. This postulate of understanding is a familiar Onettian one involving the Imaginary polarization of ideal against catastrophe, and, although there are elements of an attempt by Risso to work the two areas together into a new understanding, the story's ending does not follow through that process: the possibility of Risso's joining Gracia or of his committing suicide are left as a continued, unresolved polarization. Living on is suspended by the story's ending with Risso's disappearance from the story (echoing Gracia's earlier), and the relapse into Santa María's discourse of incomprehension with Lanza.

*

"El álbum" and "El infierno" are interestingly related by the crucial role played in each by photographs. In both cases, the photographs are the stimulus to reassessment, they are texts deriving from key female characters which disturb male characters' views of themselves. The photographs, though very different in their content in the two stories, are (indirect) indications of realities beyond what male characters had perceived or understood, and, in that sense, their mere content is not of crucial importance. In that respect, neither Carmen Méndez nor Gracia César is apparently submissive to the male character. Both women initiate the male characters into the full risks of sexual relations, but both refuse to be limited by the males, as neither of them fully see what the world is or could be. The women characters are projected as different from these male characters, who are trapped (whether willingly [Risso], or unwillingly [Jorge]) in Santa María. Hence, in both stories it is the female characters who take the decisive action – departure – , thus forcing the male characters into a position of review, though neither manages to achieve a decisive reorientation as a result: Risso is left in a profound impasse, and Jorge narrates his account largely in complicity with his younger, inexperienced self. In that way, both of the male characters cling to structures which seem to confirm them securely as "what they are" – the stimulus that they receive is not fully appreciated. That is not to deny the obvious difference between the two male characters: Jorge desires to leave Santa María, he seeks the other (something which the implied author of "El álbum" approves of), while Risso struggles even to see that, his age having restricted his potential to dream of escape. In the end, however, both are left with the split between what they desire and what they can attain, and that space, as always, is the space of Onetti's fiction. It is a split which does not find a way to a new *modus vivendi* based on awareness of the intricate relation between desire and frustration. Despite the inclusion of female characters as apparently dynamic elements in these stories, and their seemingly positive status as the locus of other values, it is ultimately *masculine* loss, lack, and the problem of coping with *masculine* desire which both stories explore. This tension is paradoxical, for at the level of the male characters' experience, Imaginary relations are disrupted as third terms are introduced (Gracia's casual lover in El Rosario, Carmen Méndez's male friend) breaking up the Imaginary dyads. And yet, at the level of the implied author's constitution of meaning, Imaginary polarizations reappear. In both cases, the split between Santa María and other places is fundamental and unquestioned. Hence, both of the women characters return to the other whence they came, and it is a remarkably mobile other – Aberdeen, Cairo, New York, Bahía, Santiago, Lima. But that polarization only reemphasizes how static and unevolving Santa María is: the geographical split makes Santa María an easy target for negation and an easy source of entrapment. The missing dimension is dialectic, a sustained living through of the diverse elements of experience without Imaginary either/or choices.

CHAPTER 4

GOSSIP AND THE OTHER IN

"HISTORIA DEL CABALLERO DE LA ROSA Y DE LA VIRGEN

ENCINTA QUE VINO DE LILIPUT"

> – Tenemos poco de qué alimentarnos – dijo –. Y todo se declara
> valioso. Pero ésta es una vieja historia. Sólo que rara vez, por lo que sé, se ha
> dado de manera tan perfecta. De modo que el testamento anterior, dígame usted,
> ¿dejaba la fortuna a curas o parientes?
> – A parientes.
> – Y esa mañana modificó el testamento.
> – Y esa mañana modificó el testamento – repitió Ferragut. (1261-62)

This passage is a quasi-enactment of the making of "Historia". In this brief

dialogue the characters both allude to the problem of understanding the two

strangers in Santa María and also override those limitations. The dearth of

information on which to base understanding is acknowledged and also the evident

necessity to make something of every detail. But that awareness is immediately

superseded by an assimilation of the situation to a well-worn paradigm – the

difficulty is reduced by recourse to a familiar model ("una vieja historia"). The

dialogue then focuses on one detail affecting the will of doña Mina, and the (false)

understanding created by the characters is that the change in the will means that

the relatives are no longer going to inherit. But a change in the will does not

necessarily imply anything so sweeping. In the dialogue, therefore, a recognized

lack of knowledge is juxtaposed with the forging of knowledge, which misleads

not only (some of) the characters but also the reader. What the characters and the reader know and do not know are two axes of "Historia", as of several other of Onetti's texts in the 1950s and 1960s. Like *Los adioses*, "El álbum", and "Jacob", "Historia" relies on a final twist which bears directly on what has and has not been learned in the development of the story. As always, there is no shortage of gossip and story-telling in Santa María, that is one of its major occupations. Its oral culture is very strong and is in no way hindered by an apparent dearth of information, quite the reverse.

The very first sentence of the story captures the dynamic process underlying "Historia": "En el primer momento creímos los tres conocer al hombre para siempre, hacia atrás y hacia adelante" (1249). This sentence contains several important elements, above all the assumption of immediate and full knowledge (past and, somehow, also future) of the man, with the collective underpinning "nosotros" that seems to secure it. But the sentence also allows for the provisionality of that knowledge in the ambiguity of "creímos". The observation of this collective witness is not neutral for various reasons, one of which is almost immediately evident:

> – Vean – susurró Guiñazú, retrocediendo en la silla de hierro – . Miren, pero no miren demasiado. Por lo menos, no miren con avidez y, en todo caso, tengan la prudencia de desconfiar. Si miramos indiferentes, es posible que la cosa dure, que no se desvanezcan, que en algún momento lleguen a sentarse, a pedir algo al mozo, a beber, a existir de veras. (1249)

The reliability of observers so amazed is immediately open to doubt.

The story presented to the reader is based on the seeing and reporting of many inhabitants of Santa María, not all of whom are identified: "Historia" is apparently composed from a myriad of observations and reports. The unknown man and woman are observed singly or together at a dance (1251), moving around Santa María (1255), in Guiñazú's office (1257-58), at "work" with doña Mina (1260), at a birthday party (1264), on the night that doña Mina dies (1265-66), and buying flowers and laying them on her grave (1270-71). The story is presented as the piecing together of a collective practice of observing and telling:

> Alguno, cualquier de nosotros, mencionaba a la pareja, y los demás
> íbamos aportando lo que podíamos, sin preocuparnos de que fuera poco o mucho,
> como verdaderos amigos. (1253)

The collective effort seems to bind them together – the community is strengthened in the reaction to the couple. Paradoxically, at one point, there is a report on how, after the couple has left a dinner, there is no discussion of them by those that remain:

> Durante la cena, nadie preguntó quiénes eran y quién los había invitado.
> Una mujer esperó un silencio para recordar el ramo de flores que había tenido la
> muchacha en el costado izquierdo del vestido blanco. La mujer habló con
> parsimonia, sin opinar, nombrando simplemente un ramo de flores de paraíso
> sujeto al vestido por un broche de oro. (1252)

And yet, it is clear that what drives Santa María is a very sophisticated network of gossip: there is usually no satisfaction with the sort of neutral description mentioned here.

The narrator's very insistent use of the verb "saber" in various forms ("supimos", "sabíamos", "se supo"), draws attention to itself and may raise doubts about veracity and reliability. Indeed, the narrator does intercalate certain negative uses of the verb which acknowledges the uncertainty of the basis of story-telling. The narrator also talks of the privileged knowledge of señora Specht, who could, he supposes, give the rest of Santa María the key to the pair (1255). But "Historia" is inconsistent, for it appears to "know" some things which it cannot really know, while it also knows things (like Guiñazú's awareness of the content of the will) which it chooses (like Guiñazú himself) not to show (at least not before some delay). The paradoxes about "knowing" are based on a collective desire to make up a version that will account for and control the couple. The recourse to imagination and untruths is welcomed, therefore, as perfectly acceptable:

> – Bailan, son bailarines, eso puede afirmarse, y no es posible decir otra
> cosa, si hemos jurado decir solamente verdades para descubrir o formar la verdad.
> Pero no hemos jurado nada. De modo que las mentiras que pueda acercar cada
> uno de nosotros, siempre que sean de primera mano y que coincidan con la
> verdad que los tres presentimos, serán útiles y bienvenidas. (1253)

There is no commitment to absolute truth – note the equivocation between "descubrir" and "formar" in relation to "verdad". What matters is whether the account that is produced fits with what the narrator, Guiñazú and Lanza expect. The question of Santa María's values and motives in this will need to be examined shortly, but the effect of its attitude is inevitably that the desire to "know" has recourse to invention. This odd combination is made manifest by Guiñazú who acknowledges his desire and the absence of security:

> "Los imagino de noche en la sala grande, sin nadie para quien bailar, cerca del fuego y rodeados por las primeras piezas desordenadas del museo. A cambio de escucharlos, le devolvería con gusto al tipo los cincuenta pesos de los honorarios y pondría otro billete encima. A cambio de escucharlos, de saber quiénes son, de saber quiénes y cómo somos nosotros para ellos." (1267-68)

This paradigmatic juxtaposition of not-knowing/knowing, in conjunction with the gap implicit in his desire, follows a perceived "accusation" from doña Mina to Guiñazú, which explicitly derides him for not understanding, in effect for being part of Santa María:

> "Los ojos de la vieja me miraban contándome algo, seguros de que yo no era capaz de descubrir de qué se trataba; burlándose de mi incomprensión y también, anticipadamente, de lo que pudiera comprender equivocándome." (1264)

Doña Mina and the couple are evidently located out of the conceptual reach of Santa María. This, however, does not prevent the narrator from imagining what the couple do with señor and señora Specht in the privacy of their home and then informing the reader as if it were true (1255). Nor does it preclude the narrator's supposedly conveying the man's private thoughts (1266, 1277) and motives (1271), which he cannot realistically know. Ironically (and this is one of the amusing elements which "Historia" flaunts), it is not just Santa María which does not know but which makes light of that through invention and speculation, since the man himself matches this practice when doña Mina dies. He reports watching the dying woman in bed:

> "Personalmente, creo que estaba disputándose algo con una amiga de la juventud. Y después de unos diez minutos de murmullo vertiginoso se hizo indudable que la amiga, una niña casi, estaba siendo derrotada y que ella, doña Mina, iba a

quedarse para siempre con el atardecer glicinoso y jazminoso, con el hombre de
párpados lentos, rizado, un bastoncito de jacarandá en la axila." (1265-66)

This flight of fancy amply matches those in which Santa María itself indulges.

Underpinning this practice of not-knowing/knowing is a value-system. The
narrator is unusually frank about Santa María's shortcomings, and makes one of
the most direct assessments of the town in all Onetti:

A pesar de los años, de las modas y de la demografía, los habitantes de la ciudad
continuaban siendo los mismos. Tímidos y engreídos, obligados a juzgar para
ayudarse, juzgando siempre por envidia o miedo. (Lo importante, a decir de esta
gente, es que está desprovista de espontaneidad y de alegría; que sólo puede
producir amigos tibios, borrachos inamistosos, mujeres que persiguen la seguridad
y son idénticas e intercambiables como mellizas, hombres estafados y solitarios.
Hablo de los sanmarianos; tal vez los viajeros hayan comprobado que la
fraternidad humana es, en las coincidencias miserables, una verdad asombrosa y
decepcionante.) (1262)

This damning assessment has the one mitigating feature that Santa María may be
no different from the rest of the world, though that opinion itself may be no more
than a reflection of Santa María's conceit and timidity. But the idea of their
judging through envy or fear may be just as significant given the relation of Santa
María to the newly arrived couple. For example, when there is a chance that they
will be evicted from the Spechts' house by the sea, Guiñazú explains to the man
that the law could protect the couple, but that the town will do exactly what it
wants regardless of the law:

"... le dije con voz soñolienta que todo lo anterior correspondía fielmente a la
teoría de derecho aplicable al caso, pero que, en la sucia práctica sanmariana,
sería suficiente que Specht hablara por teléfono con el jefe del Destacamento para
que él y la joven señora que esperaba un niño fueran trasladados desde el chalet
a un punto cualquiera situado a dos leguas del límite de la ciudad... " (1258)

The vulnerability of the outsiders is quite clear and also the hostility of Santa
María: the couple is disdained by the town because they are "known" to be living
on others' money: "Sabíamos que estaban viviendo del dinero de doña Mina; y
quedó establecido que, en este caso, el pecado era más sucio e imperdonable"
(1262-63). The town's disapproval is resoundingly demonstrated in the refusal of
its elite to go to the birthday party that the couple arrange for doña Mina (1263).

But some measure of the town's moral shortcomings is apparent when this hostility is superseded by a new attitude of hypocritical tolerance when it is thought that the couple is going to inherit from doña Mina:

> "Empezaron a ofrecerle [a la pareja] sus casas y créditos ilimitados. Especulando con el testamento, claro, haciendo prudentes o audaces inversiones de prestigios y mercaderías, apostando a favor de la pareja." (1267)

Future business may depend on good relations with the potentially wealthy couple.

In general, such acceptance is not part of Santa María's attitude to outsiders, since their value system is powerful and exclusive. The man and the woman are archetypal strangers who act as irritants to action, or, in this case, defensive reaction. On their first appearance, the narrator jokes that the man behaves as though he were a stranger on the planet (1250), and Lanza has great difficulty defining what the woman is:

> "Demasiado próxima a la perfección para ser una enana, demasiado segura y demagógica para ser una niña disfrazada de mujer." (1249-50)

These initial problems with the strangers are indirectly underlined when it turns out that the couple's contact in Santa María, the "bisnieto de Latorre", is in Europe. Their link with the town is thus absent, significantly being outside it just as they have been. There is, therefore, no internal figure to lend them recognition, and they are utterly isolated, at first at least. In confirmation of this, they live in places with connotations of outsider status. They soon move from El Plaza and into one of Specht's "casitas de techo rojo de la playa" (1254), a location which is familiar in Onetti and seems to indicate marginality on the coast outside the town. After being ejected from the "casita", they move on to live with doña Mina in Las Casuarinas, which is, however, very similar as a location to the beach chalet: "Las Casuarinas está bastante alejada de la ciudad, hacia el norte, sobre el camino que lleva a la costa" (1260). Later it is said that: "Vivían en Las Casuarinas, desterrados de Santa María y del mundo" (1262), and the notion of being exiled is echoed in various references to their disappearing from view (for example, 1258). To be invisible, to be down on the coast, is to be outside the spectrum of behaviour and acceptability of Santa María. Hence, not surprisingly, the pair are likened by the narrator to the prostitutes whose subversive invasion of the town is narrated in *Juntacádaveres* (1262).

In fact, the couple are a paradoxical mixture of invisibility and spectacular visibility. When they are seen they appear larger than life, and they seem to be playing elaborate, artificial roles. So they are described as acting the parts of servants in the Spechts' house (1255), or the man acts the part of an "invitation deliverer" (1264), and they are said to be putting on productions of the imaginary plays, *La vida será siempre hermosa* and *Farsa del amor perfecto* (1254). These ironic theatrical metaphors have more extended treatments on two occasions. When the couple move into Las Casuarinas it is as if the rehearsals are over and the full artifice of performance can begin:

> "Instalados como para siempre en la capilla de Las Casuarinas, repitiendo ahora, día y noche, en condiciones ideales respecto a decorados, público y taquilla, la obra cuyo ensayo general habían hecho en casa de Specht." (1259-60)

So, when Ferragut goes to visit doña Mina, he finds them in an elaborately posed pastoral picture:

> "Dejé el coche en la parte alta del camino y los vi casi en seguida, como en un cuadro pequeño, de esos de marco ancho y dorado, inmóviles y sorprendentes, mientras yo iba bajando hacia ellos. El en último plano, con un traje azul de jardinero, hecho de medida, juraría; arrodillado frente a un rosal, mirándolo sin tocarlo, haciendo sonrisas de probada eficacia contra hormigas y pulgones; rodeado, en beneficio del autor del cuadro, por los atributos de su condición: la pala, el rastrillo, la tijera, la máquina de cortar pasto." (1260)

The implication of these metaphors of performance is that the couple are untrustworthy tricksters, who could only convince the gullible. The other consistent element of performance which the narrator underlines in presenting them is their dancing. There are four occasions on which their dancing is mentioned and it is the subject of quite precise description on three of them (1251-52 in the Club Progreso, 1256 in the "cafetín", and 1264 at doña Mina's birthday party). It is clear that the dancing is seen as a spectacle for others to watch as well as being overtly sexual. In his description of one dance, Lanza is openly disapproving:

"Y tampoco aquello pasaba de danza tribal, de rito de esponsales, de las vueltas
y las detenciones con que la novia rodea y liga al varón, de las ofertas que se
interrumpen para irritar a la demanda... Bailaban así porque estaban los demás,
pero bailaban sólo para ellos, en secreto, protegidos de toda intromisión. El
muchacho tenía la camisa abierta hasta el ombligo; y todos nosotros podíamos
verle la felicidad de estar sudando, un poco borracho y en trance, la felicidad de
ser contemplado y de hacerse esperar." (1256-57)

As Lanza describes it, the dance overtly solicits the gaze of Santa María, but is
also only for the couple themselves, a formulation which concisely captures their
status both inside and apart from Santa María. It is the importance of dancing
which leads to their being designated with a specific role, since they are cast as
"bailarines" (1253). Such is Santa María's commitment to seeing the couple as
performing images of themselves that Guiñazú even imagines their setting up a
museum for doña Mina, in order to create a picture of her for her public to view
(1266-67).

The question is whether this "performing of images", their spectacular
visibility, is part of the couple's behaviour or merely a reaction and projection on
to them by Santa María, the elaboration of its network of defensive gossip. Given
the absence of any independent information, this "performing" by the couple seems
most likely to be Santa María's defensive projection against the troubling intrusion.
Hence their alternating invisibility and high visibility merely reflect the standpoint
of Santa María, its ignorance and uncertainty. These are registered at the very start
of the story in the doubts over the couple's substance. In their dialogue concerning
the couple, the narrator, Guiñazú and Lanza wonder whether they are real, whether,
if they stare too hard, the couple will disappear. The doubts over the couple's
reality are certainly not cleared up by the rest of the story; and it is useful to note
that Guiñazú's warning – "'... tengan la prudencia de desconfiar'" (1249) – might
be equally well addressed to the reader. This is just one of several self-referential
and demystifying remarks contained in the story: information cannot be accepted
too readily.

In fact, as the story develops, the couple are rendered bizarre by Santa
María. This is the function of the story's grotesque humour. This grotesqueness

is most apparent in the case of the woman. With her, there is much concentration on physical appearance. Her size is the first arresting characteristic, leading, as we have seen, to confusion as to whether she is a dwarf, a girl or a woman: she defies Santa María's categorization. But that oddness is compounded by both her clothes and her movement. She twice wears dresses with a degree of sexual daring that shocks the town (1249, 1256); and her dancing has great physical presence, especially as her pregnancy develops:

> ... ella aún más lenta, milagrosamente no alterada de veras por la enorme barriga que iba creciendo a cada vuelta de la danza sabida de memoria, que podía bailar sin errores, sorda y ciega. (1264)

Her walking is similarly distorted and elaborate, the foetus she carries being increasingly mentioned in the story so that it almost comes to form a trio with the man and woman (1262). The final, dismissive view of her finds her inelegantly waiting on the port, her legs splayed to accommodate the now eleven (sic) month pregnancy (1270).

The grotesqueness of the man resides more in his manner than in his physical appearance. He is noted above all for his extreme courtesy, whether directed to the woman (1250), to doña Mina (1260), to the narrator (1265), or to the women at the dance in the Club Progreso (1251). In this last example, there is a mimicking verbal play of excessive elaboration, including pseudo-stylish foreign borrowings, parallelisms and a subtle parenthetical qualification:

> En cuanto a él, lánguido y largo, lánguido y entusiasta, otra vez lánguido y con el privilegio de la ubicuidad, bailó solamente con las mujeres que podían hablarle – aunque no lo hicieran – de la incomprensión de los maridos y del egoísmo de los hijos, de otros bailes con valses, *one steps* y el pericón final, con limonadas y *clericots* aguados. (1251)

Besides this, he is striking to Santa María for his persistent optimism and smiling face (something he shares with the woman). This is seen as conveying his belief in life's indestructible happiness:

> El hombre se quitó el saco y lo puso sobre la espalda de la muchacha, casi sin necesidad de movimientos, sin dejar de venerarla y decirle con la sonrisa que vivir es la única felicidad posible. (1251)

This sort of sly comment on the man's supposed optimism is seen again in Ferragut's commentary on his gardening:

> "Había estado arañando la tierra hasta ensuciarse las uñas y ahora se las miraba preocupado, pero sin perder la confianza: 'Vamos a salvar casi todo, doña Mina. Como le había dicho, los plantaron demasiado juntos. Pero no importa.' No importaba, todo era fácil; resucitar rosales secos o cambiar agua en vino." (1260)

This cynically deflating remark captures the spirit of Santa María's resentment and insecurity. Guiñazú is much more candid than Ferragut about the unsettling effect of the man:

> "Pero cuando sentí que mi antipatía sin causa no podía sostenerse y que la iban sustituyendo la curiosidad y una forma casi impersonal de la envidia; cuando admití que lo que cualquiera hubiera llamado insolencia o descaro podía ser otra cosa, extraordinaria y casi mágica por lo rara, comprendí sin dudas que mi visitante era el tipo de la camisa amarilla y la rosita en el ojal que habíamos visto aquella noche de lluvia en la vereda del Universal." (1257)

The couple's presence profoundly disconcerts the town, and its reaction is simply a different facet of the violent reaction to the intrusion of Larsen and the prostitutes in *Juntacadáveres*: it is a defence in both cases. In addition, the aggression implicit in the grotesque projections of Santa María might be linked to narcissism insofar as it seems to result from a collective insecurity in the face of the perceived threat from the other. If in "Historia", the caricature is the sign of this perceived threat, it is one of the rare examples in Onetti where an intrusion from the outside destabilizes the whole town rather than affecting a more or less responsive and appropriately located individual (for example, "El álbum", or "El infierno").

It is not just the couple who are singled out for this grotesque treatment, for even those associated with them are included in the process. In doña Mina's case this is hardly surprising. Indeed, the obvious logic of her liaison with the couple is that she is already an outsider to the town, though living in close proximity to it. So in going to live with her, the couple find themselves close to scandal. Doña Mina is part of Santa María's elite, and her father was clearly wealthy, but she has a dubious past as far as the town is concerned. That "past" is a short period "entre la pubertad y los veinte años" (1259) when she ran away from Santa María on sexual adventures. This marks doña Mina, in the town's terms, for life: she is an unconventional outsider who almost disappeared from view. She became the subject of gossip (1259), just as the couple do. Hence she now lives in relative isolation in old age outside the town.[1] If doña Mina is therefore the element in Santa María that can recognize the couple, she acts in some sort as the replacement of the "bisnieto de Latorre". Her location close to the couple goes so far, therefore, as to allow her to express hostility to Guiñazú and the inadequacy of his understanding/conjecturing of what is going on (1264): she sets him well apart from herself with her disdain. But her will does not confirm the liaison with the couple: she does not leave all her money to them, but conventionally leaves it to her distant relatives. She may be an outsider but she maintains certain links with Santa María: she has returned to it after all. But the links are tenuous. The treatment of her dog, for example, constitutes an attempt by the town to belittle and marginalize her. The story carefully uses a variety of adjectives to describe the dog (no matter which voice is narrating in a particular passage). However varied the adjectives, they all heavily underline the dog's repulsive state. It is called "el asqueroso perro lanudo" (1260), "el perro agónico y legañoso" (1261), "el repugnante perro incontinente" (1261), "el perro hediondo" (1264), and "el perro moribundo y diarreico" (1270). Each time the grotesqueness of the dog's state is enhanced by the extreme care which doña Mina lavishes on it, seemingly oblivious to its condition.[2]

The liaison between doña Mina and the couple is further indicated by a similar multiple treatment of the names of all three. In this respect, doña Mina's treatment is restrained, but she is subjected to something of the same plurality as the others. On one page alone where her past is detailed, she is called: doña Mina

---

[1] This is similar to Moncha in "La novia robada", whose family also had money and to whose house, cut off from Santa María behind high walls, she returns having left the town.

[2] An identical state of decrepitude also characterizes doña Mina's horse (1263).

Fraga, doña Herminia Fraga, doña Mina, la muchacha, Herminia and doña Herminita (1259), before the story continues with doña Mina in alternation with "la vieja" when she has finally returned to Santa María. If the diversity of naming is a sign of the status of the outsider, then it is little wonder that the couple are given a multiplicity of names throughout. The man is called: "el hombre", "el caballero de la rosa", Ricardo, "el tipo", "el muchacho", "el hombre de la rosita en el ojal", and "el muchacho de la rosa". The woman is called: "la enana", "la mujer", "la mujercita", "la muchacha", "la enana encinta", "la enana perfecta", "la pequeña", and "la preñada". In this way, the further and detailed naming in the story's title says everything: it is bizarre and aims at exhaustion. The whole story is summed up in the title to the extent that it is about the desperate attempt to name the other so as to mitigate its effect and marginalize it. But the deep structure of "Historia" is a sliding of the referent under Santa María's signifiers and signifieds. As in other of Onetti's texts, the referent (despite efforts to the contrary) cannot be secured, and "Historia" becomes a floating tissue of contingent meanings. This is another example of the insistence of textuality in Onetti: the text that Santa María constructs out of the other.

"Historia" is, therefore, a story of foreign bodies being written over, semanticized at all costs and finally expelled, apparently in defeat. The defeat of the couple is only apparent because the "threat" that they represent is constituted from within Santa María as a function of its ideology and quest for stable identity. More obviously, the defeat is only apparent in that the couple's strategy of trying to inherit from doña Mina is assumed by the town: that is part of the "scandal" that they are represented to embody and which is the fertile ground for gossip. Their "strategy" is by no means proved even at the end when the man spends the five hundred pesos that doña Mina does leave them on the pile of flowers for her grave. The narrator describes the flowers as "la montaña insolente y despareja que expresaba para él [el hombre] y para la muerta lo que nosotros no pudimos saber nunca con certeza" (1271). However, it could be that the town's assumptions about the couple's motives are as erroneous as its assumption that doña Mina's will has been altered in order to leave everything to them. The judge, Canabal, sees the contents of the new will as a joke at the couple's expense (1269-70), but they could equally well be a joke at the expense of Santa María and its possibly misguided perceptions and gossip. Santa María assumes itself to know, but all that is certain is its commitment to a collective identity, the "nosotros", which is an Imaginary construct set up against the other (the couple). What is not in doubt is the force of the Santa María's search for a solidarity of respectability and power, which looks like a fiction built on the policing of admission to and exclusion from the town.

The paradox at the end of "Historia" (which recalls "El álbum" and *Los adioses*) is that, while deploying and ironizing the town's mistakes and insecurity, the story itself is equally reliant on producing misapprehensions in the reader. For the twist at the end to be effective, the reader must have been induced to read in a certain way and so believe that Santa María is right about the will (if not also about the couple's motives). This tactic is somewhat problematic: "Historia" ironizes the town's assumptions while also using the object of its irony to achieve its own effect. There is no shortage of story-telling in Santa María, and "Historia" itself relies on the town's own dubious telling of tales for its impact. Consequently, it is no accident that my reading repeats this pattern since the very repetition exemplifies the transferential power between text and analyst. It is only in pointing this out that the apparently transparent mirroring of the story initially assumed by analysis can be broken. This analysis has traced what it sees as the story's logic and finally reveals an internal tension (the reliance on the object of irony), and that movement is not entirely dissimilar to the story's own effort to create a sudden deepening of reflexive awareness with the twist concerning the will. The question is: once that process of reflexivity has been set in motion, can the analysis ever escape it and take a stable grasp of the story? The answer would seem to be "no", since the effort of the analysis to see its own assumptions is an example of a reflexivity which can never fully mirror itself, but only posit a movement towards such a condition.

CHAPTER 5
NEGOTIATING THE TEXT:
"LA CARA DE LA DESGRACIA"

In the first instance this analysis proposes to elaborate a reading of "Cara". But what it has ultimately to recognize is that reading is not simply a process of attempting to pinpoint and interpret intrinsic textual features, but is rather a negotiation in which networks of meaning are assembled, undermined and revised. In fact, the reading of "Cara" proposed here is particularly fluid, so that in the end the analysis is forced to confront the question not only of how to read "Cara", but of how "Cara" interrogates reading and asserts its power not to be interpreted.

*

Arturo

The narrator is formed as a character in a network of characters consisting of Arturo, Julián, the girl and Betty. Arturo is of least importance in this network, but he is useful in establishing a sense of the narrator's past since he alludes to experience that he has shared with the narrator and since they occupy the same room in the hotel. Given the signifying capacity of spaces in Onetti, the fact that the two characters initially occupy the same room suggests an equivalence between them. But there is in fact an interplay of equivalence and difference here since, although they know each other well, the narrator's reaction to Julián's death has created a break, signified by Arturo's utter incomprehension. The extent to which the narrator is changing from his past self is suggested with Arturo's departure and return to his normal life and work: he leaves the narrator behind to confront an experience in which he can play no role of equivalence. Arturo returns to his old routine of work and male chauvinism, while the narrator (as we shall see) puts himself into a wholly different space: the beach. This sort of differential relationship is central to the character network, but will need to be treated in more detail in respect of the other characters.

*

Julián

The narrator's attitude to Julián at the start of the text and apparently for some years before is of his own superiority over him. He looks down on Julián and is dismissive of what he takes to be his conformism, his quietness and his having grown old. The narrator's state of mind concerning Julián's suicide is not a break with this attitude since his acute sense of guilt derives from his feeling that he had introduced an idea to Julián with which he could not cope: Julián is seen as the victim of the narrator's worldly advice. And the idea of Julián as victim clearly maintains the hierarchy between them.

At the beginning of "Cara", the narrator is in an acute state of mourning – he is dejected, has lost all interest in the world, is indifferent to others, is unable to act, and feels tied to the fact of Julián's death by his own perceived responsibility.[1] It is through the relationship with the girl that the narrator seems to reorient himself away from the obsession with Julián. Hence the burning of the newspaper relating to Julián is a sign of his liberation from the past and corresponds to his apparently reaching a state of contentment.

However, this apparent reorientation is arrested by the arrival of Betty, a figure from Julián's past. Retrospectively she changes the whole nature of the narrator's relationship with Julián. Betty tells the narrator that he is not responsible for giving Julián the dubious idea for making money and therefore not

---

[1] See Freud 1957b, 237-58.

guilty of causing his suicide. This is because Julián had been carrying out a complex fraud with his employers' money long before the narrator had suggested his idea to him. Betty's information utterly repositions Julián and the narrator: Julián is no longer the pathetic victim worthy only to be looked down upon affectionately, for he becomes a rather cynical figure who had been living on the criminal margins for some time. Moreover, Julián's relationship with the prostitute, Betty, fits with this non-conformity – it connotes anti-familial marginality. In addition, Betty informs the narrator that Julián had laughed at his innocent suggestion about making money: where the narrator had cast himself in a position of superiority and knowledge in respect of Julián, Betty's information now places *him* firmly in the position of the naive conformist. The respective positions are completely reversed. This is characteristic of the differential mobility of the characters in "Cara". There are no fixed positions: the characters shift and redefine one another. This mobility leads to the posing of the question of "who has reliable knowledge?", for the narrator had presumed himself to know about Julián and himself, but that is a prelude to the discovery that real knowledge might be rather more complex.

Most intriguingly and paradoxically, the formation of the relationship with the girl comes to seem less like the desire to throw off the guilty obsession with Julián and more like following in his footsteps. The narrator's move towards marginality via the relationship with the girl is equivalent to the relationship of Julián with Betty: both are anti-familial, and both lead to confrontations with the law. The initial equivalence between the narrator and Arturo is replaced by the slide towards equivalence between the narrator and Julián.

*

The Girl

If the narrator's relationship with Julián is unstable and shifts radically, that with the girl is only defined clearly temporarily and deceptively. The girl is a function of the narrator's equivocal projection of desire on to her.

In her initial appearances (on the road outside the hotel and in the hotel restaurant), the girl seems to be sexually enticing for the narrator. She takes shape in the text as an object of male gazes and fantasies. Hence with Arturo she is given meaning within his childish, chauvinist categories as an "available female" (1342-43). With the waiter she is explained by a story of others' (that is, adolescents') sexual adventurism (1343). With the narrator she is chosen as an object of desire and self-recuperation.

The point is that there is no reliable, independent information about the girl. Even at the end, the police fit her into the convenient category of the abused adolescent and show paternalist horror at the treatment she has received. The girl actually appears to stand apart from all these male efforts to appropriate her. That apartness is signified by her deafness and therefore by her oblique relation to speech and communication which precludes simple contact. It is particularly significant that the narrator has to be told that the girl is deaf: his failure to appreciate this crucial fact about her demonstrates the strength of his projection on to her of his own desire.

However, the lack of knowledge about the girl does not preclude (indeed it is the basis for) the evolution of the narrator's desire. The narrator's relationship to the girl (that is, specifically not *their* relationship) progresses rapidly. Initially she is an object of visual pleasure (chapter one), and then she becomes a yardstick by which to judge the past: "Traté de medir mi pasado y mi culpa con la vara que acababa de descubrir: la muchacha delgada y de perfil hacia el horizonte, su edad corta e imposible..." (1333). The linkage between the girl and the narrator's past and guilt is a crucial step towards the establishing of an equivalence between her and Julián, an equivalence which is first mentioned as a form without the specification of its content: "Entonces... me sorprendí vinculando a mi hermano muerto con la muchacha de la bicicleta" (1340). When a content is suggested it is rather vague and sentimental: "... ambos, por tan diversos caminos, coincidían en una deseada aproximación a la muerte, a la definitiva experiencia. Julián, no siendo; ella, la muchacha de la bicicleta, buscando serlo todo y con prisas" (1341). This equivalence is established in the narrator's mind before Arturo suggests that the girl could be used to replace Julián (1343). It is as if the girl were placed in the gap left by Julián's absence. It is not that she is a simple substitute, but an object chosen to try and exorcise his acute mourning. The narrator transfers on to the present object the fierce negative emotions relating to the absent object, and in the process renders them positive. Crucially this results in the throwing off of the constricting weight of guilt:

> Era indudable que la muchacha me había liberado de Julián y de muchas otras ruinas y escorias que la muerte de Julián representaba y había traído a la superficie; era indudable que yo, desde una media hora atrás, la necesitaba y continuaría necesitándola. (1348)

The transference is achieved, his need seems to be satisfied, temporarily at least. The obsessive gaze at the girl replaces the obsessive thought about Julián.

The fixing of and investment in the girl by the male narrator is crucial to the story. For most of it she is not seen independently of his desire, but as a vehicle for the repositioning of the self.[2] His strong response to her is a function of his prior negative relation to Julián: this is what gives context and meaning to his view of the girl.[3] She is idealized and sentimentalized by the narrator as representing new meaning: "Deseaba quedarme para siempre en paz junto a la muchacha y cuidar de su vida" (1342). And yet this idealization combines with evidently sordid details. For example, their sexual intercourse is perfunctory and raises questions about whose pleasure is involved since the incident has certain undertones of rape. It seems, in fact, to correspond to the perennial fantasy in Onetti's male protagonists about the pure, female adolescent who is hardly known

---

[2] See Millington 1987, 358-77 for a discussion of this phenomenon in Onetti's work generally.

[3] In "Mourning and Melancholia" (1957b), Freud talks of the exultation and joy that can be experienced after psychic energy is redirected and bound to a new object having been previously bound negatively elsewhere (254).

and yet who is unquestioningly sexually available to the first initiative taken.[4] In
a strong Freudian reading one might speculate that the euphoric attachment of
emotions to the girl has regressive elements, since it seems to be an identification
with a symbol of the narrator's own adolescent past – an Imaginary self-image or
ego-ideal. This view would coincide with the narcissistic facet of the relationship
to which I shall return later.

However, the imposition on the girl of the narrator's desire is ultimately
revealed to have no foundation. She eludes him, she slides out of his grasp at the
end. This is the point at which her independence of the narrator becomes manifest.
The narrator's satisfaction with the relationship is fleeting and equivocal and poses
real questions about what actually happened when they were in the woods. Her
otherness to the narrator, her resistance to appropriation, is signified at the end by
her body, which has been the vehicle for so much of the narrator's thinking about
her. In death the body loses its value as an object of desire – it is unrecognizable.
Hence, the narrator barely even sees it lying in the shed – he has to be told to look
at it. Whereas before his eyes had moved across the body in an infatuated
examination, now the description of the body comes from a third party, breaking
the narrator's illusory control of it: a policeman reads out a medical description.
The terminology renders the body an alien object, it is no longer available to his
desiring gaze. Nor, crucially, does it respond to his kisses: he kissed it "por piedad
y amor", but the body "permanecía inmóvil' (1357). It is one of the possible
paradoxes at the end of "Cara" that the very effort to appropriate the girl through
sexual intercourse might be read as what destroys her.

*

The Narrator

The narrator begins "Cara" with an apparently fixed and closed relationship
to the dead Julián, but ultimately his character is as susceptible to change as the

---

[4] Clear examples are Annie Glaeson in *La vida breve*, Rita in *Para una tumba sin nombre*,
Nora in *Tierra de nadie* and Victoria in *Para esta noche*.

girl's or Julián's. At the beginning, Julián is all-important – apart from Arturo he is the only point of reference. The narrator's obsessive reading of the newspaper article about Julián's death is a sign of his intense and exclusive attachment. The minimal narrative contained in "Cara" relies on the change that takes place in the narrator, on his mobility. This involves his gradually ceasing to feel guilty about Julián and the choice of a new object of (apparently) fixed attention. The transformation that occurs as a result of the relation to the girl is quite marked. After his initial gloominess and self-questioning, the narrator reaches a state of calm and confidence (and solitude – a point to which I shall return) when on the beach with the girl. After sexual intercourse with the girl, the narrator feels transformed, energetic, in control, and above all, happy. This is the precondition for his burning of the newspaper (with its story about the flight of Julián) the following morning, which is a strong sign of his reorientation. And part of the change in him is his capacity to feel euphoric. Talking to Betty on the morning after his experiences on the beach he feels a sense of his own youthfulness: "... había vuelto a ser joven y ni siquiera a mí mismo tenía que dar explicaciones" (1352). His calm attitude in dealing with the police is consistent with this newly emerged sense of identity.

These changes in the narrator are not without problems as I shall show, but they do demonstrate the mobility of the "yo". Interestingly, the changes in him take him nearer to Julián just as they also take him further away from him. The narrator fights off his guilty obsession with Julián and in doing so he moves to follow him into marginality. The narrator is on holiday on the beach, away from the city and work, and from their binding constraints – Arturo has to leave the narrator behind in order to return to normal life.[5] And the link with the girl, especially in the sexual intercourse with her, is as marginal a relationship as that between Julián and the prostitute Betty. Revealingly, it is only after the narrator has had sexual intercourse with the girl and so decisively shifted his position that

---

[5] This change while away from the city on the beach is reminiscent of "Casa".

he receives the crucial information about Julián's real marginal status. It is as if it were only when he has moved closer to Julián that he can understand that Julián was not the dull conformist that he previously thought: his new position creates the possibility of new understanding. So the narrator moves closer to the reality of Julián just as he moves further away from emotional involvement with him. Julián and the narrator slide in their mutual relations. And yet the narrator is disturbed by the new awareness of Julián since it robs him of his feeling of superiority – it removes his hope of simply grasping Julián as he was. And that is a problem which is repeated with the girl.

Looking specifically at the narrator's relation to the girl, two psychoanalytic categories are useful for understanding its dynamic: the gaze and narcissism.[6]

The gaze   The girl is the object of the narrator's gaze, in the sense that he finds in her a focus for his desire. More particularly, the object of the gaze is the girl's body – she provides an open field for his enquiring eye. As such, "Cara" is posited on a phallocentric hierarchy. The overwhelming importance of the girl's body is evident in the opening chapter where she is described in minute detail, a description which is full of implications as to the movements of the narrator's eye. The same relationship of body and eye is repeated in chapter two in the hotel restaurant.

The sheer dominance of the male gaze is underlined by the emptiness of the girl's look. She does look at the narrator, and her look is not negligible since he does once find it hard to sustain (1342). But the eye contact of the two serves only to establish that *she* knows that *he* looks. The reader is directed by the dominant gaze of the narrator and so too of the text, and we and he know that she sees him and sees his gaze, but there is no content in her returned look. Chapter one establishes the girl as the object of the gaze, an object that registers that it is

---

[6] On narcissism see Freud 1957c. On scopophilia see Freud 1957d, and on the gaze see Lacan 1979, chapters 6-9.

seen, like a mirror which returns a gaze but devoid of all independent motivation.

The collapsing of independent subjectivity into the object of the gaze is a move to fix the object for the purposes of self-identification. The girl becomes the surface on which the narrator can fix his gaze. The emptiness of the girl's gaze is the absence of his body – this is never in question or in view in the story, it is not a field of enquiry for the girl. Here, as in so much of Onetti's writing, there is no space for female desire. The empty look of the girl is not restricting and therefore is not a disabling element for the male fantasy.

The problem arises for the narrator when he is the object of a real look which imposes itself on him. This look is that of the police at the end of "Cara". The police position the narrator as guilty, or, rather, they return him to a position of guilt, not for the death of Julián now but for that of the girl. His near-obliviousness to the police is a sign of his absorption in his Imaginary self-image mobilized via the girl. But the police's look, particularly in the hotel when they first appear (1354-55), troubles this illusion: his euphoria and quasi-regression to adolescence are restrained by the enforcers of the law, of the Symbolic.

The true dimensions of his fantasy are apparent in the final scene in the shed. Here the narrator is confronted with the dead body of the girl, but there is no gaze from him now. He virtually refuses even to look at her (1356). In death there is no object or mirroring reflection for his fantasy. The girl now unequivocally eludes his desire. And in the pressure set up by the police's look the narrator is returned to a position of tension. He is caught up between the flow of his own desire and the restraint of imposed responsibility. Despite the relation to the girl, the narrator has not overcome the on-going dialectic of desire and lack: the subject strives to fulfil itself via the appropriation of an object-world, but only reencounters its incompleteness, the resistance of the other.

Narcissism   The change that takes place in the narrator derives from the effort to find his own pleasure, and is fundamentally a move away from the real world and the characters that might be said to share it.   His euphoric contentment after sexual intercourse with the girl provides the illusion, not of a shared relationship, but of a full self-image.   Typically of an Onetti protagonist, the narrator overestimates the power of the self and its identifications.   It is no accident that "Cara" takes place in an almost complete social vacuum, a precondition of the narrator's narcissistic self-sufficiency.   That phenomenon is nowhere clearer than in the scene on the dunes when the narrator is walking alone after sexual intercourse with the girl.   It is evident that the climax of his experience is his walking, not the moments spent with the girl – the pleasure comes alone:

> Abandoné la orilla y empecé a subir y bajar las dunas, resbalando en la arena fría que me entraba chisporroteando en los zapatos, apartando con las piernas los arbustos, corriendo casi, rabioso y con alegría que me había perseguido durante años y ahora me daba alcance, excitado como si no pudiera detenerme nunca, riendo en el interior de la noche ventosa, subiendo y bajando a la carrera las diminutas montañas... (1349)

The adolescent girl has proved to be the vehicle for the idealistic new identification: the narcissistic regression to youth.   And yet her death removes her as a fixed object, and her absence unfixes the effort to create the narcissistic self-image.   As Lacan puts it: *"what I look at is never what I wish to see"* (Lacan 1979, 103).   Reality eludes desire.

*

The Ending

Betty and the Police   The narrator's relations with these two sets of characters are as disconcerting and as shifting as with the other characters in the network around him.   The narrator has certain rigid presuppositions about Betty simply because he is aware that she was a prostitute whom Julián knew.   His attitude towards her is arrogant and dismissive: "Me acerqué al sillón y ofrecí mis excusas a la mujer [Betty], a aquella desusada manera de la suciedad y la desdicha" (1350); "... estuve mirando con alegría aquella basura en el sillón, aquella maltratada inmundicia que se recostaba, inconsciente, sobre la mañana apenas nacida" (1350-51). In part his arrogance is a function of his new state of mind on the clear morning having found a way of casting off the shadow of Julián – there is a certain narcissism in his self-righteous superiority. But his presumption that he knows about Julián and Betty is utterly misplaced. Betty knows more, far more, than him of the reality of Julián's life and her knowledge reverses the positions that the narrator has assumed. When it is revealed, her knowledge destroys his pretensions to superiority and is the beginning of the disturbances to his euphoria. The only way in which he can protect himself is by rudely dismissing Betty from his room.

At first, the narrator has a strange interaction with the police. The police seem to be in agreement as to how to deal with him, and he passively complies with them. But nothing is overtly discussed, and at the hotel the police certainly do not act as if they suspect him of murder. After the reading of the medical report in the shed, however, one of the policemen suddenly becomes aggressive and accusatory, explicitly linking the narrator to the murder. This is as disconcerting a shift as that which changes the relation between the narrator and Betty. The sudden switch to aggression fits the police into a more controlling and repressive frame, as they try to position the narrator as guilty. Their identification with conventional law and respectability is emphasized now by the mention of the family and the church – one policeman crosses himself (1358). The police may be seen as the third term of the Symbolic which breaks open the Imaginary dyad of the relation of the narrator to the girl. As the agents of the Symbolic they disrupt the Imaginary unity of that relation. And this is something which the narrator simply cannot ignore or dismiss – there is no simple sidestepping of the constraints which they impose. Via the police's fixing, by their look at him, he is redefined as a guilty man, not now for Julián's death but for the girl's. The vital difference now is that he occupies the same criminal zone as Julián.

In this sort of metaphorical reading of the ending of "Cara", the girl's death might be read as the loss of the object of the narrator's desire, thus reemphasizing the absence of satisfaction and of plenitude. In death the girl's status as marginal is destroyed – her appropriation by sexual intercourse for the adult male destroys her idealization. She is destroyed for his fantasy as he tries to realize it. She is not possessed, and his desire can only slide on to other objects.

Enigma Against the grain of the normal narrative patterning of posing an enigma and then resolving it, "Cara" ends with a crucial enigma. The enigma at the end of "Cara" is "Who is responsible for the girl's death?" The story that the narrator has told in "Cara" does not indicate that he himself is responsible. It is clear from what he tells the reader that when he left the girl she was alive (1348). But the narrator also stresses that he was the only person about on the beach later. In this case the narrator does not assume the guilt as he did with Julián's death, although, in line with his newly found indifference, he does not bother to put forward any self-defence either. However, the new-found indifference does not allow him to ignore the death. His wishfulfilling relation to the girl is constrained by it and the precise nature of his final position is left open. If one takes the narrator to be guilty on the Symbolic level, one might link the sexual intercourse with the girl's death, such that the trauma of adult experience is seen to destroy what the girl represented: what the narrator wants, his regressive desire for lost youth, is precisely what destroys her. But it is in trying to read the ending in this way that the text starts to pose certain questions which undermine the reading from within.

                                        *

Reading

        The reading developed above with the use of certain psychoanalytic concepts is fundamentally and implicitly posited on the conventional critical proposition of seeking and trying to project a coherent analysis. But, in the context created by this reading, the text can now be seen as sending a signal that such a coherent analysis is problematic. The reading tries to account for and fix the meaning of the text, but it finds that the text begins to unravel such fixity and so opens up a space for rereading and revision. In other words, the critic's Imaginary does not triumph. Ultimately, the textuality of "Cara" resists meaning: like all readings (but particularly those employing the powerful strategies of psychoanalysis), the one offered here tends to lead (more or less unwittingly) to a repression of the text's textuality, its otherness.[7] What needs to be recognized is that the dynamic forces at work in the text and in reading are those of desire – the narrator's and the critic's – , desire for stability and identity. But what both the narrator and the critic of "Cara" discover is that no simple stability and identity are available.

There are certain specific difficulties with the above reading via psychoanalysis. The reading treats the death of the girl abstractly or symbolically, which is a break with its previous realistic mode, and this shift may seem arbitrary and unconvincing. In other words, the reading fails to cope with the *reality* of the death, its literality. The problem is that if the narrator did not kill the girl, it seems at the very least paradoxical that her death is read as illuminating his position and experience. In short, the reading does not get close to the main enigma of the story, namely "who killed the girl?". Not does it seem able to pinpoint why the story leaves this particular gap of information and what possible ideological explanation there might be. A different negotiation of the text would be needed to achieve that. It would require a reading of "Cara" within the socio-cultural environment of the River Plate in order to show why the concrete reality of the (possible) rape and murder of a girl are passed over in silence when a masculine identity crisis is being articulated.[8]

In the light of this faltering, the reading would be unthinking if it failed to see the inherent critique of its own practice emerging from its interaction with the

---

[7] See Felman 1977 for a detailed exploration of this phenomenon.

[8] This would not be a more convincing reading of "Cara", but it would articulate a crucial silence in the story.

text. For the objective of this reading (that is, to grasp the text's meaning) reenacts the problematic objective of the narrator (that is, to grasp the girl, to achieve the object of his desire). The desire for a full reading is frustrated by the text's refusal to mean. And this is a reality of non-grasping, such that critical "success", critical "making sense", seems to be a function of the Imaginary. The reading proposed is a product of the critic's Imaginary in that it tries to operate dyadically and reflectively. This would be equally true of a non-committal, liberal reading which chose to see this non-grasping as the story's "inherent ambiguity". This could be seen as an attempt to overlook the negotiated process of reading and to achieve mastery at a higher level. What the reading proposed above does manage to do is to undermine this pretence, to uncover a point of breakdown at which the Symbolic nature of language and reading, their non-reflective status, is perceived. Simply to "make sense" is to cover over the fact that the reading process and the text are sited within language: the third term, which divides the reflecting dyad.

The mastery of the object is as problematic for the critic as it is for the narrator. If the attempted mastery of the girl is rewarded by her mutilation and death, it seems equally likely that the attempt to master "Cara" will mean mutilation and loss. This is something which Julia Kristeva explains very succinctly: "... the propagation of psychoanalysis... has shown us, ever since Freud, that interpretation necessarily represents appropriation, and thus an act of desire and murder."[9] In other words, as Jane Gallop puts it: "... interpretation always takes place within a transferential situation."[10] It is not difficult to see why a male critic might echo the transferential experience of the narrator with the girl (though a female critic might react differently). Given the focalization and narrative strategy of the text, the implied (male) reader is aligned with the narrator

---

[9] Quoted in Gallop 27.

[10] See Gallop 27.

and will tend to react to the girl and to the text in a way which duplicates the narrator's desire. Moreover, the extended paralipsis (in the Genettian sense of an omission of known information)[11] concerning the girl's deafness strengthens the reader's closeness to the narrator's experience. The reader discovers the truth of the girl's deafness at the same moment in the sequence of events as the narrator, even though the narrator knew about it when he started narrating. In this way, the reader repeats important elements of the narrator's experience. And that repetition is encouraged by the normal operation of desire in reading a narrative, something which Bill Nichols describes in relation to film narrative. He talks of the reader's investment of desire in the delaying of resolution and closure in a narrative:

> Narrative dangles a lure before us; it promises to unfold in time, yet not run down or dissipate; to take form, to in-form. Desire – the desire to recognize a return, a closure, to enjoy pleasure as the subject-who-knows when we recognize the repetition/transformation of the beginning in the ending – snares us in these unravelling coils of events loosely called the story. Delay teases and tantalizes, like foreplay, with its promise of things to come. The beginning negotiates a contract toward us, with us: desire will be gratified, there will be a return, pleasure waits to be had. (Nichols 74-75)

The presumption to know, the pleasure of the subject-who-knows, cannot be sustained by either the narrator or the critic of "Cara". Knowledge is too defective for that. Ultimately the critic can only presume that s/he does not know. And this is not a mastery of "Cara" at one remove: it is a recognition that reading does not grasp completely, that non-meaning is not lost. This may be the first step towards understanding how reading relates to meaning and to non-meaning, and how it might avoid turning into another sort of repression. The use of psychoanalysis will be self-deceptive and a power-play if it remains content with producing a reading of the text without interrogating its own basis and without at least trying to locate its areas of blindness. If psychoanalysis can help the reading turn back on itself to uncover its capacity to select and deceive, and if it can thereby uncover the text's capacity to elude and subvert the pretence to mastery, the critic's

---

[11] See Genette 93.

self-understanding may be enhanced. At best the text may return a message telling the critic something about what s/he has been saying without being able to hear it.[12]

---

[12] This is a notion that both Felman and Gallop explore in the works cited above.

CHAPTER 6

MASCULINITY AND THE FIGHT FOR IGNORANCE:
"JACOB Y EL OTRO"

The fact that Onetti's writing in "Jacob" is dense and allusive can be immediately corroborated by a curious and resistant textual detail.[1] On two separate occasions (1376 and 1394), one of the characters mentions the canvas of a wrestling ring and alludes to the existence of two words to refer to it, "tapiz" and "alfombra". The purpose of this double designation and the double mention of it is far from clear, though just how one might respond to this detail in reading is something to which I will return when the question of reading itself is explicitly addressed. In terms of the content of the reading of "Jacob" offered here, there is an insistence on the importance of sexuality, and more specifically on the problems of masculinity. In highlighting the importance of masculinity in "Jacob", I seek to open up the story to something of its own hidden logic: in other words, the analytical approach to the story seeks to uncover what the story itself is not explicitly saying but which is nonetheless crucial to its discourse. Not that this could ever be the last word on "Jacob" – merely a word which "Jacob" may not be able to speak itself.

*

---

[1] I should like to thank Bernard McGuirk and the students in a seminar at the University of Michigan for their helpful reactions to earlier versions of this chapter.

The Logic of the Story

For all but its final page, "Jacob" seems to encourage the reader to follow Orsini's point of view on Jacob and the fight. Orsini's pessimism, reinforced by the doctor's in chapter one, strongly stresses the inevitability of Jacob's defeat. In that sense, the operating theatre is simply the extension of the ring: a locus of physical vulnerability. Central to this process of shaping the reader's expectations are periodic assessments made by Orsini of Jacob's physical condition. He perceives the decline which has taken place beneath the surface:

> "Toda esta carne – pensaba Orsini... ; los mismos músculos, o más, de los veinte años; un poco de grasa en el vientre, en el lomo, en la cintura. Blanco, enemigo del sol, gringo y mujer. Pero estos brazos y esas piernas tienen la misma fuerza de antes, o más. Los años no pasaron por allí; pero siempre pasan, siempre buscan y encuentran un sitio para entrar y quedarse. A todos nos prometieron, de golpe o tartamudeando, la vejez y la muerte. Este pobre diablo no creyó en promesas; por lo tanto el resultado es injusto." (1383)

There are three points to be made about this. Firstly, Orsini is the principal focalizer of the story and as such his assessment is almost always the dominant one. Secondly, Jacob's body is a major focus of attention in the story: it is read as a source of signs about the future. The body is seen to be caught in a process which is controlled by time and age, and the crucial thing is that the story's other important body, Mario's, is much younger and therefore brings Jacob's condition into sharp focus. Thirdly, it is worth noting that the problem of putting on weight and therefore losing fighting edge is indirectly related to feminization: this is a hint at a nexus of concerns which I shall develop later.

Matching Jacob's physical decline, Orsini also deduces a mental decline. Jacob's violent and unpredictable behaviour and his excessive drinking are signs of a profound inner crisis:

> El gigante movió la cabeza para mirarlo; los ojos azules estaban turbios y parecía usar la boca entreabierta para ver. "Disnea otra vez, angustia," pensó Orsini. "Es mejor que se emborrache y duerma hasta mañana."...
> "Ahora empieza – continuó Orsini – , la última vez fue en Guayaquil. Tiene que ser un asunto cíclico, pero no entiendo el ciclo. Una noche me estrangula y no por odio; porque me tiene a mano..." (1367)

This combined physical and mental deterioration in the ex-world champion is matched by Orsini himself who is also rather weary with the situation he finds himself in. Orsini devotes much of his energy to fighting off the truths consequential on his perception of Jacob's condition, and is committed to trying to negotiate a course around Jacob's decline. He is also committed, come what may, to happiness, which seems like an investment in illusion:

> Había nacido también para la felicidad, o por lo menos para creer obstinadamente en ella, contra viento y marea, contra la vida y sus errores. Había nacido, sobre todo, lo más importante, para imponer cuotas de dicha a todo el mundo posible. (1364)

But this position clearly inserts him in the contradiction of desiring against his own knowledge: this is the story's apparent metaphysical framework. The consequence for Orsini is that he is propelled by this contradiction to minimize the effects of his knowledge, to try and avoid it, and this means constant movement and constant pretence.

The movement and pretence are perceptible as a continual performance of the self for others. Both Orsini and Jacob (to some extent) put on a display of themselves for others as supremely confident and in control. Their exhibitionism is apparent from the very first moment of their presence in Santa María: it is the first thing that the doctor remembers about them in chapter 1. They appear in the central square parading ceremoniously in an ostentatious display of themselves:

> Avanzaban indiferentes a la curiosidad que hacía nacer la bestia lenta de dos metros; sin apresurarse pero resuelto, el movedizo marchaba con una irrenunciable dignidad, con una levantada sonrisa diplomática, como flanqueado por soldados de gala, como si alguien, un palco con banderas y hombres graves y mujeres viejas, lo esperara en alguna parte. Se supo que dejaron la coronita, entre bromas de niños y alguna pedrada, al pie del monumento a Brausen. (1364)

This performance continues as long as they remain in Santa María. Jacob performs himself as heavy-weight wrestling champion of the world, in which role his body is the supposed transmitter of a message of power and control, although Orsini is well aware that Jacob's body is no longer capable of being read in this way: " – Ciento diez animales abriendo la boca porque el campeón salta a la cuerda, como saltan, y mejor, todas las niñas en los patios de las escuelas" (1380). But not all of Santa María is deluded by Jacob's performance, for that is precisely what Orsini cannot control: Adriana for one reads a very different message transmitted by Jacob's body and perceives the imminence of defeat.

While Jacob performs his role, Orsini performs another as manager, and he does this even more elaborately than Jacob. He is massively courteous, externally self-confident and pretentious. He continually smiles and pretends, especially when it comes to the need to deposit the five hundred pesos as the guarantee for the challenge. In his case, the bigger the problem he faces the bigger the smile that he produces to minimize it. But his performance is the symptom of the gap between what he knows and his desire for things to be otherwise. The excess in the performance is the sign that he knows the gap cannot be filled in. For much of the story Orsini proposes his knowledge as superior to Jacob's – for example:

> "No puedo decirle que alguna vez tuve éxito amenazando y también pagué para que la cosa no durara más de treinta segundos; pero acaso no tenga más remedio que decírselo." (1386)

But in fact the story's ending suggests that Jacob knows the same thing about himself as Orsini, he knows that the gap between knowledge and desire cannot be overcome.

It is important that this masculine exhibitionism is undercut by the narrator of chapters 2-5, important because this consolidates the strength of the underlying knowledge being proposed. The narrator of chapters 2-5 occasionally reminds the reader that the truth lies elsewhere than in Orsini's games:

> Tal vez las burlas, nunca dichas en voz alta, rodearon todo el día al príncipe Orsini, a sus ropas, a sus modales, a su buena educación inadecuada. Pero él había apostado a ser feliz y sólo le era posible enterarse de las cosas agradables y buenas. En *El Liberal*, en el Berna y en el Plaza tuvo lo que él llamaría en el recuerdo conferencias de prensa; bebió y charló con curiosos y desocupados, contó anécdotas y atroces mentiras, exhibió una vez más los recortes de diarios, amarillentos y quebradizos. Algún día, esto era indudable, las cosas habían sido así: van Oppen campeón del mundo, joven, con una tuerca irresistible, con viajes que no eran exilios, asediado por ofertas que podían ser rechazadas. (1371-72)

And Adriana is also part of this deflationary tendency: with her terseness and directness she cuts through and denies all purpose to Orsini's pretence.

The "knowledge" of the story is, therefore, carefully placed and creates an almost inevitable position for the reader: the narrator, Adriana and Orsini all know the same thing. Add to this certain other details and the manipulation of the reader is quite marked. Not only does Orsini constantly anticipate defeat, but the badly injured body in chapter 1 is unidentified, and the doctor describes Jacob as "el gigante moribundo" twice in that chapter (1364 and 1365). Orsini anticipates that Jacob will be subject to an autopsy (1392) and he also describes Jacob as "difunto" (1394) just before the fight. The whole situation of their staging exhibition fights in obscure Latin American locations after the renown of the world championship reinforces the idea of imminent defeat, and Orsini's own "defeat" at the hands of Adriana in trying to "buy off" the challenge looks like a pre-echo of the actual fight. All these details lead the reader to the almost inevitable conclusion that Jacob will lose catastrophically in the fight. That this is not so should lead to the reconsideration i) of the story's tactic of manipulation, and ii) of all the framing "knowledge" that is carefully put in place. Rather than simply accept the metaphysics of Jacob's and Orsini's situation, on the grounds that it too may be a manipulation of the reader, it seems appropriate to reread the story, and I want to propose that a possible focus of rereading should be gender, and specifically masculinity, which is something about which, I would suggest, the story itself does not seem consciously to know.

*

Rereading for Masculinity

Rereading "Jacob" is crucial because Jacob does not lose the fight, although it is not clear that he wins it in any real sense (something to which I shall return). The fact that he does not lose seems to cut against the very strong logic set up by the story. By breaking the rules Jacob seems able to eliminate the threat of opposition, as if the decline of his body could be kept at bay. But the strongly resisting attitude of the crowd (they express extreme disapproval at what happens) suggests that there is no simple victory for Jacob. Rereading will reveal that there is an important textual and political unconscious in play here. And to begin the rereading process the nature of space needs to be investigated.

The fight takes place in a ring, a delimited space and, moreover, a space within which Jacob can be isolated from others while remaining at the same time in full view. What happens at the end is that Jacob survives in that space: he emphatically avoids the need to leave the ring and negotiate with those outside it (as his manager, Orsini has done throughout the story). It is as if Jacob were trying to reaffirm what he has been in the past: a unique individual, the world champion. In the space of the ring Jacob seems to seek to stand alone, literally (and metaphorically) unchallenged. His ejection of Mario from the ring is a theatrically obvious *re*jection of any doubts or questions about himself. The ejection of the challenger leaves Jacob as the monadic male, so characteristic of Onetti's fiction. And this position is strongly narcissistic, seemingly seeking to affirm self-sufficiency. One might go further in unravelling the importance of the ring as the space for Jacob's identity and see it as the image of his desire for clear-cut ego-boundaries. The importance to masculinity of such boundaries is well documented in psychoanalysis and studies of gender, being contrasted with an ability to empathize and negotiate with others.[2] The connotations of the ring's outside – the Other, the cultural and social world of Santa María – are significantly rejected by Jacob's act. The narcissism of masculinity is also characteristically associated with aggressiveness: the aggression against the other (the individual Mario) is suggestive of Jacob's desire for extreme control over his identity. In Kleinian terms, one might argue that the ejection of Mario is (by implication) a defence against the depressive feelings of recognizing that he is not in complete control. The (apparent) win over his opponent is reminiscent of a manic defence

---

[2] See Sherrod 222-25.

to protect his identity against the challenge of Mario and Santa María. In her commentary on Melanie Klein, Hanna Segal explains the nature of manic defence:

> The manic relation to objects is characterized by a triad of feelings – control, triumph and contempt. These feelings are directly related to, and defensive against depressive feelings of valuing the object and depending on it, and fear of loss and guilt. Control is a way of denying dependence, of not acknowledging it and yet of compelling the object to fulfil a need for dependence, since an object that is wholly controlled is, up to a point, one that can be depended on. Triumph is a denial of depressive feelings of valuing and caring; it is linked with omnipotence... (Segal 83-84)

Hence the violence against Mario can be seen to take on crucial psychological connotations. And in that respect, Orsini's acquisition of the narrative voice may be the equivalent of Jacob's "success", in that he takes control of language in the final chapter. In the same way one might also see consistency in the story in that the doctor in chapter 1, in his operating to save Mario's life, seems to acquire a certain masculine control and heroism in the eyes of the other male characters, even though he ironizes their reaction to him as part of his class role of superiority and condescension.

Returning to Jacob in the ring, it is important to note the sort of performance he gives. From his viewpoint, training and fighting in public view are a way of soliciting a look, he puts himself forward to be seen, *not* as an object of desire, but as the source of signs that bespeak power and control. The problem for him is that his body may be read in ways which he does not seek, and his inability to control the reception of the message of his body points to the inevitable dialectic of identification that Jacob tries to reject by his treatment of Mario.

Before the fight in the ring there occurs the crucial long scene between Orsini and Jacob in chapter 5. During that scene, a shift in power takes place whereby Orsini's view of their situation is rejected and Jacob refuses to take his advice and leave Santa María. Before this scene the relationship between the two characters is already complex. Orsini is variously cast as protector of Jacob (1366-67), as nursemaid (1385), and even as a sort of "lion-tamer" (1367), since Orsini tries to guide him but needs to contend with his fear of Jacob's volatile aggression. In general, Orsini acts as Jacob's interface with the world, and so he is the one to deal with the public, the newspapers and any challengers who appear. He is the one to assess the nature of reality and the best strategy to adopt in responding to it. Even though he treats Adriana with disdain, he can read the clear message that Mario's body is sending to her, and he knows immediately that he must bargain with her in order to save Jacob.

By contrast, Jacob is not verbally interactive with the world, and barely even with Orsini. He simply tries to dominate the Other, which is a source of potential challenges to be overcome. He makes no effort to modify his view or behaviour in order to accommodate any aspect of reality which might prove problematic; tacitly, this function is delegated to Orsini. There is a clear demarcation between himself and others. In this contrast with Orsini, the true nature of their interdependence is manifest: it is not so much that there is a bond or communication between them (of a physical or emotional sort), but that they fulfil different functions which complement each other. Which is not to deny that certain adjustments need to be made: though Orsini appears to be the manager, his position is precarious, and his judgement is subject to Jacob's veto, since Jacob is in a position to make their hotel room another sort of "wrestling ring" and impose his view on Orsini physically.

The complementarity of Orsini and Jacob can be seen in (at least) two ways. Firstly and most simply, the relation can be seen to be less that of two individuals and more that between the mind and the body: the one who thinks and the one who acts, though this division is somewhat simplistic given Jacob's ultimate imposition of his will on Orsini. Alternatively, one might see the relation in terms of the psychic apparatus. In this description, the two characters could be taken to represent different areas of complementary function within one subjectivity. In this sense, Orsini has certain attributes of the ego, negotiating with the world, projecting a clear personality, building up the standing of the pair, and Jacob has certain features of the id, the source of drives and energy. Again it is worth emphasizing that any absolute limit drawn around these functions would be misleading: the division is a way of highlighting general tendencies. In both these descriptions, however, the pair can be usefully seen as parts of one figure, interactive and mutually dependent, though not necessarily working in harmony. If one does choose to read the relationship in psychoanalytical terms as being that between elements of one subjectivity, it might help to give perspective on the problematic and unresolved outcome of the fight, to probe beneath the manifest content.

In the long scene before the fight, the interactions and the struggle between the two are seen most revealingly. In this scene the revolver (as elsewhere in Onetti[3]) is of some significance in locating the shift in power through the scene. The revolver is prepared by Orsini in anticipation of Jacob's hostile reaction to the suggestion that they should run away from Santa María before the fight. The revolver is an equivocal sign of the nature of the relationship between them: on the one hand, it suggests Orsini's recognition of the urgency to extricate themselves from what he feels to be a lost cause; but, on the other, it is a clear sign of the fragility of his control over Jacob. Throughout the scene the revolver is periodically mentioned as a reminder of both these aspects. But it becomes clear that, despite Orsini's attempts to conceal it, Jacob is well aware that he has it in his pocket. By the morning after the scene, the revolver has been unloaded as a definitive signal of Orsini's powerlessness.

Running parallel with the revolver motif, is the shift that occurs in the location of the smile in the scene. Orsini is conspicuous almost throughout the story for the smile which he presents to the world, but in this scene it is Jacob who, after expressing his determination to stay on in Santa María and fight, acquires possession of the smile and even of laughter. This change underpins the apparent rejuvenation of Jacob, which runs counter to the logic of his physical condition: it is as if in reacquiring the smile and laughter he were going back in

---

[3] Other important revolvers in Onetti appear in *El astillero* and "Tan triste".

time: "Van Oppen se puso a reír y el sombrero cayó sobre la cama. Su risa había sido descuidada por los años, era la misma" (1392); and: "Me bastó verlo – los ojos aniñados, limpios y sin nada; la corta curva de la sonrisa – para entender que no quería hablar conmigo, que no deseaba prólogos, nada que lo separara de lo que había resuelto ser y recordar" (1394). Quite how this happens is far from clear.[4] But it seems evident that at this point there becomes visible the underlying textual logic cutting against the logic of the body previously set up. The rejuvenation is underpinned by the *deus ex machina* resolution of Orsini's seemingly insuperable problem of providing the five hundred peso guarantee for the fight when Jacob simply produces it from the savings concealed in his shoe (1393): all seems to become possible.

This question of the rejuvenation of Jacob is closely linked to masculinity and its crisis in "Jacob", the context for which is signalled early in the story in Jacob's self-assessment during his bout of heavy drinking with Orsini. Summing himself up he says: " – Nadie... El *footing* las flexiones, las tomas, Lewis. Por Lewis; por lo menos vivió y fue un hombre. La gimnasia no es un hombre, la lucha no es hombre, todo esto no es un hombre. Una pieza de hotel, el gimnasio, indios mugrientos. Fuera del mundo, Orsini" (1368). Jacob's doubts appear to vitiate his wrestling career, which by the end comes to look like a desperate attempt to fill the gap in gender identity. And the image of the champion is crucial here. Jacob's reimposition of boundaries, his casting aside of the doubts and the challenge to him signals the drive to coincide with the plenitude of the identity of champion. Here the designation "champion" (repeated several times) has a particular significance. One can see Jacob pinning his ideal of identity on the apparently neatly circumscribed public title – the title is as delimiting as the ring he stands in. Ellie Ragland-Sullivan clarifies this particular, precarious nexus of Imaginary and Symbolic in the identificatory process:

---

[4] Other rejuvenations of this sort in Onetti occur in *El astillero*, *Los adioses*, "Cara", and "El infierno".

In adult life subjects constantly reconstitute their identities within a synchronic, cultural signifying context – a Symbolic order – to secure themselves a fixed value in terms of their Imaginary "self"-fables. A subject represents him- or herself to another person as signifying something cultural (a title, a profession) within a given Symbolic order, or something more basic and personal in terms of his or her own narcissism, and tries to confirm the merit of the Symbolic and Imaginary aspects of identity in light of Real events. When a subject's Imaginary ideal is confirmed by Symbolic labels and approved by Real events, the accompanying feeling is one of wholeness or *jouissance*. But the ever-jostling, power-bent signifying chain of society continually threatens the constancy and fixity of any subject's Imaginary, Symbolic, and Real constellation of joy. (Ragland-Sullivan 223)

Jacob's effort to impose boundaries and to pin identity on the title is also illuminated by recent research into the psychology of sport in men's lives. Sport acts as a key source of identification for many men; it becomes a means of achieving self-validation.[5] But this research into sport makes clear that this is a hazardous and ephemeral process, so that the key question is how to go on winning, how to sustain the source of identity, how to ward off threats and challenges. The desire for perpetual success and stability is just that: desire, which cannot be definitively satisfied.

This perspective might be productively applied to Jacob. At first sight it does appear that he gains a triumphant victory – Mario is emphatically overcome and physically damaged. Indeed Gabriel Saad talks of Jacob and "el milagro de su resurrección" (Saad 104). But, on close inspection, this is neither a clear victory nor a resurrection. There are three crucial elements which render Jacob's win rather equivocal. Firstly, Jacob appears to have to break the rules in order to beat Mario: "Contra todas las reglas, Jacob mantuvo los brazos altos durante diez segundos", and "No habíamos llegado a los cincuenta segundos y el campeón había ganado o no, según se mira" (1395). The suggestion of cheating reinforces the sense that what is primarily in play here is desire. The unwritten logic appears to be that Jacob can only afford to follow the rules as long as he is sure of winning. When winning is doubtful the rules are infringed just enough to permit an

---

[5] For a survey of this work see Messner.

unchanging desire to be acted upon. I would suggest that by implication Jacob seems to know that he will not (perhaps cannot) win fairly, hence he cheats: he will at least avoid defeat. In this implicit tension between desire (to win) and knowledge (of probable defeat), Jacob is clearly opting against knowledge. The knowledge is of unstable identity, an identity that is decentred and incomplete, perhaps (following the metaphor) removed from the illusion of control in the ring. What seeks to cover over this knowledge is a desire to perpetuate the narcissism and ignorance of apparently fulfilled and stable masculinity. Not that the two are exclusive positions since the ignorance of full masculinity is interdependent with the forgetting of the knowledge of its unattainability.

Secondly, the reaction of the crowd, its utter hostility to Jacob (1395-96), seems to refuse him all recognition. But the status of the regained identity as unquestioned champion is equivocal if it is not recognized by others, and this is a strong element undermining the significance of Jacob's win. While Jacob seems not to pay attention to the hostility, the crowd's reaction underlines his retreat from any negotiating with the Other.

Thirdly, seen in its full context, this win is only one in a long, indeed in an endless, series. The question then is how Jacob can continue to win. And the question must be posed and reposed in each town and with each challenge. Jacob and Orsini are on a tour which signifies continual movement, and the outcome of any one fight is temporary: the tour is inherently unstable. In fact, the tour represents an endless chain of desire, with each town as just one more link. In Lacanian terms, Jacob's desire is unending, it cannot be controlled and fulfilled in the ring in Santa María. Its logic is of constant striving and non-fulfilment, of excess to any attempt to satisfy it.[6] The very fact that Jacob and Orsini have left Europe means (implicitly) that they have *already* lost. By touring obscure parts of Latin America, they have moved to evade any prospect of a real challenge. And the very fact of touring means a lack of permanence: it is a constant sliding, a

---

[6] On desire in this sense see Ragland-Sullivan 68-89.

constant repetition of the desire to hold on. All that Jacob and Orsini can do is to talk and delude themselves about the prospect of a return to Europe and to the status of champion of the world, and about the possiblity of sustaining the identity of masculinity. Whence, in part, the significance of the song that Jacob forces Orsini to sing: *Lili Marlen* is strongly nostalgic.[7]

In this context, the "win" over Mario is significant in ways that Jacob and Orsini do not wish to recognize. Superficially, Jacob wins over "el otro", over Mario. But one might also say that it is an attempted win over "lo otro", the Other: in other words, over the Symbolic and all that is liable to make a demand on the individual.[8] Jacob's attempt to impose his desire for (narcissistic) victory would therefore seem to put Orsini's efforts to negotiate survival with the Other into the domain not of realism but of "weakness" and "non-masculinity". In addition to these aspects, I would also argue that Jacob's win is over "la otra", Adriana, and so has further crucial gender implications. In the first place, Mario fights in the ring as the representative of Adriana: they are to marry and she has decided to try and secure their future by this means. In this context, Jacob's ejection of Mario from the ring is a refusal of Mario's position: the male body in the service of a woman and marriage. All that conventional behaviour is rejected and held at bay outside the ring. At a more abstract level, Adriana's putting up of Mario to fight goes beyond the wish to secure their future: it is like a challenge to masculinity and the patriarchal order. In that light, one might see Adriana and Mario as an indivisible pair cognate with Jacob and Orsini, with Adriana as the managerial figure and Mario as the body given credit for no brains (1374). And the stereotypical characterization of Adriana underpins this: she is made of iron (1370), and is a tough, calculating manipulator of Mario – she goads him with her nails when Orsini applies pressure on him to back down (1377-78). Hence also the

---

[7] See Geyman 36-37.

[8] On the Other see Ragland-Sullivan 15-16.

characterization of her in chapter 6 as almost crazed with resentment against the defeated Mario (1396): it is significant and belittling that her reaction to the badly injured Mario omits the marker of loyalty to her future husband. In overcoming Adriana and Mario, therefore, Jacob maintains a gender hierarchy: in part, what Jacob survives is the direct challenge to his masculinity, and Rius' scorn for Adriana at the hospital consolidates the sense of male solidarity against the "scheming" woman (1362). With the woman finally reduced to the condition of a screaming, spitting and hysterical caricature there is no need to negotiate with her any more, and Orsini's earlier efforts to do so come to appear rather unnecessary. In this characterization of Adriana, the implied author is evidently writing in complicity with hierarchical masculinity. By stressing the gender aspects of "Jacob", I am trying to go beyond its implicit invitation to read it as a story about the problem of human ageing and loss. The dilemmas faced by the characters might begin to look rather different and perhaps more politically freighted if they are seen as partially (or even largely) based on problems of masculinity and gender relations. This is one way of trying to promote a resisting reading. With that objective of demystification, "Jacob" might be seen as a narrative about a crisis of masculinity and its bid for exclusivity and power. In not questioning the nature of Jacob's and Orsini's understanding of their actions, "Jacob" tends to overlook the way in which it reproduces certain notions to do with gender. In recreating a certain myth of masculinity, "Jacob" is close to the deep structure that Teresa de Lauretis claims for all narrative:

> in its "making sense" of the world, narrative endlessly reconstructs it as a two-character drama in which the human person creates and recreates *himself* out of an abstract or purely symbolic other – the womb, the earth, the grave, the woman... The drama has the movement of a passage, a crossing, an actively experienced transformation of the human being into – man... (de Lauretis 121)

This is a broad statement but it does reveal a certain fundamental tendency in narrative, which is not simply a formal structure but which serves cultural and social purposes. Applied to "Jacob", it emphasizes how Jacob strives to recreate himself in a certain image against what is represented by Adriana and Santa María, which is seen as contemptible and debilitating. Jacob tries to project on to them those inherent problems within himself which he does not wish to recognize and then to destroy them. As in all Onetti's fiction, there is a profound (and contradictory) reliance on the function of women characters in enabling masculine narrative and action. By contrast, in "Jacob"'s own terms, what Jacob does is seen to have less to do with myths of masculinity, potency and control than with the inevitability of human (men's ?) ageing.

What I am proposing in my reading of "Jacob" is that there is rather more involved here than the story seems to know.[9] This may appear a paradoxical position given what the story actually tries to *do*. In setting up a certain knowledge only to undermine it and so surprise the reader, the story may seem to suggest its own ultimate mastery in controlling information. But just as Orsini's knowledge is not complete and he is taken aback by the outcome of the fight, I want to suggest that the story itself at the end does not know everything either. I propose that the story's structure (the movement from knowledge established to knowledge reformulated) does not connote the story's mastery, but the fact that no knowledge is substantively whole, that there is always more, always another reformulation, always an ignorance within knowledge, a knowledge that "Jacob" itself cannot see. I have insisted on gender issues as a way of widening understanding of the mechanisms of meaning involved in "Jacob". That is not an attempt to treat it as a delimited space (as a circumscribed ring) for critical muscle flexing over "definitive" meaning, but rather an attempt to open up the gaps and silences in the story. It is an attempt to deny clear, conscious boundaries to the

---

[9] Hence, for all his useful insights into "Jacob", Matthew Geyman remains content to work within the logic of the story, and to celebrate its complex of ambiguities as controlled not merely by an implied author but by Onetti himself. So he sees the reader in (apparently) man-to-man combat with (again) Onetti: "These ambiguous clues represent a struggle between Onetti and the reader. This figurative wrestling match nicely parallels the struggle between Jacob and the Turk" (p.42). The gender problem in this stance for "the reader" and the implication of engaging in a struggle with the text, presumably to get the upper hand through some critical muscle flexing, are precisely what I want to avoid by not accepting the story's own terms — by refusing to see it as offering a challenge to be overcome.

story and to politicize what on the surface is a somewhat idealized thought process. Here one might draw an analogy from within "Jacob". In Orsini's discourse, Jacob's body has the status of an empty signifier to which he attempts to attach a certain signified, but it turns out that Orsini has not foreseen certain attributes of that signifier. In this way, Orsini is seen to fill that signifier only to discover that in it there is a strength of desire which is in excess of what he had allowed. It is not that he was wrong, but simply that he did not know this desire. In a sense, therefore, at the end Jacob insists bodily and, in so doing, reveals some of the blindness of Orsini's discourse, how its signifiers cannot be held to the signifieds. Precisely the same partial emptying also takes place in chapter 5 when Orsini's revolver is unloaded by Jacob. In reverse, one can see the double designation of the canvas in the ring ("tapiz", "alfombra"), to which I alluded at the start, as an allusion to this slippage of signifiers over an apparently single referent – in reverse, but connoting the same notion of multiple relations between signifiers, signifieds and referents. To consolidate this idea of multiplicity, one might also draw an analogy between reading the story and the encounter of Jacob and Mario in the ring. It is possible to see Jacob and Mario as performing in the ring as signifiers circumscribed by the framing of the ropes: they constitute a figure in the carpet/canvas. But the story emphasizes that the carpet/canvas itself is not fixed: it vacillates between "alfombra" and "tapiz". And moreover, the apparent containment of the mens'/signifiers' movement is shown to be illusory when Jacob ejects Mario from the ring and into the public. The "private" nature of the contest, of reading, of this "analytical session", is thoroughly disturbed and the ring is revealed as not the only scene of encounter, but as one link, one moment, in a potentially endless chain of signification. The figure in the carpet is not constant. Hence, by ejecting Mario, Jacob is making space for the next contest, the next reading, the next "analytical session".

    The underlying proposition of my reading is that the story needs to be negotiated and renegotiated endlessly, on the analogy with interminable psychoanalytic interpretation.[10] As with Jacob, Orsini and their tour, there can only be a series of encounters, never a single, final coming together of reader and text. Rather than my trying to draw a boundary, to establish a clear division between the inside of the text and its outside, between what it does and does not mean, what I want to suggest is that the story is teaching an unconscious lesson about relations between subjects and objects, and about the internal workings of both. What it teaches might be that a subscription to myths of control and dominance is the inherent, crucially unacknowledged, contradiction and source of ignorance within masculinity. Such a subscription is a lure that a regendered mode of reading might learn to be aware of and to question... if not to avoid.[11]

---

[10] On interminable reading and its parallel with psychoanalysis see Felman chapter 4.

[11] On reading and gender in general see Flynn and Schweickart.

CHAPTER 7
OBJECTS AND OBJECTIONS:
"TAN TRISTE COMO ELLA"

"Tan triste" is a dense and difficult story. It is particularly tricky to negotiate in view of the fact that there is little interpreting carried out within the story itself. The writing of "Tan triste" places a stress on reference to objects and physical movement as if it were simply "raw material", simply registered as being or happening. I propose to confront this difficulty of reading explicitly, and to begin with an examination of certain of the story's recurrent objects. This will allow me, on the one hand, to make an initial opening in the story, and, on the other, to begin to see the implications of such a search for a system of coherent meanings. What I will ultimately attempt to establish is an open, interactive reading which is alert to the problems of trying to control and objectify the story.

*

Symbolic Readings

The density of reference to objects in "Tan triste" is such that it seems a worthwhile strategy to concentrate first of all on the possible ways of negotiating them. The most obvious, if necessarily speculative, way of reading these objects is as symbols.[1] There are a number of them to which repeated reference is made: the garden, the "cinacinas", the revolver and (arguably) the dream, and it is worthwhile considering each separately.

The garden is notably wild and unruly, "salvaje y enmarañado" (1309), and those characteristics are linked with the woman's childhood: this seems to be the same garden she knew as a child. In fact, the garden appears to have been a place of refuge in which she hid from the world: "Y cuando el mundo vino a buscarla, no lo comprendió del todo, protegida y engañada por los arbustos caprichosos y mal criados, por el misterio – a luz y sombra – de los viejos árboles torcidos e intactos, por el pasto inocente, alto, grosero" (1312). The garden is a place of enchantment and plenitude set up against the world. Her "stability" of identity in it is disrupted when she is summoned by the world outside.

Crucially, the woman now clings to the same view of the unruly garden. For instance, even when the cement has been spread over it she walks on it as if the paths through the garden were still there (1315). And this clinging to the past brings her into direct conflict with the man's plans: " – Puede quedar cerca, cerca de los ventanales, un rincón para estirarse y tomar cosas frescas cuando vuelva el verano. Pero el resto, todo, hay que aplastarlo con cemento. Quiero hacer peceras" (1312). The man's decision to build the fish tanks could be seen as a crisis in their relationship in two respects: firstly, he takes no account of her wishes; and secondly, the garden to which she attaches such importance is destroyed for "commercial" reasons.

The woman rationalizes his action in transforming the garden, in destroying her past, as an attempt to take revenge on her. To destroy the garden is to destroy

---

[1] In fact, precisely this way of reading forms the backbone of M. Ian Adams' discussion of "Tan Triste" (Adams 37-80). His reading of symbols could be characterized as positivistic. The same practice is also part of the basic project of Jack Murray's careful analysis of the story. Two of Murray's phrases are particularly clear in that respect: "... [Onetti] strews details along the path which virtually beg for analysis" (80); and: "... a masked, though calculated, intellectual order that the reader is invited to unravel" (81). Both phrases are revealing of the critic's desire to be mirrored in the text. This practice is one from which this analysis will ultimately aim to distance itself.

her. And that is linked to the dispute about the parenthood of the child. Hence, in his bitterness about the baby, the man takes away the only thing that really matters to her (1318). In the absence of the garden the woman continues to desire the rebirth of the past; she even asks the first workman if the garden could grow again (1322-23).

In this elaboration, the garden becomes readable as a sign of the woman's Imaginary relationship with the world. She is drawn to try and seclude herself from its demands, to pursue images of former fullness, and the implied author seems to naturalize this articulation of her position with a symbol loaded with positive connotations: like so many other literary gardens, this one connotes free growth and pleasure. This implicit support is part of the ideological position of "Tan triste" to which I shall return.[2]

A second recurrent object, the hedge of "cinacinas", has clear links with the garden. The attributes of the hedge are rather precisely figured in the story: the "cinacinas" are all round the house like a "cerco", and the trunks have an adolescent slimness (1316). These two attributes enable a link to be made with the garden as a place of entrapment in the past. The story makes it clear that the woman could get out of the house and garden but that she chooses not to:

> Podía marcharse por el gran portón de hierro que usaban los poceros, las imaginarias visitas; podía escapar por la puerta del garaje, siempre abierta cuando el coche estaba fuera.
> Pero elegía, sin convicción, sin deseo de verdad, el juego inútil y sangriento con las cinacinas... (1317)

She chooses this "game" with the "cinacinas", and it is as if even in choosing, in being active, she were lacking in energy and will ("sin convicción, sin deseo"). Furthermore, the search for a way through the hedge seems oddly perverse and doomed to failure: if she could leave by the iron gate why choose the hedge? The effort to get through the hedge constitutes precisely the "game", and that can hardly be read literally – "making sense" of this motif is necessarily highly

---

[2] For his treatment of the garden see Adams (63 and 66-67), where he is prepared to read rather more in to the object than I am.

abstract. The "game" might be read, for instance, as a sign of her psychological state in which she chooses to inflict pain on herself, or as a sign of the pain inflicted by her imprisonment in a male world.[3] But the "game" is not really projected as negative in this way within the system of the story. This game of extracting blood with the thorns of the hedge (a sort of self-inflicted crucifixion), produces pleasure (1328), as if the important thing is that this is at least a sign of life, a minimum affirmation, even though its form and its repetition seem numbing and entropic. It may be best to read this "game" as an enactment of the death instinct: it is one of the few things which she has chosen to do, though by clinging to this restricted space she prevents herself from engaging with the otherness of the world – she very precisely cannot find a way through the thorns.

Balanced with the space of the garden is the space upstairs in the house. The woman's seclusion and isolation in an Imaginary world is also suggested here. It is from the upstairs windows that she watches the activities of the men in the garden. Frequently in Onetti upstairs locations associated with women characters connote withdrawal from adult engagement with the world.[4] Hence the sexual relation with the first workman which fails occurs upstairs where she has insisted it take place (1323-24), and her suicide occurs there also (1329-30). By contrast the pleasurable sex with the second workman occurs downstairs in the garden shed (1328), which might be read as the equivalent of the idealized "casitas" of fulfilment and subversion in other Onetti texts – "Casa", for example.

A further recurrent object is the revolver, which has one striking attribute: on its first appearance in the hands of the man it does not work, and at the end it

---

[3] This perspective is similar to Murray's.

[4] See the discussion of this motif in the chapters on *Para esta noche*, *Para una tumba sin nombre*, *El astillero*, and *Juntacadáveres* in Millington 1985. It could be noted as well that the withdrawal of women characters into secluded places upstairs is associated with "madness" and/or religiosity. Julita in *Juntacadáveres*, Angélica Inés in *El astillero* and Beatriz in *Para esta noche* are all relevant points of reference here. In "Tan triste" the woman thinks that she is "loca": "'Estoy loca, o estuve y lo sigo estando y me gusta'" (1323), and before committing suicide she prays (1329).

fails again three times for the woman. In this light a possible reading of the revolver is as a sign of their failed relationship, of the absence of a sexual relation. Clearly one could argue that this failure or absence leads to the woman's death. And it is precisely the revolver which is the instrument of her suicide.

One final "object" that seems to allow this type of symbolic reading is the dream which the woman experiences near the start of "Tan triste" and again in the moments of her dying. It seems to encapsulate the futility of her life, as it figures her progressing slowly towards nothing:

> Soñó, al amanecer, ya separada y lejos, que caminaba sola en una noche que podía haber sido otra, casi desnuda con su corto camisón, cargando una valija vacía. Estaba condenada a la desesperanza y arrastraba los pies descalzos por calles arboladas y desiertas, lentamente, con el cuerpo erguido, casi desafiante... Casi desnuda, con el cuerpo recto y los pequeños senos horadando la noche, siguió marchando para hundirse en la luna desmesurada que continuaba creciendo. (1308)

The dream first occurs after the refused vaginal intercourse with the man before they were married. That failure is followed by the dream of the woman alone in the tree-lined urban landscape, so different from the garden motif of her regressive desire. This dream seems not to be one of wish-fulfilment, but rather a metaphor of her current, isolated state. What sustains her is "el gusto del hombre" (1308), a point repeated in the dream's reappearance: "creyó que volvía a tener derramado en su garganta el sabor del hombre..." (1329-30). The obvious suggestion is that the sexual relation on their first attempt turned into fellatio when the woman refused to allow the man to penetrate her: "Pero un miedo que nada tenía que ver con el dolor antiguo la obligó a decir no, a defenderse con las manos y la rigidez de los muslos" (1307). Hence there is a certain symmetry at the end when the penis is replaced in her mouth by the revolver which finally fires and kills her.

What I have done so far is to transpose into symbols all these specific objects in the text, to homogenize them into more or less stable and coherent meanings. At a more general level, the quantity of reference to physical objects could be read as suggesting inertness, as creating a mood of resistance and lifelessness in the couple's experience. And this would fit with the emergent pattern of meaning of the specific objects.

*

Sexuality and Object Relations

This question of objects and their possible meaning in the story can also be seen to be relevant at the level of character. So the notion of the object can be taken further and used to develop a reading of "Tan triste" which will eventually be more flexible and less homogenizing than the simple assigning of meaning above. It will also start to enable a reading against the textual logic, which is what I am initially establishing. This notion of the object is useful in respect both of the self as object of a reflexive hyperconsciousness, and of the relation to the other.

The woman's orientation in the world is seen as one of passivity. She thinks at one point that life is not made by people but is simply "there" beyond human will: "la mujer empezó a encontrar consuelo, a creer que la existencia está como una montaña o una piedra, que no la hacemos nosotros, que no la hacían ni el uno ni el otro" (1311). There is little in her by way of an active engagement with the world. In Lacanian terms, by choosing to cling to the Imaginary in the garden the Symbolic is held at bay: she tries to avoid the demand of the social world and articulates her view of herself as a victim (1318). By this logic, the woman's end, her suicide, is inevitable even before the concrete is laid on the garden: "en la mitad del verano, llegó la tarde prevista mucho tiempo antes, cuando tenía su jardín salvaje y no habían llegado poceros a deshacerlo" (1329). So the dream suggesting her death first occurs before she is married and well in advance of anything which the marriage produces to cause it.

Turning to the man, in the time covered by the story, he relates to himself as to one who is changed, one who has lost all that mattered. At thirty-two, he feels that he has no more illusions about his position in the world (1310). He sees no hope of improvement in his life because it is too arbitrary. And yet he looks for a sexual relation outside the home in a systematic way, which is clearly a search for a new object against which to fix himself. In contrast to the woman's passivity in relation to the world about her, he is active in his recognition of the importance to him of the lost object (the woman's younger self). Underpinning that activity, the man has the world outside the home to provide an area in which to move: it gives him stories, it rings him up, it allows him the distraction of making money. By contrast, the woman has no other space, and eventually renounces what little space she has altogether.

The man and the woman can also be considered in their relating to each other. If the man feels changed he also views the woman as having changed – he can no longer take her as an object for sexual relations. This is the nub of the problem in the story for the man. When the woman confronts him near the end with the demand for an explanation as to why he married her, he eventually responds by asking if she wants to hear the whole of his point of view:

> – ¿Todo? – se burló el hombre – . ¿Más todo? – hablaba hacia la copa en alto, hacia momentos perdidos, hacia lo que creía ser – . ¿Todo? Tal vez no lo comprendas. Ya hablé, creo, de la muchacha.
> – De mí.
> – De la muchacha – porfió él...
> – Eso dije – continuó el hombre, despacio, vigilante – . La que todo tipo normal busca, inventa, encuentra, o le hacen creer que encontró. No la que comprende, protege, mima, ayuda, endereza, corrige, mejora, apoya, aconseja, dirige y administra. Nada de eso, gracias.
> – ¿Yo?
> – Sí, ahora; y todo el maldito resto... (1327)

The woman is no longer the girl. She is no longer the object which he had desired. Hence his wish to replace her. The mysterious Másam is the main figure of this fantasy of replacement. Appropriately, it is far from clear whether Másam is real or just a figment of his imagination since she is only referred to in a piece of the man's writing which the woman comes across by chance: "Al pie de Másam el hombre había escrito con tinta roja: 'Tendría dieciséis años y vendrá desnuda por encima y debajo de la tierra para estar conmigo tanto tiempo como duren esta canción y esta esperanza'" (1319-20). The man longs for the return of the girl whom he considers the woman once to have been – an Imaginary projection of adolescent plenitude: "El, en cambio, esperaba el milagro, la resurrección de la chica encinta que había conocido, la suya propia, la del amor que se creyeron, o fueron construyendo durante meses..." (1314-15). In fact, both the man and the woman desire a return to the Imaginary plenitude of the past. For them time is loss, not movement forward. But the retrospective desires of the man and the woman refer to different sorts of past: she clings to an idealized image of her younger self before she even met the man, while he clings to an image of her in order to enable a narcissistic fantasy of a self which has not aged. Both, in other words, are suffering from a loss of object, and struggle with their wish not to accept their present identities.

These strongly solipsistic attitudes, with their divergent utopian desires, pinpoint the lack of relation between them. The title of the story and the sentence within the story which the title partially quotes ("Tan triste como ella, acaso" [1317]) propose an equivalence between them, but not something shared. In fact, the very opening of the story figures the gap between them quite graphically. It presents a sort of cameo, especially as it concentrates upon sexual contact:

> [Ella] quería ir, deseaba que ocurriera cualquier cosa... cualquier cosa útil para su soledad y su ignorancia. No pensaba en el futuro y se sentía capaz de negarlo. Pero un miedo que nada tenía que ver con el dolor antiguo la obligó a decir no, a defenderse con las manos y la rigidez de los muslos." (1307)

Even at the very start there is a fundamental discrepancy (perhaps even an inexplicable one since the "un miedo" is highly imprecise) between what she wants and what they can actually achieve.

The man seeks to emphasize this discrepancy in his attitude towards the baby, which appears not to be his but Mendel's. There is a strong irrational strand in his attitude: "Pero, ¿por qué tuvo que nacer varón? Tantos meses comprándole lanas rosadas y el resultado fue ése, un varón" (1313). Further, this irrational resentment that the woman could not produce a daughter is the basis for his casting himself in the role of "caballero" and "pobre diablo" because he is supporting the baby financially when he believes that it is not his, and for casting the woman in the role of "putita astuta" (1313). The baby and Mendel both appear to be elements used by the man to separate him from the woman, to drive a wedge between them. They are third terms which break up the Imaginary dyad which he projects them as having formed in the past. The baby and Mendel epitomize that present triadic relation in the Symbolic which both the man and the woman find so hard to bear.[5]

Much of the discrepancy between them is articulated at the micrological level in the dynamic of the look.[6] At this level their asymmetry is constantly apparent. The woman looks at the man, she passively observes him and waits for his actions. Her looking at him connotes her dependence, since he is where things happen. The man, on the other hand, either avoids looking at the woman or simply allows his eyes to be seen:

> A escondidas ella le miraba los ojos. Si puede darse el nombre de mirada a la cautela, al relámpago frío, a su cálculo. Los ojos del hombre, sin delatarse, se hacían más grandes y claros, cada vez cada mañana. Pero él no trataba de esconderlos; sólo quería desviar, sin grosería, lo que los ojos estaban condenados a preguntar y decir. (1308)

> Durante aquellas mañanas él no trataba, en realidad, de mirarla; se limitaba a mostrarle los ojos, como un mendigo casi desinteresado, sin fe, que exhibiera una llaga, un muñón. (1310)

He shows her his eyes, he allows them to be seen, but he does not look at her. Repeatedly his refusal to look at and see her is a denial of her existence; he gives

---

[5] It is far from clear if Mendel really exists and if the woman really had a relationship with him that produced the baby: he may simply be a device used by the man which the woman does not bother to refute. On the one hand, there seems to be a story about Mendel (presumably told by the woman) (1314). But, on the other hand, some statements about him are rather ambiguous: "Por la tarde, luego del rito con las espinas y las perezosas líneas de sangre en las manos, la mujer aprendió a silbar con los pájaros y supo que Mendel había desaparecido junto con el hombre flaco. Era posible que nunca hubieran existido. Quedaba el niño en la planta alta y de nada le servía para atenuar su soledad. Nunca había estado con Mendel, nunca lo había conocido ni le había visto el cuerpo corto y musculoso; nunca supo de su tesonera voluntad masculina, de su risa fácil, de su despreocupada compenetración con la dicha" (1319). It is not clear here who has not been with Mendel, whether it is the woman or the baby. If it is the woman who has never been with him, then the physical description of him must derive from the narrator-focalizer.

[6] The look is often important in Onetti. See, for example, my analyses of "Cara", "Jacob" and *La muerte y la niña*.

her no confirmation, no hint of reciprocity, and this might be read as part of the
implicit logic of her suicide. By humiliating her and refusing her his look, the man
contributes to her elimination. There is, in this context, a very telling moment
when the man does look at the woman, after she has asked the fundamental
question of the story:

> [La mujer] estaba de espaldas cuando dijo:
> – ¿Por qué te casaste conmigo?
> El hombre le miró un rato las formas flacas, el pelo enrevesado en la
> nuca; luego caminó hacia atrás, hacia el sillón y la mesa. (1326)

Here, momentarily, the structure of power between them falters and he occupies
the weaker position, hence he looks at her. But he quickly recovers and things
continue as before.

In sum: the absence of the look from the man is a sign of the lack of
reciprocity, the absence of sexual relation. What is enacted is a dual and discrete
search to cling to images and fantasies of the self. The link between the man and
the woman is perceived by him as broken and that leads him into a crisis. The
break with the woman creates a breach in the horizon of his sense of self, the
beginnings of an awareness of the lack of correspondence between his desire and
its object. It turns out that the desire is in excess of the object that he has chosen
and so he seeks out new ways to fix an idealized image of the self. This involves
him in a nostalgic mystification. And the implied author of "Tan triste" is
complicit here with the character. So the man looks elsewhere for a place to attach
his desire, precisely to Másam, whose name connotes her exotic difference from
the woman. This is a sort of disavowal of the division he has discovered with the
woman and in himself (between his view of his present and past selves): he seeks
another idealized object to try and restore a sense of plenitude. But the fact of the
mobility of his desire is a sign of the extent to which his fantasy is attached to
images, to an idea of "woman", and not to a specific person. Hence, the woman
or Másam are more like symptoms than realities, since neither can be said truly to

exist for him as independent subjects.[7]   And the woman, revealingly enough, does not react to this crisis in the man by trying to break out of her Imaginary circle and by looking to alternative roles (to motherhood, for example, though that is potentially heavily idealized, of course).   In the absence of the man to maintain her present state, the woman opts for regression to an image of herself in a secluded childhood.   And it should be noted that it seems to be *his* crisis and withdrawal that trigger *her* problem.

Now "Tan triste" is not mounting (even implicitly) a critique of these characters: it is fixed in an entropic view of the pain of discovering non-correspondence.   This is the nub of its negative metaphysics.   The understanding of "Tan triste" that I want to propose, which underlines the problematic nature of its representations, comes from a position that is articulated through psychoanalysis and which resists the metaphysical grain of the story.   To elaborate that understanding is to uncover the unspoken sexual politics of "Tan triste" which show themselves through the formulation of the crisis itself and through the different reactions to that crisis.

*

Implicit Sexual Politics

The man moves outside the space shared with the woman in order to reappropriate and restore an identity which he is conscious of having lost. He can articulate his problem, though with difficulty. By contrast, the woman remains almost throughout in the space shared with the man and reacts by internalizing her situation passively. Hence the importance of her dream as an articulation, but hence also the relation to two of the workmen as crucially disruptive (something which I will discuss later). These contrastive responses begin to sketch in the conventional sexual hierarchy which is not posed as problematic by the story. A phallic economy underlies the whole structure and the dynamic of all movement.

---

[7] See J. Lacan, "God and the *Jouissance* of The Woman" in Lacan 1982.

But there are ample grounds for contesting that economy and that hierarchy, and there is a moment in the story that seems to enable both that close questioning and a radical shift and reengagement with the story. I refer to the moment of the suicide.

> En el dormitorio, envolvió en [la bolsa de agua caliente] el *Smith and Wesson*, aguardando con paciencia que el caño adquiriera temperatura humana para la boca ansiosa.
>   Admitió, sin vergüenza, la farsa que estaba cumpliendo. Luego escuchó, sin prisa, sin miedo, los tres golpes fallidos del percutor. Escuchó, por segundos, el cuarto tiro de la bala que le rompía el cerebro. Sin entender, estuvo un tiempo en la primera noche y la luna, creyó que volvía a tener derramado en su garganta el sabor del hombre, tan parecido al pasto fresco, a la felicidad y al verano. (1329-30)

In the story the revolver is first associated with the man: it is part of his family history in which it has been provided for the protection of women – it is a sign of male power when men are absent. It is not just a phallic symbol, that is, a symbol of the penis (though its failure to fire (1309 and 1329) is connotative of the failure of the sexual relationship between the man and the woman).   Above all, the revolver may be seen as a symbol of the phallus, that is, in Lacanian terms, of the Symbolic power of the Father, of patriarchy.   In that sense, one can read the woman's suicide as a privileged moment revealing the implicit power structure in place in "Tan triste".   With the revolver in her mouth, the woman can no longer speak.   On one level, this alludes to the act of fellatio that may have occurred on the occasion of the first sexual encounter (1307-08), but on another this blocking of the mouth with the revolver can also be read as a silencing of the woman, as her destruction by patriarchy.   Her weakness is the result of a position made available to her in the patriarchal system, which "Tan triste" inscribes but does not articulate consciously.   It is above all this socio-sexual, phallic economy which underpins the workings of the story.   In this way, the woman's death comes as the extension of her prior silence and dependency, that is, the fact that her situation in the story is determined as a reaction to the man's withdrawing himself and belittling her.

In this way, "Tan triste" can be seen as a text of male desire: it contains not a woman's crisis but a man's, and the title of the story reinforces that view since the point of reference is the man, the woman ("ella") being merely a term of comparison. The dynamic desires derive from the man: the woman's death simply enacts the realization which the man makes at the start relating to the lost object – the woman is no longer the girl. In Lacanian terms, this realization is the Symbolic tear in the man's Imaginary which he tries to repair via other women/girls.[8]

Here, I would claim that I am beginning to articulate something which is not consciously known by the implied author of "Tan triste". The story works at the level of the operation of desire but without talking about it – the story registers movement and tension but cannot *explain* aetiology or structure. Nor, above all, does it assess the potential destructiveness of the forces it represents. But a psychoanalytic frame can help to make sense of the underlying structure. In these terms, the suicide is not a moment of emotional sadness or defeat: it is a textual nexus which reveals ideology. Further to this, I would say that it is crucial that the woman cannot be simply silenced by the underlying sexual economy. And this is because she represents a danger to it. This insight might lead to a further questioning of and reengagement with the story.

Firstly, the man's neglect and abandoning of the woman is already a sign of a problem: she does not coincide with the man's Imaginary scheme, she has a certain specificity and independence which are excessive to his control. Secondly, there is a faltering of the dominant phallic economy in the woman's relation to two of the workmen. The relation with the first workman is a failure, but it does begin to release something. When the two are alone together she makes a discovery:

> Nunca había imaginado que un hombre desnudo, real y suyo pudiera ser tan admirable y temible. Reconoció el deseo, la curiosidad, un viejo sentimiento de salud dormido por los años. Ahora lo miraba acercarse; y empezó a tomar conciencia del odio por la superioridad física del otro, del odio por lo masculino,

---

[8] See Gallop 60.

por el que manda, por quien no tiene necesidad de hacer preguntas inútiles.
(1324)

Her mixed reactions include hostility to the male, which is the beginning of the
possibility of demarcating an independent space. Also of interest with the first
workman is that the woman seems to be in charge of the relation: "Lo llamó y
tuvo al pocero con ella, hediondo y obediente" (1324). It is likewise the woman
who takes the first step to initiate the relation, and in this sense she appears less
passive. It is significant that the implied author terminates this first relation
seeming to view its failure as inherent, as a matter of principle or destiny: "Pero
no se pudo, una vez y otra, porque habían sido creados de manera definitiva,
insalvable, caprichosamente distinta" (1324). The use of the word "creados" here
may lead to the question "who is it that has created this determination in the story
if not the implied author?". In which case the word "caprichosamente" seems
revealing and potentially overdetermined.

Interestingly, between the relationships with the first and second workmen,
the woman's switch out of passivity affects even the relation with the man. Very
unusually, the woman confronts the man about their marriage at that point
(1326-27), and the man is weakened by this and unable to respond very adequately.

With the second of the workmen, the woman again takes the initiative, and
this leads to a far stronger and potentially subversive relation. She is dominant and
positive, even sadistic, with the second workman, who is little more than a boy,
and who is a willing victim of her violence and humiliating behaviour.

> Desnudo, [el segundo pocero] se hacía niño y temoroso, suplicante. La
> mujer usó todos sus recuerdos, sus repentinas inspiraciones. Se acostumbró a
> escupirlo y cachetearlo, pudo descubrir, entre la pared de zinc y el techo, un
> rebenque viejo, sin grasa, abandonado.
> Disfrutaba llamándolo con silbidos como a un perro, haciendo sonar los
> dedos. Una semana, dos semanas o tres. (1328)

Not only is the story's underlying power structure shifted here, but these activities are a source of pleasure, as if this were the excess, the unacknowledged, which the phallic economy cannot control.[9]

However, if the story allows this shift of power, it is only a glimpse since the woman decides to give up the relation with the second workman:

> Sin embargo, cada golpe, cada humillación, cada cobro y alegría la introducían en la plenitud y el sudor del verano, en la culminación que sólo puede ser continuada por el descenso.
> Había sido feliz con el muchacho y a veces lloraron juntos, ignorando cada uno el porqué del otro. Pero, fatalmente y lenta, la mujer tuvo que regresar de la sexualidad desesperada a la necesidad de amor. Era mejor, creyó, estar sola y triste. (1328)

This is an absolutely vital moment in the textual logic of "Tan triste". The woman decides to give up her activities with the workman and to resume her previous position. Characteristically the story explains remarkably little of this decision. Fundamentally one may suspect that the story simply needs to reappropriate her for the phallic economy. It does not explain adequately why she abandons the pleasure she has found – it becomes vague and mystificatory by stating what it proposes simply in the form of principles: "en la culminación que sólo puede ser continuada por el descenso", and "la mujer tuvo que regresar de la sexualidad desesperada a la necesidad del amor". What the story does at this point is to open out to a possible subversion of its system, only very quickly to close up the gap thereby created. It is not clear why the pleasure she experiences with the workman is incompatible with the other parts of her experience: "Era mejor, creyó, estar sola y triste". She is made to opt for love, although, as so often, that term is unanalyzed and, in this context, simply suggestive of the nostalgia for Imaginary unity with the man. Given that she does not now possess that unity with the man

---

[9] It is difficult to adjudicate, without falling into banal moralizing, on the humiliations the boy receives. But I find it hard not to retain some doubts about the nature of the momentary shift of power to the woman which involves such violence, although it is clearly legitimate to see it as a reversal of the habitual violence done to her by the phallic economy. On the other hand, given the location of the story within masculine discourse, this brief release of violence could be seen as a further sign of male fear of the "uncontrollable" and "threatening" nature of women's sexuality.

(she is after all "sola y triste") it is hard to see why she abandons the pleasure she finds with the workman which cannot be said to be endangering what remains of her marriage. In short, the overriding need here seems to be to reinstate her within the phallic economy.

"Tan triste", therefore, seems to offer a glimpse of a subversive potential only quickly to repress it and reinstate the woman's subservience. "Tan triste" cannot accommodate either the power of the woman's pleasure or the pleasure of her power: those excesses are recontained. Her opting for "love" and the "belief that it is better to be alone and sad" are tell-tale signs of the textual logic which lacks an entirely credible causality. Her choices are contrived to homogenize with the story's dominant entropic metaphysics. And it is worth noting that metaphysics is also discernible in the narrative structure of the story. Barely anything in the story happens in a clear, causal sequence. Time is homogenized and generalized via a notable amount of temporal juggling. The dominant devices controlling time in the story preclude any secure sense of linear development. "Tan triste" mixes the temporal techniques of summary, iteration and random scenes in moving back and forth across a barely defined period of time between spring and summer. The impression created is that nothing *can* happen, so that everything inevitably remains where it started within the structure of the phallic economy: the woman still wants to be wanted by the man, and even her suicide was inevitable before the whole transformation of the garden began (1329).

Ultimately, therefore, there is an underlying intuition in the story that the disposition of the Symbolic may create certain problems, but the reaction to that is not to seek some new possibility but is rather retroactive and Imaginary. There is no rechannelling towards a new future. Hence "Tan triste" cannot explore the woman's choices but can only state that she makes them. So the story finds a formal ending (the woman's suicide) which is actually mystificatory since it suggests its inevitability (hence the repetition of the dream), but it is unable to say why this particular ending had to occur. That is the ideological crux. My analysis seeks to suggest that there is rather more involved here than the implied author seems to know. The objective is to show "Tan triste" to be a more complex object than it thinks itself to be.

*

Reading

The position that reading has now reached is rather different from the one in the second section (Symbolic Readings); the third section (Sexuality and Object Relations) begins to undercut the second section working as a corrective to it, and the fourth (Implicit Sexual Politics) consolidates that process. The strategy of reading for symbols in the second section "dematerializes" specific objects and renders them abstract. In that sense the garden was transformed into a coded meaning, or, at a more general level, the quantity of physical objects in "Tan triste" was read as suggesting inertness, the resistance and lifelessness of the couple's "experience". But there is another object in the story which can be read so as further to consolidate the undermining of this way of reading for essential meanings. I refer to the suitcase in the dream. On its first appearance it is registered in this way: "Soñó al amanecer, ya separada y lejos, que caminaba sola en una noche que podía haber sido otra, casi desnuda con su corto camisón, cargando una valija vacía" (1308). And on its other appearance it is registered in this way: "Avanzaba pertinaz en cada bocacalle del sueño y el cerebro deshechos, en cada momento de fatiga mientras remontaba la cuesta interminable, semidesnuda, torcida por la valija" (1330). There is an obvious "existential" reading of the suitcase in both these dream sequences which may seem very attractive, namely that the suitcase is a burden weighing the woman down and preventing her from moving with complete freedom. But the problem there is clearly that the suitcase is "vacía", which cuts against the idea that the suitcase is a burden.[10] What I want to propose is the avoidance of simply forging

---

[10] For his treatment of the suitcase see Adams 70-71 where he reads it as a positivistic symbol of sexual deficiency. The suitcase can also be seen more interestingly as undermining this reading.

substantive "fillings" for the suitcase. The alternative is to try and signal something of the Real of the text and so produce a more interesting response which examines reading itself and what is involved in *making* sense.[11] In other words, the suitcase can be seen as a privileged moment in which the deceptiveness of the objects within the story is manifested, and any too rapid an attempt to render those objects transparent vehicles of meaning is preempted. This suitcase seems to have no *necessary* symbolic freight or content. Perhaps, by extension, all the objects have an empty centre. In this (suit)case the materiality of the object seems to insist, to resist the Imaginary presumption on the part of the critic to turn it rapidly into the "freight of life of the woman". If reading, on the other hand, aims not to dematerialize these objects, how might it proceed?

The answer to that question has already begun to take shape in section four (Implicit Sexual Politics), which aims to see "Tan triste" as a sort of empty suitcase, as a structure with space and gaps within it, as a process of constructing meanings, as a form of making sense within certain cultural and ideological limits. The fourth section tries to uncover the form of the limits, the form of the space within the patriarchal structure underlying the story: what those inner spaces and gaps seem to signify. This shift in strategy between sections two and four is crucial in order to keep in view the productive process of recreating "Tan triste" as an object in reading. And the use of the term object here is a helpful reminder of the framework of object relations discussed earlier in respect of the characters within the story, and a salutary reminder therefore of the libidinal aspect in the reading process – a sort of return of the repressed.

There is more than one way in which "Tan triste" itself can be seen as an object. Firstly, its verbal densities and opacities render reading a slow and consciously achieved process. There is also a calculated vagueness of terminology and a notable difficulty about the collocation of certain words which creates a sort

---

[11] On the interactions of the Lacanian concepts of Real, Imaginary and Symbolic, see Ragland-Sullivan 187-89.

of material obstruction to the rapid formation of sense. The prose tends to use abstract nouns in strings and to avoid adjectival attribution which leaves sense rather vague and generalized. And the story is very reluctant to provide pointers about the articulation of meaning: there is little internal point making, and few interpretative signals. All these features create a strong verbal surface and stress the story's material status: a sort of resistance of the Real prior to any attempted appropriation by the Symbolic and Imaginary in reading.

Another way of viewing the object status of "Tan triste", and so of engaging it not as a virtually transparent tissue of symbols which just need "working out", can issue from the ideas in the story's epigraph. This epigraph is a very brief piece of text which does not form an integral part of the story material, but which if not inside the story is clearly not outside it either since it is located beneath the title.

Querida Tantriste

Comprendo, a pesar de ligaduras indecibles e innumerables, que llegó el momento de agradecernos la intimidad de los últimos meses y decirnos adiós. Todas las ventajas serán tuyas. Creo que nunca nos entendimos de veras; acepto mi culpa, la responsabilidad y el fracaso. Intento excusarme – sólo para nosotros, claro – invocando la dificultad que impone navegar entre dos aguas durante X páginas. Acepto también, como merecidos, los momentos dichosos. En todo caso, perdón. Nunca miré de frente tu cara, nunca te mostré la mía.

J.C.O. (1307)

The story is addressed as a woman. It is as if the story had been the lover of J.C.O. And the separation of J.C.O. and Tantriste parallels that of the man and the woman in the story. Similarly, the refusal to look at Tantriste or to show his face to her echoes the asymmetrical play of looks within the story itself. Moreover there is no rancour in J.C.O. but a good deal of self-justification: *he* takes the initiative and measures his distance from *her*. This controlling of the positions by the male is perceptible within the story too where the implied author is also male. At the start of the story, the man and the woman are both objects of focalization, but after page 1314 the man becomes much less important. Thereafter, for the bulk of "Tan triste", the woman is the central object. There are certain brief moments that derive from her focalization but almost always she is the object of focalization whether from within or (mostly) from without. This mode of representing her clearly helps in manipulating her for the underlying phallic economy – it tends to preclude her own independent position.

This framing of the story from a masculine position prompts an urgent question. If the story is structured from such a standpoint, how is the reading this analysis proposes gendered? I would suggest that the initial attempt to read the story "into symbols" and to provide substantive interpretations of characters (even though not in the terms provided by the story) is a way of trying to frame and control it. Rather like J.C.O. with Tantriste, that first reading is redolent of masculine control. But the later move towards resistant critique may start a reexploration and repositioning of reading that allows the story much more complexity and independence. The superseding of that first reading suggests the need not to idealize the story into a neat object which the (masculine) critic can easily manipulate for "triumphal" insights. The story's opacities and gaps need to be stressed in order to contain that tendency, otherwise the story becomes a mere tool for the critic's method and a mirror for self-reflection. The return of the text, of the repressed, undermines that pretension to stability, that effort to objectify. Cynthia Chase states this point with some lucidity:

> To "plunge into the minutest details" of a text and context, in quest of the "hidden meaning", is indeed to *transfer* onto the text in such a way that its modes of expression and condition of knowledge – its transferences or tropes, and its status *as* trope – may never come to be known. Instead the text will be experienced as a message in which we have an interest; not read as a set of mechanisms and process of displacement, but seen or heard like a dream or a voice. The transference "peremptorily demanded" by the *hermeneutic* enterprise of interpretation, in short, conflicts with the *poetics* of the enterprise of textual analysis, which would have to trace, by means of displacements or transferences, not the meaning but the *devices* of meaning, the transferential process, of the text. (Chase 212-13)

Hence it may be necessary to carry out the problematic enterprise of interpretation in order to see the possibilities and the limits of analysis, of not being able simply to seek meaning. That, in any case, is the logic of my analysis. Hence, at the end of this chapter, "Tan triste" is no longer quite the object it seemed to be in its early pages. The relationship between analysis and story has shifted and diversified. And the heterogeneity of responses precludes the illusion of a transparent object relation: precisely the problem within the story's phallic economy. The final question is: can that heterogeneity ever be anything but a series of attempts at some sort of (deceptive) mastery? That danger (or perhaps just that simple reality) may be the transferential logic of all reading, the inevitable libidinal investment, unless one can also commit oneself to trying to find some of the countertransferential potential, the disruption of the transferential system, in the text and in the text of reading.

CHAPTER 8

HER STORY/OUR STORY:

THE TEXTUALITY OF "LA NOVIA ROBADA"

Textuality

> Esto, tan largo, en la imposibilidad de contar la historia del inadmisible
> vestido de novia, corroído, tuerto y viejo, en una sola frase de tres líneas. (1421)

"Novia" is a story that insists in a variety of ways on its own textuality.
It bends the logic of "common sense" by flouting contradictions, by using
repetition and variation to fracture any univocal version of events, and by its
allusiveness and lack of precise definition. As the above quotation makes clear,
the narrator insists on the impossibility of simplicity which makes necessary the
complexities of the text that is "Novia": "esto".

Some examples will demonstrate the variety of its textual devices.

> Esto, la ignorancia de las fechas de los seguros regresos, la validez
> indudable, inconstable de la palabra o promesa de un Insaurralde, palabra vasca
> o de vasco que caía y pesaba sin necesidad de ser dicha y de una vez para
> siempre en la eternidad. Un pensamiento, apenas, tal vez no pensado nunca por
> entero; una ambición de promesa puesta en el mundo, colocada allí e
> indestructible, siempre en desafío, más fuerte y rotunda si llegaba a cubrirla el
> mal tiempo, la lluvia, el viento, el granizo, el musgo y el sol enfurecido, el
> tiempo, solo. (1410-11)

This heavily elaborate paragraph appears to fulfil the function of a summary of the
situation in which Moncha and Santa María find themselves. But it is a summary
that teases and alludes rather than spelling out with clarity. The very first word

seems to gesture vaguely back at the complexly evolving detail of the complicity of Moncha and the town which has not been defined precisely. Then the summary renders itself open to question by showing that it relies on no more than ignorance and the credibility of an Insaurralde. The allusiveness of the formulation of the general situation is compounded by the fact that both sentences are grammatically incomplete (neither has a main finite verb), which tends to remove any clear focal point. Rather like its own content, the summary relies on an assertion of will over reality: just as Moncha and Santa María are complicitous in trying to impose their desire on the reality of what is actually happening to her, so the summary seems to provide definition without ever clearly doing so. Nowhere is that more apparent than in the final link between the "ambición de promesa" and the weather, which, in mingling the abstract and the concrete, is hardly self-explanatory.

This example of the idiosyncrasy of textual logic is characteristic of the disconcerting effect of much of the story. The idiosyncrasies of presentation operate at both the microtextual and macrotextual levels, and I shall look at some examples of both. Firstly, I want to analyze some verbal details which call attention to themselves. These give a sense of the intricacy and density of certain formulations in the story which block any smooth process of reading off a transparent meaning.

> Nada sucedió en Santa María aquel otoño hasta que llegó la hora – por qué maldita o fatal o determinada e ineludible – , hasta que llegó la hora feliz de la mentira... (1403)

The reason for the choice of the adjective "feliz" is not explained, and the context of moving through a series of alternatives hardly suggests much conviction with the final selection, especially in view of its rather unusual linkage with the word "mentira". The arbitrariness of the play with these adjectives draws attention irresistibly to the textual formulation. A second example is distinctly aberrant grammatically:

> Si hay nardos y jazmines, si hay cera o velas, si hay una luz sobre una mesa y papeles vírgenes en la mesa, si hay bordes de espuma en el río, si hay dentaduras de muchachas, si hay una blancura de amanecer creciendo encima de

la blancura de la leche que cae caliente y blanca en el frío del balde, si hay
manos envejecidas de mujeres, manos que nunca trabajaron, si hay un corto filo
de enagua para la primera cita de un muchacho, si hay un ajenjo milagrosamente
bien hecho, si hay camisas colgadas al sol, si hay espuma de jabón y pasta para
afeitarse o pasta para el cepillito, si hay escleróticas falsamente inocentes de
niños, si hay, hoy, nieve intacta, recién caída, si el Emperador de Siam conserva
para el vicerrey o gobernador una manada de elefantes, si hay capullos de algodón
rozando el pecho de negros que sudan y cortan, si hay una mujer en congoja y
miseria capaz de negativa y surgimiento, capaz de no contar monedas ni el futuro
inmediato para regalar una cosa inútil. (1420-21)

This paragraph is inserted in the story with scarcely any clear link to its context.
It is grammatically striking since it appears to be the highly complex beginning of
a conditional sentence, but no balancing phrase for the conditions ever arrives.
This is paradigmatic of the verbal density of the story, and of the lack of
conceptual stabilization: without a main idea tied to these initial conditions the
verbal string is left hanging completely unresolved. Moreover, the series of
conditions itself is extremely disparate, suggesting no common thread and
precluding the reading of them in terms of a single principle or idea. The
paragraph resists reading into a simple meaning – it demonstrates the insistence of
textuality, a constant movement across a chain of slipping signifiers.

If the above are examples of localized verbal idiosyncrasies resisting
translation into transparent sense, my next examples are of conceptual oddities or
incompatibilities. The first is quite simple – it refers to Moncha's appearance and
behaviour with Barthé:

... el largo insecto blanquecino recorría los habituales grandes círculos y pequeños
horizontes para volver a inmovilizarse, frotando o sólo uniendo las antenas, sobre
las promesas susurradas por el *tarot*, sobre el balbuceo de los naipes de rostros
hieráticos y amenazantes que reiteraban felicidades logradas luego de fatigosos
laberintos, que hablaban de fechas inevitables e imprecisas. (1416)

Here the strangeness of the formulation derives from the insistent mixing of the
physical and the abstract. The elaborate reference to the insect is a metaphor for
a combination of a physical appearance (Moncha's wedding dress) and a tenuous
emotional equilibrium (in the absence of Marcos Bergner). It also combines with
a highly characteristic use of abstractions ("promesas susurradas", "felicidades

logradas", "fatigosos laberintos") and allusive references ("fechas inevitables e imprecisas"), which do not settle easily into a focused meaning. Other examples also involve paradoxical formulations and quasi-contradictions:

> ... no me inspiraste otro deseo posible que el de escribirte algún día lejano una orillada carta de amor, una carta breve, apenas, un alineamiento de palabras que te dijeran todo. La corta carta, insisto, que yo no podía prever cuando te veía pasar...
>   La carta, Moncha, imprevisible, pero que ahora invento haber presentido desde el principio. (1404-05)

She inspired a desire to write a letter, a letter which simultaneously and paradoxically cannot be foreseen, and for which the narrator retrospectively invents an anticipating desire. The contradiction is simply flouted by the overt reference to it. This is a bending of common sense similar to another later in the story: "Todo posible, hasta lo físicamente imposible, para nosotros..." (1414). Such is the power of fiction.

Another disconcerting passage which seems to underline the independence of the textual logic comes with the set-piece description of Santa María. This is a self-contained description constituting a separate section of the story and receives no contextualization at all. It seems to be directly addressed to the reader ("usted") and his/her imaginative response to the text. However, the motivation for its location seems almost completely arbitrary:

> Santa María tiene un río, tiene barcos. Si tiene un río, tiene niebla. Los barcos usan bocinas, sirenas. Avisan, están, pobre bañista y mirador de agua dulce. Con su sombrilla, su bata, su traje de baño, canasta de alimentos, esposa y niños, usted, en un instante en seguida olvidado de imaginación o debilidad, puede, pudo, podría pensar en el tierno y bronco gemido del ballenato llamando a su madre, en el bronco, temeroso llamado de la ballena madre. Está bien; así, más o menos, sucede en Santa María cuando la niebla apaga el río. (1417-18)

The references to the river, the boats and their sirens, to the bather and his family and to the mist have little apparent relation to the rest of the story. Indeed, the permutations on the verb "poder" in the fifth sentence strongly suggest a certain verbal arbitrariness here. And, if congruence with the rest of the story is being sought, the assertion in the final sentence that this is what happens in Santa María when there is fog may only leave the reader somewhat bemused. The point is that any attempt to unify this passage with the rest of the story via a metaphorical or allegorical recuperation would tend to dissolve the textual density that I have been describing. No doubt it could be done, but the point is that the text itself seems to be stretching such conventional procedures.[1] "Novia" will not conform to comfortable cultural expectations and reflect back to the reader a homogeneous position for understanding. Its linguistic and conceptual twists continually disrupt any such expectation, challenging the reader to question a reading practice that might rely exclusively on common sense structures or consistent referentiality.

This is true also at the level of the story's global organization. The features that I have examined so far are local and specific, but there are certain contextual and structural idiosyncrasies which also underline the textuality of "Novia". The context of the opening three pages, for example, is only hinted at minimally. In particular, it is not clear for some paragraphs that the narrator is addressing the dead Moncha after having attended her wake. At most, fragmentary references and remarks can be pieced together to grasp the underlying situation. The whole of the opening three pages is rather lacking in explicit grounding, and its paragraphs seem barely consecutive. This is not a systematic exposition, but a halting, heterogeneous progress through an emotional space which links the narrator with Moncha (though possibly not vice versa).

The presentation of Moncha's condition is similarly tenuous. The reaction by Santa María to her condition precedes any naming of the condition itself, and, characteristically, is heterogeneous:

> Era inevitable, Moncha, que nos dividiéramos. Unos no creíamos y pedíamos otra copa, naipes, un tablero de ajedrez para matar el tema. Otros creíamos desapasionados y dejábamos arrastrarse las ya muertas tardes de invierno al otro lado de los vidrios del hotel, jugando al póker, aguardando con la cara inmóvil una confirmación esperada e indudable. Otros sabíamos que era cierto y flotábamos entre la lujuria imposible de entender y un secreto sellado. (1406-07)

Even having mentioned the confused reaction of some of Santa María, the story does not rush to specify what is the matter with Moncha. For a further page it

---

[1] See Ludmer 201-02.

hints at her strange activities, while avoiding the details of her general condition. It is content to describe her nocturnal rituals and her seclusion behind the walls of her father's house, rather than spell out that she is mad. Often as here, "Novia" prefers to explore the facets of information or reactions in arborescent detail and permutations, eschewing any pretence to fact or univocal statement.

Having gradually established that Moncha is locked away from the gaze of Santa María in madness, the story proceeds, even more gradually, to supersede that view. It becomes difficult to tell whether Moncha is locked away or not, since the reader is also told that she spends much of her time visiting old acquaintances (1418). It seems that barely has the story established the beginnings of a framework of understanding than it is fractured into almost incompatible permutations. Indeed, the passage describing her visits to the respectable citizens of Santa María is followed by a (not uncharacteristic) allusion to how things can be permutated or shuffled afterwards, presumably in the (re-)telling:

> Todas las cosas son así y no de otro modo; aunque sea posible barajar cuatro veces trece después que ocurrieron y son irremediables. (1418)[2]

Given the logic of this text, it is hard to see how anything can be said to be fixed or certain.

A second type of structural idiosyncrasy in "Novia" concerns the infraction of perspectival consistency. The story begins by setting up a "yo" narrator who quite quickly opts to merge his voice into that of a collective "nosotros". Despite this shift, the reader might assume that he is an extra- and homodiegetic narrator,[3] but subsequent information clearly poses problems for that assumption. It is unclear, for example, how a homodiegetic narrator can have access to the richness and meaning of the mad Moncha's fantasies (1407-08). Likewise, it is far from self-explanatory how this narrator knows so precisely about Díaz Grey's direct

---

[2] This passage is toying with the metaphor of card playing: four multiplied by thirteen is fifty-two, the number of cards in a pack. The use of such a metaphor is reminiscent of Díaz Grey's nocturnal games of solitaire in *El astillero* and *La muerte y la niña*.

[3] For this typology of narrators, see Genette 251-59.

thoughts concerning Moncha during her consultation with him. The same applies to the intricate "goings-on" of the three characters (Moncha, Barthé and the youth) in the pharmacy, and even the snippet of direct speech from Barthé (1416), suggesting that he has spoken to the narrator about Moncha, does not entirely account for the sheer wealth and allusiveness of the information: no oral account would have taken this form. In short, the narrator begins by appearing to be extra- and homodiegetic, but in practice acts more like an extra- and heterodiegetic narrator, such is the degree of authority that he assumes.

In terms of the temporal organization of the story, there are further idiosyncratic features. The period encompassed seems to be three months (1418), but that period is not covered in anything like a chronological way. The narrator mentions that a particular ordering has been suggested to him: to start at the end and then to return to the beginning and work through in sequence. This relatively conventional textual order does not suit the narrator, who explains what he will do instead:

> Pero tú y yo, Moncha, hemos coincidido tantas veces en la ignorancia del escándalo, que prefiero contarte desde el origen que importa hasta el saludo, la despedida. (1404)

Quite what this order will mean is very hard to judge, since it is based more on an unspecified, emotional logic rather than a conventional cultural one. The form of the story as it stands is somewhat elusive, with little integration or dovetailing of large spans of narrative time. So Moncha's early visits to Díaz Grey and Mme Caron (to obtain the bridal dress) are narrated after the references to her subsequent mad behaviour when she is locked away while already wearing the dress; and Barthé and the youth are abruptly introduced though their relevance to Moncha's story is not initially mentioned. In fact, the narrator creates a complex temporal landscape in multiple and repeating fragments. This elusive and idiosyncratic structure is summed up near the end by the statement of the impossibility of containing the story of the dress with which I opened this analysis. The story cannot be told in a phrase of three lines, and the implication is that "Esto, tan largo..." (1421), this complex narration, is the only choice: this is an acknowledgement of the idiosyncrasies that I have been describing. What the structuring of the narration ultimately produces is a greater emphasis on local textual detail rather than on an emergent global structure.[4] In terms of events, there are few global structures, which is not surprising since there is hardly any sense of story time. In accordance with the stress on the textuality of the story, it is text time, the time of the narrating itself, and its logic, which predominate. And that time and that logic create a strong sense of simultaneity and of lack of selectivity. These features are apparent in the text's reliance on repetition and variation. "Novia" is full not only of repetitions, but repetitions modified by small variations and slight expansions. By relying on these devices the story appears relatively static – it seems to explore a terrain rather than moving forward chronologically. The repetition and variations involved are of various sorts.

In the first place, there are repetitions at the level of content. On the one hand, that involves Moncha explicitly as one of many who have tried to get away from Santa María only to return:

> Pero la vasquita Moncha Insurralde o Insaurralde volvió a Santa María. Volvió, como volvieron todos, en tantos años, que tuvieron su fiesta de adiós para siempre y hoy vagan, vegetan, buscan sobrevivir apoyados en cualquier pequeña cosa sólida, un metro cuadrado de tierra, tan lejos y alejados de Europa, que se nombra París, tan lejos del sueño, el gran sueño. (1405-06)

This is a general pattern, explicitly invoked by the story, which underlines the difficulty of getting away from the town, and also the sheer difficulty of coming back and adapting to it. Appropriately, the sentence itself is woven around repeating words and phrases. On the other hand, and more important for the writing of the story, there are repetitious presentations of its own content: incidents and activities which are written and reelaborated through several paragraphs with

---

[4] Even possible literary parallels (that is, the similarity of Moncha with Miss Hathersage in *Great Expectations*, or of the whole story with Faulkner's "A Rose for Emily") hardly provide global, structural blueprints. At most they suggest a certain intertextuality. For the links with Faulkner see Ludmer 193 n.7.

slight changes and additions of detail. There is an example of this on pages 1407-08, where Moncha's nocturnal ritual in the garden is described and redescribed. (As a whole, this lengthy, densely written passage is also full of repetitions of words and phrases.)

> Sabíamos, se supo, que dormía como muerta en la casona, que en las noches peligrosas de luna recorría el jardín, la huerta, el pasto abandonado, vestida con su traje de novia. Iba y regresaba, lenta, erguida y solemne, desde un muro hasta el otro, desde el anochecer hasta la disolución de la luna del alba... La mujer, en el jardín que ahora hacemos enorme y donde hacemos crecer plantas exóticas, avanzando implacable y calmosa, sin necesidad de desviar sus pasos entre rododendros y gomeros... (1407)

The story is not only characterized by such localized elaboration, but also by periodic returns to material already dealt with – a continual retracing and rewriting of elements. The very opening of the story is an obvious example of this rewriting. The first three paragraphs present and re-present the static situation to which Moncha returns. The first paragraph reads:

> En Santa María nada pasaba, era en otoño, apenas la dulzura brillante de un sol moribundo, puntual, lentamente apagado. Para toda la gama de sanmarianos que miraban el cielo y la tierra antes de aceptar la sinrazón adecuada del trabajo. (1403)

Nothing is happening before she returns, and very little happens after she does: events are anathema to "Novia". Curiously, for all its repetitions, they are essentially repetitions of very little. Appropriately, therefore, the season is a moribund autumn. The second paragraph reiterates the inertia and also suggests a minimal disturbance:

> Sin consonantes, aquel otoño que padecí en Santa María nada pasaba hasta que un marzo quince empezó sin violencia, tan suave como el Kleenex que llevan y esconden las mujeres en sus carteras, tan suave como el papel, los papeles de seda, sedosos, arrastrándose entre nalgas. (1403)

It is not insignificant that the hint at a disrupting event is quickly overwhelmed by the elaboration of two metaphors as if returning the narrative opening to the state of initial inertia. The same process of blocking an opening is demonstrated by the third paragraph:

> Nada sucedió en Santa María aquel otoño hasta que llegó la hora – por qué maldita o fatal o determinada e ineludible – , hasta que llegó la hora feliz de la mentira, y el amarillo se insinuó en los bordes de los encajes venecianos. (1403)

The preterite seems to give the event a potentially sharper focus, but it is soon subsumed by the repetition of time and place and by a parenthesis which delays the definition of what did happen. When the event seems about to be described it is ushered in by another internal repetition and is then left unclarified by the reference to a detail concerning the lace of Moncha's dress which can have no meaning yet for the reader. In short, the opening refuses to move forward: it remains statically with the same material and deflects the arrival of anything new. This is deeply characteristic of the whole story. A similar proliferation occurs in the description of Moncha's dress (1411-12). There are four different descriptions of it which cannot define a single dress, and indeed they appear to be little more than hypothetical versions, which ultimately say more about the rhetoric of describing wedding dresses in general rather than Moncha's dress in particular.[5] Attention is also drawn to the surface of the writing by the repetition of the references to the absence of Marcos Bergner and Padre Bergner, and to the complicity of sections of Santa María in supporting Moncha's delusion that she is about to get married.

These repetitions litter the text, creating the impression of an arborescent proliferation rather than linear forward movement. That same process is seen in miniature in the passage dealing with Barthé and the youth. Here certain elements appear and reappear almost like the shuffling of cards in a pack. In the course of pages 1413-16 certain details are reiterated and refined continually from slightly varied angles. These elements include: the physical appearance of Barthé and the youth; the relationship between them and their business "partnership"; Barthé's framed pharmacist's certificate; his extreme left-wing political position; the

---

[5] The dress is not singular in any way, since it also functions as a "salto de cama, camisón y mortaja" (1421).

contents of the pharmacy; the tarot cards; and finally Moncha's wedding dress, which is elaborated into extensive repeated metaphors concerning a mermaid, and then an insect (1416). The passage dealing with Moncha in the pharmacy is rich and suggestive, but is remarkably uninformative about what the three characters are trying to do. They may be using the tarot cards to see into the future (presumably to find out whether Moncha's bridegroom will return), but it is never explained why she decides to see into the future with these two characters. One might surmise that the three share a marginal status within Santa María, but that explanation is never made explicit. Moncha's visits simply happen, and they are then treated en bloc and as a series of images and descriptive repetitions.

In addition to these devices which stress repetition over movement, the story at various points includes global summaries referring to Moncha's return to Santa María, her activities (the garden ritual, the visits to the pharmacy and courtesy calls), and to Santa María's reaction and its attempt to indulge Moncha in her illusion. In this respect, the most striking of the repetitions in the story is that involving her visit to the restaurant. It is the narrator who imagines the visit taking place again forty years later with Moncha as an old lady (1419-20). There is no assumption of referentiality here: the repetition is purely invented, and as such amply demonstrates the underlying tendency of the story to thicken its textures and accumulate rather than move forward. In that way, this invention underlines how these repetitions in the story may insinuate an underlying ideology of no escape, since forty years later the same things may still be happening. There is no progression, no seeing beyond the same; on the contrary, there are fatalistic circles within "Novia" and within Santa María, which is precisely why Moncha, like so many before her, has returned to it.

The question of repetition is also relevant to the play of subject pronouns in the story, especially in relation to the use of "nosotros" and the status of knowledge. The story insists quite heavily on the link between "nosotros" and "saber". And the "nosotros" is also linked fundamentally with Santa María and its values. These two links are made clear near the start with the narrator's condescending attitude towards "returnees", those who left Santa María for something more interesting but who inevitably come back. Referring to the returnees, the narrator explains the reaction to their complaints about being back in the town:

> Pero nos aburrimos, sabemos que mascarán con placer el fracaso y las embellecidas memorias, falsificadas por necesidad, sin intención pensada. Sabemos que volvieron para quedarse y, otra vez, seguir viviendo. (1406)

Santa María knows that life goes on, that there is no escape, and the insistence on knowing better seeks to bolster authority, something that also derives from references to the narrator's group as "los notables" (1413) and "los viejos" (1417, 1420, 1421).

The insistence on knowing might suggest that there is a stable, underlying framework of information, but my analysis so far clearly demonstrates that there is no such framework. And frequently knowing exists in complex and tense relation with ignorance and forgetfulness, "ignorancia" and "olvido" (1407, 1410-11, 1417, 1420). The intimate relation between knowing and not-knowing is well demonstrated in one brief passage:

> La crónica policial no dijo nada y la columna de chismes de *El Liberal* no se enteró nunca. Pero todos sabíamos, unidos en la mesa de juego o de bebida, que la vasquita Insaurralde, tan distinta, se encerraba de noche en la botica con Barthé... y con el mancebo manceba que ahora sonreía con distracción a todo el mundo... Los tres adentro y sólo quedaba para nuestra curiosidad avejentada, para adivinanzas y calumnias, el botón azul sobre la pequeña chapa iluminada: Servicio de urgencia. (1413-14)

This passage first sets up others' lack of knowledge against the fact that "nosotros" do know, but it then shows that all that "nosotros" know is that the three characters meet in the pharmacy. What happens inside is only available, it seems, through guesswork (or slander). Despite the passage's initial assertion to the contrary, all that is visible is the emergency button: significantly, the curiosity of "nosotros" is reduced to panic, to an emergency, in other words, their absence of knowledge. There is a split here undermining the telling of the "nosotros".

That tenuous base for the assertion of knowledge and the role of invention are alluded to again in another remark made by the narrator:

> La vasquita Insurralde estuvo, pero nos cayó después desde el cielo y todavía no sabemos; por eso contamos. (1406)

To tell the story fills the gap left by the lack of knowing, hardly the surest foundation on which to build trust in the reader. There are further references to invention (1407, 1410), and it seems clear that if the "nosotros" are prepared to collaborate with Moncha in the fiction of Marcos' and Padre Bergner's return, then there is also room to wonder if they do not also create the fiction of Moncha that constitutes "Novia".

The essential problems for knowledge in the story are distance and otherness. In the first place, when Moncha returns she does not apparently speak to "nosotros" (1406), and furthermore she proceeds to lock herself away behind the walls of her father's house which shuts out the whole of Santa María. And that separation is partly willed by "nosotros" since they want to be apart, not implicated, "a salvo" (1407): they are other to her, just as they are also intrigued and observe from a distance. There is, therefore, another division within the narrating position.

Moreover, Moncha is an irritant, a foreign body that does not fit in Santa María, and "nosotros" can only cope with that in a certain number of ways: they are certainly not united in their reaction to her. There are those who prefer not to know about her and opt for the simplicity of ignorance (1411, 1412), and there are others who would protect her from the truth, but who do that only in order to preserve Santa María's peace and routine (1408). In either case, Santa María lacks the imagination to cope adequately with the challenge that Moncha poses. There is even a suggestion, for all Santa María's apparent stability and its wish to be the possessor of knowledge, that the fundamental problem lies with it, in its pretence and inflexibility. Using the metaphor of poker and the expressionless face assumed in playing it, the town's repression and lack of emotional reaction seem to incapacitate it:

> Pero al matar toda expresión que pudiera trasmitir alegría, desencanto,
> riesgos calculados, grandes o pequeñas astucias, nos era forzoso, inevitable,
> mostrar en las caras otras cosas, las que estábamos resueltos, acostumbrados a
> esconder diariamente, durante años, cada día, desde el final del sueño, todas las
> jornadas, hasta el principio del sueño. (1414)

Significantly, the town's repression is sandwiched between dreams, a byword in Onetti for desire, precisely what seems to drive Moncha and the narrator too, before he hides himself behind the mask of the "nosotros". As elsewhere in Onetti, the dream is linked explicitly with what is not Santa María – Europe or Paris, in this case (1405-06).[6] The repression of desire may therefore explain the doctor's insistence (in the death certificate that he writes for Moncha at the end of the story) that the cause of her death is Santa María and certain representative individuals involved with it: "Estado o enfermedad causante directo de la muerte: Brausen, Santa María, todos ustedes, yo mismo" (1422).

*

Textuality and Sexuality

The story contains little information about Moncha, and what there is derives exclusively from male viewpoints: "yo", "nosotros", Díaz Grey and Barthé. The only direct quote of her words consists of a strange account of her travels in Europe (1412-13). Her story, albeit rather minimal, provides the important context of her return to Santa María. She was born into a rich family and becomes a rebel, going to live in the phalanstery down on the coast (1408). Díaz Grey sees her (perhaps in fantasy) defying Santa María (1409) in the role of "muchacha", which may be read as symbolizing her innocence. Her subsequent departure for Europe extends her rejection of Santa María and seems to be the attempt to enact a dream of fulfilment elsewhere (1405). Her return to the town at the beginning of "Novia" is therefore a reversal, but, although Moncha does return physically, she is still an outsider, locked away behind the walls of her father's house and of her own madness. That continued outsider status may be confirmed by her close contact

---

[6] The distance of the dream (again located in Europe) is also the basic problem for Kirsten in "Esbjerg".

with Barthé and the youth. In their homosexual relation, Barthé and the youth are stigmatized by Santa María, including the narrator, and their outsider status seems to give them a certain equivalence with Moncha. So her return is hardly complete, and it is linked with desire just as her departure was: she comes back to marry Marcos Bergner. Although she returns for this conventional purpose, she is still locked in frustrated desire because of Marcos' death. The logic of desire continues in her story: there is no escape into fulfilment with Europe or with Marcos. Hence, Marcos is the "otro ausente" (1418), the missing object against which she wants to fix herself. But interestingly, in talking to Díaz Grey, she equates marriage with death, as if the realization of her desire would mean the end of life (1408).[7] Hence, in the logic of the masculine discourse she goes mad and commits suicide – she becomes a "trágica loquita" (1409) like Julita Malabia[8] –, and that is a further sign of her marginality to Santa María, of her refusal of its reality of simple, continuing life (1406). The typing of Moncha in this way is a highly characteristic move in Onetti and is yet another example of the objectification of a female character. It is apparent too in the use of the wedding dress which Moncha constantly wears. The dress (with its colour slowly changing from white to yellow, and its lace decorations) is referred to as a whole or in fragments quite frequently, and indeed sometimes appears to become an independent entity ageing and moving on its own. The dress is used as both a synecdoche for Moncha (for example, 1418), and as a device locking her into a single, specific role: the mad, desiring and frustrated *novia*.

The fixing and stereotyping of Moncha show another, more significant functioning of desire in "Novia". That aspect is related to the narrating "yo" and its relation to the "nosotros". The first three pages are exclusively narrated by the "yo", though it would be more accurate to say that the first three pages sketch an

---

[7] That incompatibility of life and fulfilled desire might also be said to be manifested in "Sueño".

[8] See *Juntacadáveres* (1964).

emotional landscape with a logic of their own and create a context for the rest of the story. Even with the switch to the "nosotros" the initial framing by the "yo" is not entirely superseded – it is, rather, displaced.

The opening sequence is notable for the "yo"'s direct address of Moncha, as if he were writing a letter to the dead woman:

> Dije, Moncha, que no importa porque se trata, apenas, de una carta de amor o cariño o respeto o lealtad. (1403)

These emotions bulk larger in the narrator's mind than sheer events: the story is not original, though the feelings may be:

> Me dijeron, Moncha, que esta historia ya había sido escrita y también, lo que importa menos, vivida por otra Moncha, en el sur que liberaron y deshicieron los yanquis, en algún fluctuante lugar del Brasil, en un condado de una Inglaterra con la Old Vic. (1403)[9]

This lack of interest in the mere events is particularly important given the circumstances of the "yo"'s writing: he writes after attending Moncha's wake (1404), and hence her living reality is even more distant – she becomes a purely mental object for him. And this leads the "yo" to the insistence that, despite others' suggestions for the ordering of the story, he will structure it in his own way: "... prefiero contarte desde el principio que importa hasta el saludo, la despedida" (1404). It is not so much her story as herself that will be written, and that derives from two desires: his love for her, which it appears may have been unreciprocated – "Siempre supiste, creo, que te quería..." (1403); and his wish to gain respect for her – "... y yo contribuía sin palabras a crear e imponer un respeto que se te debía desde siglos por ser hembra y transportar recatada e ineludible tu persona entre tus piernas" (1405). It seems clear that the wish to create respect by the use of such objectifying formulations is contradictory, since Moncha's dignity is severely compromised by this reductive attitude. And this is indicative of the problematic nature of the narrator's framing of Moncha.

---

[9] The allusion to the south and the yankees may well be to Faulkner as Ludmer suggests, but the general pattern of relocating the story is also reminiscent of the opening gestures of Borges' "Tema del traidor y del héroe".

That masculine framing is by no means superseded when the "yo" assimilates itself to the collective "nosotros" of Santa María's establishment:

> Por astucia, recurso, humildad, amor a lo cierto, deseo de ser claro y poner orden, dejo el yo y simulo perderme en el nosotros. Todos hicieron lo mismo. (1405)

Despite the fact that the "yo" continues to be used in the next paragraph, the rest of "Novia" is narrated by the "nosotros". There is an apparent disguising of the personal in this switch, but it is clear that the "nosotros", for all its plurality, is singularly masculine in the way it acts as the constituting subject of enunciation. The result is that the ensuing "story" is not so much Moncha's as Santa María's, and above all the story of the establishment men who observe and react to Moncha – it is "nosotros"' story about her. And that is significant in the absence of any direct access to her (except for her brief account of being in Europe, whose source is not explained).

"Novia" is a text constructed on masculine desire, hence any investment by the reader in the narrator and the "nosotros" as one(s)-supposed-to-know is flawed, as not-knowing and desire are in important ways constitutive of the text. So "Novia" tends to reveal more about the "yo"/"nosotros" than about Moncha and her desire. She is a type constituted in male desire and against which the anonymous "nosotros" constitute themselves. However, she continually eludes and irritates them; even her name is unstable: she may be called Insurralde or Insaurralde, and the uncertain "a" is a sign of her lack of fixity, or incipient insurrection.

Hence, what is projected as Moncha's desire is actually the "yo"'s and the "nosotros"'s desire for her desire, which cannot in practice be held steady. Hence also the lack of relation: the "yo" desires Moncha who desires Marcos – the objects of desire are both in some way absent (dead) and unreciprocating. Desire does not coincide with its object, and demands more than the object can give. The *fracaso* in "Novia" is apparently the continuing of desire in Santa María, the antithesis of fulfilment or the dream of it. It is notable that the desire is for an apparently minimally socialized object, as if the thrust of desire were always away from the rootedness in a social structure, though a social structure necessarily precedes its rejection. The madness of women in Onetti and the desire to get away from Santa María always have this negating and Imaginary push to reject the Symbolic shared in the town.

In the absence of narrative line in "Novia", a structure is created by a crossing back and forth over an emotional terrain, the space of a certain masculine desiring subjectivity. And that space is one of textuality, the textualizing of desire, where words fill or try to fill the gap of the absent relation. Hence the dynamic of desire is textual production, the metonymic shift from word to word. The "novia robada", therefore, is not so much the bride stolen or taken away or abducted, as the bride constituted by masculine desire and denied the power of its own enunciation.

CHAPTER 9

A CASE OF LETHAL PATERNITY:

LA MUERTE Y LA NINA

The title of *La muerte y la niña* proposes a tension – between new life and its end – , and this is indicative of the novella's constant deployment of material that never resolves or settles into clearly defined relations. *La muerte y la niña* does not contain a narrative of easy cohesion, on the contrary, it is extremely fluid in its changes of focus, definition, time and detailing. It is constructed out of a mutating play of centrifugal and centripetal forces which reading cannot stabilize satisfactorily. The novella opens itself to but resists the reader, and the potential falsification of analysis is to reduce the complex surface to transparent "sense". In fact, in one respect *La muerte y la niña* disrupts its own logic by attempting to stabilize meaning, an inconsistency which I will analyze and try to counteract by re-insisting on textual density.

*

Centrifugal Forces

La muerte y la niña appears to be written as a narrative but its form is somewhat idiosyncratic. The result is that it creates a strong sense of its own textuality, of its own writing practice. This is highly characteristic of late Onetti, witness for example "Novia" and *Cuando entonces*. The novella contains twelve chapters which span a long period: it is hard to delimit that period precisely though it seems to be approximately forty years, covering the first part of Augusto Goerdel's life. To say "covering" is misleading because the novella's concentration is rather sporadic, mostly being focused on specific dialogues. The chapters are not presented chronologically; if they were their order would be: 3, 4, 8, 1, 2, 5, 6, 7, 9, 10, 11, 12, showing an apparently more conventional narrative progress in the later chapters. But that impression is less obvious in practice given the temporal gaps between the chapters, matching those between earlier chapters. So chapters 3, 4 and 8 take place several years apart, the gap between chapters 4 and 8, for example, omitting the whole of Goerdel's university years. Chapter 2 follows directly from chapter 1 but begins with an analeptic passage from a year before, when Díaz Grey examined Helga Hauser. This expansive and irregular coverage of time is in contrast with chapters 5, 6 and 7 (which probably take place a little more than the length of a pregnancy after chapter 1): here a single conversation spans three chapters.[1] Chapters 9 and 10 move forward to a period considerably in the future from chapters 5-7: Goerdel has been to Europe and returned. Chapters 11 and 12 leap forward from chapters 9 and 10 and seemingly contain yet another return of Goerdel from Europe.

The temporal dislocations are the more striking in that most chapters focus on a single conversation which therefore figures as a point of time in a long expanse: chapters 1, 2, 4, 5, 6, 7, 9, 11 and 12 are either wholly or largely focused on one dialogue. Only chapters 3 and 8 seem to summarize (briefly) a number of years, and chapter 10 (briefly) a number of months. Hence, there is an extreme contrast between broad spans of time (hardly mentioned or described) and the detailed treatment of single dialogues within those spans. This sort of contrast is found again in *Cuando entonces*. Both texts stretch causal chronological ordering, so that they are striking for the absence of a clear, global narrative framework. *La*

---

[1] In the interview between Goerdel and Díaz Grey in chapter 1 concerning the danger of pregnancy, it is implicitly understood that Helga Hauser is not yet pregnant, otherwise there seems to be little point in discussing the danger of such an eventuality and how to avoid it. By chapter 5, Helga Hauser has died in childbirth.

muerte y la niña is constituted by a series of moments across a span of several decades, but without a consistent causal chain: the interconnections in the series depend far more on recurrent characters (who in turn are not all stable in their identity), and on repeated references to key information (for example, the death of Helga Hauser). The attenuation of narrative form is further achieved by the stress on dialogue: there is very little action in *La muerte y la niña* and hardly any reports of its occurrence in the periods of time not covered. This is a novella of story-telling and interaction of values, and even the summaries in chapters 3, 8 and 10 tend to render action remote.

A further centrifugal effect in the novella derives from the fact that the narrator-focalizer is not constant throughout. The main narrator-focalizer is an unidentified figure who is (mostly) extra- and heterodiegetic, but who also personalizes his account by occasionally referring to the self as "yo" and inserting personal experience and opinion. The other is Díaz Grey, and at certain moments it is not possible to tell which is in control. The anonymous narrator-focalizer is apparently a figure of authority, able to report characters' private actions and thoughts, or to make general comments. It is also this narrator-focalizer who can move the text's focus around in time. However, this narrator-focalizer is not so impersonal that he refrains from passing comment on or deflating characters. His authority is slightly undermined by occasional self-references which hint at not knowing, at his status as just another citizen of Santa María. For example, in considering the changes to Brausen's statue:

> Nadie lo notó, nadie me lo dijo. Tal vez los antiguos no vieron el cambio por la costumbre de mirar la cabeza casi todos los días; los nuevos, porque siempre la vieron así... Miraré mañana, en el sol. (50)

The narrator-focalizer's position as citizen of Santa María leads to the few moments of slight confusion with Díaz Grey, when the narrating voice uses the "nosotros", the collective voice of Santa María. Two examples will show the difficulties of identification. Chapter 9 opens with general comments on time using the "nosotros" voice, but the identity of the narrator-focalizer is hinted at by a reference in the second paragraph to "las agendas que repartían generosos los laboratorios médicos" (91), suggesting a special interest, in other words that of doctor Díaz Grey. But that suggestion is over-ridden when the name Díaz Grey is mentioned in the third paragraph and the anonymous narrator-focalizer proceeds to recount the interview between Díaz Grey and Padre Bergner neutrally. By contrast, chapter 11 also opens with an unidentified narrator-focalizer in a scene involving Díaz Grey and Jorge Malabia, but here the identity is revealed to be that of the doctor, though this is only deducible slowly.

Díaz Grey is the narrator-focalizer in certain passages, but only when he participates in a scene, and not always then. He is an extra- and homodiegetic narrator. In chapter 5, for example, Jorge visits Díaz Grey and the latter is (mostly) the narrator-focalizer: his voice and values condition the communication of information. However, in the continuation of that scene in chapters 6 and 7, the narrating and focalizing switch to the anonymous narrator-focalizer, though the scene does continue to be closer to Díaz Grey's viewpoint than to Jorge's (with the exception of the opening of chapter 7).

These variations and slight blurrings in narration and focalization are compounded by more unsettling switches. For example, in chapter 11, the narrator-focalizer is Díaz Grey throughout pages 111-22, but by page 126 Díaz Grey is referred to in the third person and he does not appear to resume narrating for the rest of the chapter. The most extreme examples of the switches in narration and focalization come in chapter 5 where they occur in the course of one page (53), and even in the course of one paragraph; note the ambiguity of voice at the start of the third sentence here:

> Dos herencias, pensó [Díaz Grey], que servirían algún día para unirnos o separarnos. Angélica Inés, su mujer [la de Díaz Grey], dormía babeando en el piso de arriba. Jorge se estiraba en el suelo, desperezándose, henchido por la noticia que lo empujaba hacia mí, que lo obligaba a esperarme, entrar, poner para siempre en algún rincón del consultorio o de la sala, dentro de mí en todo caso. (55)

The final example of centrifugal forces in the novella is the characteristic practice of introducing a detail or element without full explanation. This creates gaps or disjunctions as possibly important contextualizing or framing information may be delayed for some time or even completely omitted. An example of this comes in the opening pages where Goerdel visits Díaz Grey and tells him that he may be about to kill his wife (9). This publicizing of a future death/murder (which may actually happen but which is not therefore a recognized crime in legal terms) is striking, though not focused on directly, as the novella only starts when Goerdel has *finished* telling his story. Hence it is only fragmentedly in the course of the first ten pages that it becomes clear that this "crime" has a very particular circumstance, that is his wife's medical condition which puts her in danger if she has more children. The point is that the narrator-focalizer does not explain this: the information reaches the reader dispersed in the characters' conversation.

Goerdel's identity is another example of how the novella avoids linking information explicitly, and so stretches cohesion. Character continuity is a basic device of narrative integration, but *La muerte y la niña* can be remarkably sparing with it. In the whole of chapter 1, the patient who visits Díaz Grey is given no name. Chapter 3 introduces a character named Augusto Goerdel and outlines the salient details of his early life, particularly his education with Padre Bergner. It is only on page 59, when Jorge tells Díaz Grey that a woman has died giving birth and calls it murder, that the information of chapter 1 is referred to again. Subsequently, it is only on page 65, in chapter 6, that Díaz Grey finally makes the explicit link between the name Goerdel and the patient who came to warn him of his impending "crime" in chapter 1. So virtually half the novella is completed before this important link is confirmed.

Towards the end of *La muerte y la niña*, Goerdel twice returns unexpectedly to Santa María. His first return is at the start of chapter 9, though it has never been made clear that he had *definitively* left the town, indeed chapter 8 ends with him busily engaged in the Colonia and facing the prospect of marriage to Helga Hauser. The reason for his permanent departure and the link with the death of his wife has to be surmised: he apparently flees for his life from Santa María at the end of chapter 6. At the start of chapter 11, it again seems that Goerdel returns, although chapter 10 ended with Goerdel and Padre Bergner visiting the Insauberrys to request the hand of their twelve-year-old daughter for Goerdel. How that episode finished (Goerdel apparently does not marry the girl) is not explained, and neither are the reasons for his now living in East Germany. Indeed, the motivation that he provides for his second return to Santa María – that he wants to clear his name of the unjust suspicion of being responsible for the pregnancy which killed his first wife and so claim that he was cuckolded – seems rather improbable.[2] Moral sensitivity and abhorrence of the apparently surviving adulterer in Santa María hardly explain why he made no effort on his first return (in chapter 9) to establish his innocence, nor why it is necessary for a man now living in East Germany to return for this purpose.

In the context of these gaps in information, it is hardly surprising that the novella ends without resolution. In chapter 11, Goerdel makes his claim for innocence (albeit in a rather dispersed and minimalist fashion) and leaves the photos of the letters which he claims will prove his case. And then in chapter 12, Díaz Grey and Jorge examine the letters in detail and decide that they prove nothing. Hence the novella ends with the guilt of Goerdel undecided: two points of view confront each other, as contrary views so consistently do in *La muerte y la niña*. In addition, Goerdel finishes by precisely counterbalancing his own position in chapter 1: he begins the novella by announcing his possible murder of his wife, and he ends it by categorically denying his guilt, which at least gives the novella formal balance.

Something of the challenge posed by the writing of *La muerte y la niña* and its general subversion of conventional practice is alluded to metatextually by Díaz

---

[2] Examples in literature of male characters accusing themselves of cuckoldry appear to be somewhat rare.

Grey in comments he makes about his own sense of history. There is not a little similarity about the stretching of simple chronology and explanation in Díaz Grey's approach to history at school and in the writing of *La muerte y la niña*, of which he is one of the narrators:

> Mis notas en Historia, cuando era estudiante y ambicioso, siempre fueron pobres. No por falta de inteligencia o atención; lo supe mucho después y sin necesidad de análisis. La falla estaba en que no era capaz de relacionar las fechas de batallas militares o políticas con mi visión de la historia que me enseñaban o intentaba comprender... Innumerables datos, a veces contradictorios, se me ofrecían en los libros y en las clases. Pero yo era tan libre y tan torpe como para construir con todo eso una fábula, nunca creída del todo, en la que héroes y sucesos se unían y separaban caprichosamente. (117-18)

The substitution of fiction ("fábula") for history appears particularly revealing in this formulation, suggesting as it does a lack of concern with facts which is normally alien to the study of history. In addition to this, what is striking in Díaz Grey's understanding of history is repetition – a profoundly non-narrative force which homogenizes information and events, and inhibits narrative impetus:

> Siempre sentía la reiteración: los héroes y los pueblos subían y bajaban. Y el resultado que me era posible afirmar, lo sé ahora, era un ciento o miles de Santa Marías, enormes en gente y territorio, o pequeñas y provinciales como ésta que me había tocado en suerte. Los dominadores dominaban, los dominados obedecían. Siempre a la espera de la próxima revolución, que siempre sería la última. (118)

All seems to be indistinct and blurred into a single form, and that lack of differentiation is also essential to *La muerte y la niña*'s writing practice.[3]

*

Centripetal Forces

There are certain patterns in the novella which do tend to act as centripetal forces, whether formal or thematic. For example, religion is a frequent point of reference, which is unusual in Onetti, but the nature of the references is hardly orthodox. Virtually all religious references are to Juan María Brausen, the creator

---

[3] It is also evident in *Cuando entonces* where there is a lack of focus on any single thematic core and where no conventional distinction is drawn consistently between foreground and background information.

of Santa María in *La vida breve* (1950), and virtually all are ironic and disparaging.[4] Padre Bergner does refer to Brausen respectfully, but in general the religious strand is used to associate Brausen with the attributes of the Christian God only to distort them. So, for example, the Lord's Prayer is invoked only to be subverted (10), and Díaz Grey tells Padre Bergner to trust in Brausen who may surprise him with some illumination (102). Díaz Grey also mentions that Brausen is copying the tradition of the Christian God by allowing his creatures – that is, Díaz Grey – to die slowly cell by cell: Brausen is apparently devoid of originality even in his cruel treatment of the inhabitants of the town. The critique from Díaz Grey is pointed: he resents the arbitrariness of his creator who simply thrust him into the world of Santa María at thirty or forty years of age with no past. This is a blatant metatextual joke, since Díaz Grey arrived in Onetti's fiction at this age in *La vida breve* and the character is therefore referring to his own fictionality. *La muerte y la niña* is quite unusual, in fact, in alluding to events involving Díaz Grey's daughter which could antedate his "birth" at thirty or forty years. Díaz Grey's black humour is employed consistently and his resentment over his nonexistent early years culminates with a strong curse on Brausen, which sees him as a deity subject to a more powerful deity:

> [Las muchachas] siempre lejanas e intocables, apartadas de mí por la disparidad de los treinta o cuarenta años que me impuso Juan María Brausen, maldita sea su alma que ojalá se abrase durante uno o dos pares de eternidades en el infierno adecuado que ya tiene pronto para él un Brausen más alto, un poco más verdadero. (25)

The religious references are then a sort of intermittent humorous touch-stone, and none more so than those concerning the statue of Brausen: not only is it unorthodox for a sort of Christian God to have a statue, but this one is equestrian and developing bovine features (49-50).

---

[4] There are also references to "Diosbrausen" in "Novia".

In a more formal vein, there is a simple centripetal pull in the interview format which is used in all but four chapters (chapters 2, 3, 8 and 10). The interview is an element which contributes to the attenuated narrative impetus since key events are not directly recounted so much as verbalized and attitudinized over. Díaz Grey has interviews with Goerdel (twice), Jorge Malabia (twice), and Padre Bergner (once), and they have all chosen to consult him. In addition, Goerdel and Padre Bergner have one extended conversation, and, given the latter's authority, it also has the hierarchical structure of a formal interview. In these interviews Díaz Grey is hardly ever consulted for his medical opinion. On the contrary, each of them seems to represent a way for characters to demand recognition, and Díaz Grey is therefore implicitly invested with authoritative opinion, although he rarely approves of or cooperates with his visitors. Interestingly, insofar as *La muerte y la niña* casts him in this role, it too imbues him with authority, a point to which I shall return. One particular characteristic of the interviews is their forcefulness, and occasionally even hostility: characters do not find common ground easily, and Díaz Grey is suspicious and dismissive of others' motives. These discords help to articulate disparate positions: the clash of values and viewpoints seems to be one of the main purposes of the interviews. Not that the differences are predictable. *La muerte y la niña* has a rather unstable set of subject positions, and, although a Santa María/other polarity is in play, it is difficult to locate characters absolutely or consistently. In fact, the sheer restrictedness of the man-to-man interview format is in direct inverse proportion to the clarity and stability of the information that the interviews produce about the characters. Centrifugal and centripetal tensions are simultaneously in play here, and Goerdel is particularly elusive in this respect.

*

Goerdel

Augusto Goerdel is a character with little homogeneity, and the changes in him hardly follow a consistent trajectory. Even in chapter 1, he is difficult for

Díaz Grey and Santa María to understand. In the doctor's eyes, Goerdel appears a self-publicist in announcing the risk of his "murdering" his wife, performing a part for him and Santa María and making them complicitous with his actions. Díaz Grey distrusts him, seeing him as cynical and calculating (9-10), the sort of clarity of view which characters aspire to in their judgements but which the novella rarely justifies. However, near the end Díaz Grey seems to know that clarity is inadequate when he says about Goerdel: "Nunca pude saber si estaba improvisando el infortunio o si recitaba un discurso sabido de memoria" (120). Goerdel goes to the doctor to ask for advice about avoiding the risk to his wife of another pregnancy (11), but, on receiving Díaz Grey's severe recommendations about how to reduce his sexual urge (14-15), Goerdel announces that he and his wife have already decided to take precautionary steps of quite a different sort (17). Goerdel's elusiveness is therefore registered at the very start, and the mixing in him of conformity with non-conformity is constant. This heterogeneity is underpinned by the consistent presentation of him from others' points of view: he is continually seen by other eyes and by other criteria, and this precludes any centring of the character.

The very origins and location of Goerdel are undecidable – it is, for instance, unclear whether he was conceived inside or outside the Colonia: "Augusto Goerdel había sido engendrado en la Colonia suiza o ya venía dentro del vientre de la madre durante el largo viaje de nuestra bamboleante 'Flor de mayo'" (29). His early life is spent in poverty in the Colonia, a place which is not inside Santa María and yet not outside it either: the Colonia is a Swiss Catholic community which is built up as a sort of extension of the town. His ambiguous location inside/outside Santa María (which is sustained throughout with different intensities) is paralleled in his relation to religion, this time perceived by Padre Bergner. Goerdel acquiesces in Padre Bergner's selection of him for special training within the church. This is significant in that he expresses no will in the matter, which might connote desire or identity, but passively accepts a role provided for him: he is to become Padre Bergner's instrument (34). His selection relocates him outside the Colonia and within the church in Santa María, and the narrator-focalizer explicitly tells the reader that the poverty and restrictions on him created by the Colonia have been left behind (34). This is a major shift for the character. However, Goerdel's very acquiescence raises doubts: Padre Bergner sees him as intelligent and ambitious but as merely using the church to satisfy his will to succeed. Hence, Padre Bergner believes that he is only playing a part as a future priest, pretending to believe and to be devout. This is brought into focus when Padre Bergner witnesses what he takes to be a cynical performance of religious devotion:

> Y allí, en camisón y arrodillado, golpeándose el pecho para acompañar el llanto, Augusto Goerdel.
> "Debe hacerlo todas las madrugadas – pensó Bergner – ; sudoroso o helado, tenaz y puntual, apostando sobre la ley de probabilidades, seguro de que alguna vez tendré que verlo, sorprenderlo en su pieza de bravura y creer en él."
> (38)

In chapter 4, at the end of Goerdel's studies in Santa María, Padre Bergner confronts him with their joint play-acting over years, their shared, though hitherto unacknowledged, hypocrisy. And Padre Bergner claims that they have both always known that Goerdel will never be a priest. As with Díaz Grey, there is an attempt at a clear view of Goerdel, but the latter does not acknowledge Padre Bergner's "truths", only finally acquiescing with them ambiguously: " – De acuerdo – dijo [Goerdel] –, de acuerdo en todo. Ahora y aquí. Escucho y obedezco" (47). The suggestion here is that he is merely deferential to the priest's authority without admitting anything of substance. And Goerdel is prepared to shift position again when Padre Bergner offers him a new role as the church's representative in the secular world. It appears that the role playing continues, and the character's diversity is reaffirmed. The elusiveness of Goerdel continues when he returns to Santa María after university to carry out his "religious" mission in a very secular world of legal and financial problems in the Colonia (83-84), because, while ostensibly helping to protect Padre Bergner's flock from religious infiltration, he also makes a lot of money for the priest (84-85). By doing that he becomes rich himself, in sharp contrast with the poverty of his childhood and student years.

Goerdel is sufficiently orthodox to marry and have children, something which is extremely rare in Onetti's protagonists; but that very orthodoxy leads to the "unorthodoxy" of his possible shared responsibility for his wife's death in childbirth. At that point, his ambiguous position in relation to Santa María would seem to be resolved as the town simply ostracizes him. The clarity of the "expulsion" is consistent with the attempts of others in *La muerte y la niña* to adopt clear views of him. And that effort seems to be confirmed reciprocally by Goerdel himself when he reappears in chapter 11 and writes an assessment of Santa María for someone unconnected with the town. He insists on Santa María's inhospitable attitude to strangers and outsiders (as epitomized by Jorge's behaviour towards him [114-15]), and its arrogant assumption of superiority over the rest of the world, its desire for power (115-16). But Goerdel's presence throughout the novella puts such attitudes and the assumption of clear knowledge deeply in question, for he fails to be controlled and accounted for by the town. There is no simple view of his position possible.

The desire for clarity in Santa María's ostracism of him is questioned by Goerdel, firstly via his return (chapters 9 and 10) with the dream of marrying the twelve-year-old daughter of the wealthy Insauberrys (the sincerity of which creates a typical division: Padre Bergner is uncertain about it, Díaz Grey is not); and secondly via his later return (chapter 11) in order to refute the town's belief that he was the father of the child that killed his first wife. This puts in question the very foundation of his ostracism, and his guilt. In opposition to Goerdel's attempt, Díaz Grey seems in little doubt that he is untrustworthy and Jorge seems to share that view, dismissing Goerdel as "loco" (111), and thereby othering him. The unresolved nature of Goerdel's relation with Santa María is compounded at this late stage by further elements of heterogeneity and oddity in his identity. In chapter 11, Jorge tells Díaz Grey that Goerdel is now a Catholic priest, so that regardless of the change of Padre Bergner's early plans it seems that Goerdel has in fact fulfilled the initial objective. Despite this reversion, Jorge also claims that Goerdel is married with children, which hardly fits the normal blueprint for a Catholic priest, though Jorge speculates (somewhat improbably) that he may have papal permission for this unorthodoxy (112). Regardless of this new identity as priest, Goerdel himself signs a letter to Germany as "student" (117). Furthermore, he has changed his name to Johannes Schmidt. And in the quoted letter which he sends to Germany, he seems to eliminate his early years of connection with Santa María and the Colonia by describing the town as if he had only just got to know it: "'De manera que después de conocer a Santa María personalmente, no vierto tantas lágrimas por este país como antes'" (115). These new elements evidently continue to destabilize the character, so that no focused motives can be ascribed to him. Díaz Grey (uncharacteristically close to Santa María orthodoxy) sees Goerdel as simply set against the town, as a negative: "El hombre parecía resuelto a cruzar como demente todas las murallas de los cuerdos; a violar, lúcido, todos los obstáculos que construyéramos nosotros, herederos de la locura del bienestar, del variable ser en la pasividad" (119). Consequently, Díaz Grey is not convinced by Goerdel's attempts to clear his name. He feels that the desire to prove his innocence in respect of his wife's death is another example of play-acting (120). And indeed, Goerdel's explanation is at odds with the logic of discrepancies and ambiguities in *La muerte y la niña*, which would deny all simple resolution. In fact, having made the bid for the simple truth of his own case, Goerdel rather undermines himself by revealing to Díaz Grey that he has lied to Santa María about his earliest memories of Europe: "'Fíjese: mentí siempre... Engañé también al padre Bergner'" (125). His bid to establish his innocence, to prove that the fatal child was not his and perhaps to take revenge on Santa María for its ostracism (126-27), is exactly counterbalanced by Díaz Grey's and Jorge's refusal to believe his evidence (134-35).

The novella is a web of undecidability and permutation. It shifts identity/-
ies and denies the availability of any univocal truth: it foregrounds the dialogic
play of different views and values. In that sense, it is a more public piece than
much of Onetti's work, though it is akin to "Historia". In neither text is there the
usual Onettian centring of the textual tension within the consciousness of one
character, but there is a shared interest in the ways in which Santa María deals
with the outsider. Paradoxically, Goerdel's identity is as open and shifting as that
of many of Onetti's protagonists but for reasons not linked to his own desire or
relationships (unlike the case of the protagonist of "Cara", for instance). So, far
from this character smoothly performing a normal role in narrative – as a stable
focal point – , it is blurred, fragmented and contradictory.

*

Jorge

It might seem that for most of the novella Jorge is diametrically opposed
to Goerdel in values, location and consistency. In most details this is so, but even
Jorge seems to share something of the novella's general shifting of positions, as
we shall see.

Throughout the novella Jorge is the system's forceful, even crude,
representative, a role that becomes an exaggerated performance in Díaz Grey's
view. So he goes to see the doctor in chapter 5 on horseback despite the fact that
he has two cars (53-54).[5] This display of himself is consolidated by his
conspicuously wearing a gun, the shirt of an "hachero canadiense" (55) and long
hair. In adopting this appearance, Jorge is conforming to certain fashions and
seems to be soliciting a look, an identification by others, and the early pages of his
presence in the novella are heavy with references to Díaz Grey's seeing him. This
visual performance is complemented by a forthright verbal performance of his view
of Goerdel's involvement in Helga Hauser's death: he fulminates against him.

---

[5] Jorge starts to ride a horse around Santa María on his return from Buenos Aires in *Para una
tumba sin nombre* (1959).

Now Díaz Grey undercuts this performance, not taking it at face value but diagnosing it in terms of a life trajectory. Díaz Grey sees Jorge ageing and growing fatter (a term of abuse in Jorge's vocabulary in *Para una tumba sin nombre*), and as devoted not only to identifying himself with the stupidity of the town but also to an empty future of making money: "Le dolía [a Díaz Grey] que Jorge ofreciera su futuro a la nada, a ganar dinero sin esfuerzo ni propósito. Le dolía que el otro engordara, que se mezclara, tan inocente, con la estupidez y la mugre del porvenir que le ofrecía la ciudad" (69). Díaz Grey contextualizes this transformation (in this case the reader sees the end of the process only) in relation to family events – Jorge has lost his metaphysical preoccupations and replaced them with material ones:

> El, Jorge Malabia, había cambiado. Ya no sufría por cuñadas suicidas ni por poemas imposibles. Vigilaba caprichosamente "El Liberal", compraba tierras y casas. Ahora era un hombre abandonado por los problemas metafísicos, por la necesidad de atrapar la belleza con un poema o un libro. (55-56)

This is an assimilation to the values of Santa María, which (in "El álbum", for example) he once despised. Jorge is now a spokesman for the town, speaking for it with the "nosotros" voice (59), and it is in that guise that he condemns Goerdel. So Jorge has changed: he has shifted location to be squarely within Santa María, where previously he had sought an exit from it (unlike Goerdel whose relation with the town never seems to be one of voluntarily seeking release from nor entry into it). This shifting of Jorge brings him into alignment with the general logic of *La muerte y la niña*. It is as if Jorge had resolved the Oedipus positively, arriving in the position of the father after earlier futile rebellion against it.[6] Hence, Jorge is now writing the very leading articles which he despised his father for writing in "El álbum", and he enforces Santa María's viewpoint, rather histrionically performing the town's moral outrage at Goerdel. In Díaz Grey's view (and it is his view which dominates in this respect and so tends to fix Jorge's identity), the price that Jorge pays for his delayed accession to the position of the Father is very

---

[6] On the Oedipus see chapter 21 of Freud 1957a.

high. Díaz Grey's reaction to Jorge throughout chapters 5-7 is to try to cut through what he sees as Jorge's performance, his contemptible assertions of outrage (66-67, for example). Hence, when Jorge refers to Goerdel as "'ese asesino judío'" (67), Díaz Grey is overtly dismissive:

> – Goerdel es más ario, probablemente, que tú y yo. No debe haber un solo judío procedente de la Colonia. Arios suizos, católicos, alemanes. Pero aquí, en Santa María, ninguna de esas palabras sirven para insultar. Entonces, el judío Goerdel. (68)

There is a subtext of disappointment in Díaz Grey's view of Jorge, a disappointment deriving from references to a past which saw Jorge much closer to Díaz Grey's position. And that past closeness is echoed in the format of Jorge's visiting Díaz Grey as he does so often in *Para una tumba sin nombre*. But the judgemental authority of Díaz Grey in *La muerte y la niña* is evident from the very start of this sequence when the doctor looks out of his window and *down* on Jorge stretched on the grass (55). The sheer disapproval of the doctor is striking and parallels the harshness in the equivalent relation of mentor-disciple between Padre Bergner and Goerdel. It also poses a fundamental question about why Jorge goes to Díaz Grey in the first place. At no point in their interview in chapters 5-7 does Jorge ask for information about the whereabouts of Goerdel, and it is Diaz Grey who offers what he knows as a way of deliberately frustrating Jorge's search for him (71).

Given that this interview exposes a whole series of concerns and judgements related to Díaz Grey's view of Jorge's modified identity, it is ironic that the only piece of information that Jorge asks of the doctor is precisely who Díaz Grey is (71). This is a sudden shift of ground and exposes the doctor himself to scrutiny. Until that point the very format of Jorge's visit and Díaz Grey's strong opinions have invested the doctor with authority, and that may imply the reason for the visit, but Jorge's question not only changes the focus of attention but also undermines the authority attaching to Díaz Grey. Chapter 7 is occupied by the doctor's account of his relationship with his daughter and finishes the interview without referring back to the issues discussed in chapters 5 and 6.

In this context, it is notable that in the final chapter a further shift apparently occurs by which Jorge seems to revert to something like his earlier self, as Díaz Grey suggests: "Repito que gracias al resucitado Jorge irónico y casi alegre, pasamos varias madrugadas con la botella de J. B. y la dicha inseparable de todo paraíso de tontos" (132). His shift is certainly corroborated by his agreeing with Díaz Grey in his condemnation of Goerdel, but without the earlier play-acting. If Jorge shifted to reach the position he occupies in chapters 5-7, here he apparently shifts again, so that, although still polarized with Goerdel, he does share something of his mutability. But *La muerte y la niña* does not rationalize his shift back nearer to Díaz Grey, it is simply asserted by the doctor.

A shifting of identity and a heterogeneity of traits characterizes many aspects of the novella: it is a text whose focus is constantly blurring. This is evident, for example, in Padre Bergner with his ambiguous ambitions for Goerdel, involving the striking contrast of a "religious" mission with strongly materialist methods, a mission to strengthen the church which promotes hypocrisy, cunning and capital accumulation. Heterogeneity and instability of identity are also apparent in Brausen's statue. It is an equestrian statue, but its face (though it is not always clear if it is the horse's or the rider's or both) begins to acquire bovine features. At first it is Brausen's face which is acquiring these features (49-50), but later it is clearly the horse's head that is taking on the look of a cow, as well as the rider having a dubious appearance (93-94). Not satisfied with the bizarreness of a deity on horseback in a public square and one with bovine tendencies, Díaz Grey speculates to Padre Bergner that the hybridity may go even further: " – Y si vuelvo al jinete, Padre, considero posible descubrir una cabeza de caballo, el hocico de un asno testarudo, la frente achatada de un perro dogo, el morro bestial de un cerdo, el perfil estúpido de un buey" (95). The joke is exploited to maximum, profane effect.

Ultimately more germane than this is the equivocation over the sex of the child that kills Helga Hauser during birth. When Jorge announces her death to the doctor, he is clear about its sex, but interestingly refers to Helga Hauser's contrary preference: " – La mató – gritó Jorge – . La mató a medianoche con un varón. Ella había pensado siempre en una hembrita" (59). Goerdel, the presumed murderer, refers to the child as "el niño" much later (127), and so do the letters (six times) which Goerdel shows to Díaz Grey (132), though these might be generic references. Despite the clear assertion by Jorge that the child is male, the novella also asserts that the child is female: Goerdel calls the child "la hija asesina" (121-22), Díaz Grey calls it "una niña" (122), and the very title of the novella is quite clear about the child's female sex. However, despite these discrepancies, *La muerte y la niña* neither alludes to the undecided identification nor provides final and decisive evidence. The question is simply left open.[7]

*

Díaz Grey

Within *La muerte y la niña*'s heterogeneity Díaz Grey acts as a double stabilizing focus: his presence at the start and at the end of the novella corroborates that. He is important for his textual function and for his discursive positioning, and these aspects interact. However, there are tensions in the character's constitution deriving from the disparate pulls of heterogeneity (centrifugal) and stabilization (centripetal) which need to be pinpointed.

As far as his textual function is concerned, Díaz Grey, as so often in Onetti, is a device to enable others to talk while he watches and assesses. He is also a means of articulating certain values. This function is highlighted very clearly in the opening and closing chapters of the novella. In both of them Díaz Grey's function is to assess and judge Goerdel. His is a demystifying role, whereby he appears to read through the other character's surface and bluntly or ironically speak

---

[7] This is not dissimilar to some of the undecidable identifications in *Cuando entonces*.

out the "underlying truth". He is not convinced by Goerdel and his view is that the latter is trying to fool Santa María. Díaz Grey may or may not be right: what is clear is that he sets up a critical denial of another character, and that is part of the novella's almost constant process of unsettling. Díaz Grey passes harsh judgements on Goerdel, Jorge, and Brausen, and is amused and sceptical about Padre Bergner. None of the other characters can establish himself securely when set within the authority of his judgements, and all open themselves to that by visiting him. But here already is an internal difference: Díaz Grey proposes a critical knowledge which is not directly challenged or unsettled as the views and positions of the other characters are.

In terms of his discursive positioning, he is not so much a device, but more a focus of values and experience. Díaz Grey is projected as the fulcrum of authority within the novella's discourse. In fact, authority has two sources in *La muerte y la niña*: Padre Bergner and Díaz Grey. The two characters are set off against each other in chapter 2 in tracing the background of Goerdel. Their professional activities take them to the Colonia and into contact with the young Goerdel (32); they are analogous in caring, Padre Bergner for the spirit, and Díaz Grey for the body; and they are counterposed as enemies (32). Padre Bergner's authority is consolidated in chapters 3 and 4 in his relationship with Goerdel as spiritual mentor. But ultimately Padre Bergner is weakened and *La muerte y la niña* valorizes Díaz Grey: he remains in the novella more consistently and longer than the priest; and Padre Bergner goes to the doctor to ask for his opinion.

Díaz Grey is positioned quite carefully as the fulcrum of the discourse. At the start of chapter 5, this status is signalled physically in some interesting detail: Jorge visits the doctor and the latter forces the former to wait outside his house, below him on the grass. Díaz Grey is on the first floor and Jorge has to climb the stairs to visit him (58). By contrast, Díaz Grey's mentally unstable wife, Angélica

Inés, living in a dream world of her own, is located on the floor above him (55).[8] Díaz Grey is, therefore, between them, having access to both worlds: Santa María/Jorge and Angélica Inés/madness. The chapter also associates him with purgatory, another "between" position (58). To underline his link with madness, Díaz Grey is later located in the great armchair of Jeremías Petrus, Angélica Inés' mad father with dreams of greatness in *El astillero* (76). This double quality in Díaz Grey is further stressed by what happens to him at the start of chapter 5: Jorge's early arrival and whistle seem to summon him from his dreams (53). Rather than respond immediately to Jorge, Díaz Grey decides to return to his dreams. This balancing between dream and wakefulness is important in building the connotative frame around Díaz Grey. It is also significant that while Díaz Grey tries to return to a pleasant dream it is unattainable, while another dream overtakes it which is disjointed and sad: again elements are in balance in relation to him. That the area of dreams is linked to Angélica Inés is apparent later in the novella (132), just as Jorge and Santa María are linked to wakefulness by disturbing Díaz Grey's sleep and threatening to do the same to Angélica Inés (58). This "between" position – between Jorge and Angélica Inés, between sanity/Santa María and dreams/madness, between wakefulness and sleep – is implicitly related to authority at the start of chapter 5 by Díaz Grey's own thoughts about his work as a doctor and the investment in him by patients (57-58).[9]

In disparaging Jorge's and Santa María's narrow mentality and stupidity, Díaz Grey clearly sets himself up as standing for other values, and indeed he claims that he would have helped Goerdel to escape if he had been asked. He is contemptuous of Santa María's zealous imposition of conformity and its complacent, petit-bourgeois self-satisfaction. This contestatory role for Díaz Grey is not uncommon in Onetti. However, *La muerte y la niña* is also striking in

---

[8] Angélica Inés is also linked to prostitution in Díaz Grey's games of fantasy with her (131-32).

[9] See Terry 56.

giving an experiential dimension to his stance to underpin his centrality to the novella's values. This dimension emerges through his relation with his daughter. The key to the introduction of the information about this relation is a question from Jorge, when he asks about the doctor's identity and past (71-72). This introduces a complex and relatively untouched area in the character of Díaz Grey, about whom little personal information is given in Onetti, a situation that Jorge alludes to explicitly when considering Díaz Grey's preparations to speak: "... aquella vez, acaso la primera, en que aceptó hablar de ella [la hija], reconocer ante otro su existencia... " (75). The immediate response to Jorge's question is for the doctor to fetch two packs of playing cards and an envelope full of photographs and letters. As will become apparent, the two sorts of item correspond to Díaz Grey's present and past respectively. All of the photographs are of his daughter, from the period when she was a baby through to her separation from Díaz Grey at three years and on to adolescence. Now, paternity is rare in Onetti, and this is the second example in the novella.[10] Children and parents are hardly ever referred to in his writing. It is significant therefore that Díaz Grey answers Jorge's question about his identity by in part describing his relation to his daughter. The man defines himself via the girl. This is indicative of the patriarchal discourse in *La muerte y la niña*, which is very much a story between men and in which the women characters (with the very brief exception of Helga Hauser [21-22]) are never seen directly, but act as reference points or stimuli to male identification. This gender hierarchy is graphically clear in Díaz Grey's present, where he is mentioned in routine couplings with a woman who has no identity:

> Todos los jueves, salvo la luna, tenía en el crepúsculo una mujer en la camilla chirriante o en la alfombra inapropiadamente espesa y que mezclaba decenas de olores indefinibles, o por lo menos era indefinible su conjunto...
> Las mujeres no le importaban de verdad: eran personas. (22-23)

With this woman there is no relation: women are neutralized here by being seen merely as persons, and in his daughter's case by being denied the right to grow up.

---

[10] Padre Bergner's "paternity" is clearly somewhat different from Díaz Grey's and Goerdel's.

The photos that Díaz Grey keeps of his daughter are precisely an attempt to counter her "loss", her growing up. For the key element in the relation is the split at three years and her absence since then except for the sending of photos and letters. But the split only serves to underline the difference: the photos prove that she ceases to be who she was, so that Díaz Grey wants to cling to the images of her as a young child.[11] Each new photograph of the changing daughter becomes more incomprehensible and further removed from what mattered to him. The logic of Díaz Grey's present seems to be that in the absence of the idealized child there is little to reconcile him with life. Hence the games of solitaire are a way of passing time.[12] So again Diaz Grey is located "between", because the current reality is punctuated by his games of alternative solitaire with the photos from the past: he lays them out on the table just as he lays out the cards. The point of the second solitaire he says is to help him to suffer better (78-79): it is a sort of structured, controlled way of being open to loss, as well as a way of reconfirming an illusion. And this is the interesting thing, because the control and the illusion coexist in Díaz Grey. He claims to be aware of the trick that he is playing on himself: "'Era, es, la única trampa que me permito. Era, es, siempre el llamado suave, irresistible de una necesidad viciosa'" (77-78). He apparently appreciates his own predicament, allowing his desire to fix an image of the past but also seeing it as fatally flawed: it can provide no fulfilment, his daughter is now different. In this way, Díaz Grey appears as authority to himself, suffering and analyzing his own suffering: he is analyst and analysand.

There is then a tension in the representation of Díaz Grey in combining desire and disillusion: running counter to the novella's transformational logic and Díaz Grey's refusal to confirm others' identities, there is a desire in him towards

---

[11] The title of the novella might refer not only to Helga Hauser's death and her daughter, but also to Díaz Grey, in the sense that Díaz Grey's daughter metaphorically dies as she grows up and ceases to be a "niña". Her separation from Díaz Grey could be read as a metaphor of death from his point of view.

[12] These card games had already started in *El astillero* (1961).

a stable identity via the relation to his daughter which is simultaneously a denial of her reality. On the one hand, he tells Jorge that he will burn all the photos of his daughter dating from after their separation (being unable to bear her independent existence and so clinging to an Imaginary relation to her):

> "Y alguna noche que no será más triste que las otras, quemaré todas las fotos cuya edad pasa los tres años. Si me decidí a pensarla mujer sin cara no fue porque ella se estuviera convirtiendo en una mujer distinta, año tras año, un remiso correo tras el otro. Lo hice porque no tuve fuerzas para tolerar que ella fuese una persona." (80)

But, on the other hand, he is the character who goes on with his games (this time chess) with Jorge at the end, the character who allies himself with Jorge (and by implication with Santa María) in not accepting Goerdel's claim to innocence, as if asserting secure knowledge. In doing that, he explains why he will not accept Goerdel's photos of the letters supposedly proving that Helga Hauser had a lover (132-34). But that is the same character who clings to his own photos of a child with whom his relation can have no reality: that is the scope of the division in him. He is heterogeneous and divided *between* insight and illusion, and yet there is no challenge to his claim that he can be in control of illusion, which seems a little naive: the extent of his insight is clearly open to debate. The risk is in the text's Imaginary investment in Díaz Grey as the one-who-knows: the combination of heterogeneous elements in Díaz Grey's character is consistent with the discourse, but that does not link convincingly with the will to invest in him as source of insight into others and into the self: heterogeneity and centring do not coexist comfortably.

In trying to make Díaz Grey a stable point, the novella seems to undermine its own discourse. Díaz Grey is one investment that *La muerte y la niña* does not convincingly demystify. The novella has a consistent practice of cutting through a false surface to expose a reality beneath. So there is demystification of Goerdel by Díaz Grey (chapters 1 and 12), of Goerdel by Padre Bergner (chapters 3 and 4), of Jorge by Díaz Grey (chapters 5 and 6), of Goerdel by Jorge (chapter 11), of Santa María by Goerdel (chapter 11), of Brausen by Díaz Grey intermittently, and even of Padre Bergner's humbug by Díaz Grey (chapter 10), but not of Díaz Grey in any complete sense.[13] At the start of chapter 5, the doctor does underline his own pretences with his patients, but this is simply another way of investing in his authority as demystifier and also asks the reader to credit a model of self-consciousness being transparent to itself, which is hardly sustainable. Hence, even the explanation of his problematic relation to his daughter derives from him and explicitly announces its own perceptiveness. The discourse does not explore a position from which to demystify Díaz Grey, so it ends with him: his routine and his "in-between" privilege simply go on. It is as if the novella cannot know that investment, it is too fundamental to risk. Interestingly, there is potential for demystification with the arrival of his daughter – her reality might destabilize Díaz Grey's balancing of dreams and the discourse of authority, but that arrival is only mentioned as occurring months after the end of the main events in the novella (131).

At the level of content, *La muerte y la niña* has a major preoccupation with the brittleness of the characters' surface pretences, with their permutations of identity and self-presentation; at the level of textual logic, the equivalent of that is the sliding of signifiers over signifieds, the toying with the arbitrariness and the blurring of stable meaning. With Díaz Grey, the sliding stops or pauses: he is (at least partial) anchor. So in order not to replicate that sort of effect in my analysis, I want to end by emphasizing a destabilizing element in the novella.

At the end of chapter 5, Díaz Grey introduces a religious metaphor, by alluding to the story of Cain and Abel. But it turns into much more than a metaphor. On the one hand, the religious reference aims to denigrate Brausen and

---

[13] Lovers are also strikingly demystified: "Aquel pasajero, rápidamente olvidado momento en que uno de los dos [amantes] logra ver, sin propósito, con un adelgazado deseo de pedir perdón, excusarse, bajo la piel de la cara ajena, abrillantada por el amor o el vino, a través de la piel de la cara que se quiere.   Cuando uno de ellos tropieza con, traspasa sin desearlo la piel tan lastimosamente indefensa, tensa o blanda de la cara del otro. Y ve durante un segundo, adivina y mide la dureza y la audacia de los huesos, el candor de los pómulos, la fragilidad o el inútil grasoso atrevimiento del mentón" (24-25).

so is consistent with one of the centripetal forces analyzed at the start of this chapter. But, on the other, the nature of the reference and its relevance are rather tantalizing. In the first place, the Cain and Abel roles fit the characters in at least two ways. The metaphor is introduced by Díaz Grey immediately after Jorge's threat to kill Goerdel for having "murdered" his wife: "¿Y no veía – no se veía – su grotesco Abel muerto, resucitado por camaradas, conocidos del villorio?" (59-60). The subject of "veía" is most likely to be Jorge following as it does his threat, and the "no se veía" would therefore consolidate Díaz Grey's prior critique of Jorge's lack of awareness of his own behaviour. In this reading, Cain is Jorge. Hence, "su Abel muerto" would be the potential victim Goerdel, and the two male characters in the novella would match the male characters in the biblical story. This seems convincing, but, interestingly, the outcast in the novella is actually Goerdel, and if there is any guilt over a "murder" then it would attach to him as a result of his wife's death. The reference to Cain as forced to commit murder (60) also coincides with Goerdel's expression of helplessness in preventing his wife's pregnancy/death in chapter 1. On these grounds Goerdel could be seen as Cain, though in that case the gender match of metaphor and plot fails since the victim would be a woman. So there are possibilities for a double fit between plot and biblical metaphor.[14]

The elaboration of the metaphor is also intriguing. Certain elements coincide with the biblical text (Genesis 4). Brausen saves his "Cain" from human justice for his "murder" by threatening a sevenfold imposition of justice if he is pursued (compare Genesis 4:15), and he therefore attaches a sign to "Cain" to set him apart from other people (the mark of Cain, Genesis 4:15). These echoes of Genesis are given a modern inflection:

> Pero Brausen, cumplió su propósito inexplicable para siempre y para nosotros, actuó como un caudillo político. Amparó a Caín ante el juez de instrucción, advirtió a la policía que cualquier castigo al homicidio acarrearía siete

---

[14] Omar Prego and María A. Petit assert that Goerdel is Cain.

veces la repetición de justicia y venganza. Y colocó al matador un letrero de
prevención e inmunidad. (60)

In addition, "Cain" appears to stand up to Brausen, whose surveillance and testing
of him (60-61) are equivalent to the biblical Cain's exile and suffering (Genesis
4:14). But there are divergences from the Bible too in that it is stated that Cain
was *obliged* to kill (60), which is not accurate, and also in that Cain does actually
kill Abel whereas (strictly speaking) there is no murder in *La muerte y la niña*.
Furthermore, in Genesis, Cain goes into exile and founds a city (Genesis 4:17),
whereas in *La muerte y la niña* "Cain" is isolated in a cave under a strict surveying
eye. In fact, as the metaphor progresses it develops its own hermetic logic which
is mostly to do with Brausen; what ultimately links it to the Bible is a concern
with guilt and punishment. So the end of chapter 5 elaborates a situation in which
the isolated "murderer" confronts his God/Brausen and criticises him for his unjust
treatment. Hence, the religious metaphor (developed, it must be stressed, in Díaz
Grey's perspective) turns into a vehicle for a critique of a cruel God/Brausen: he
provides no relief to a suffering "Cain" because it does not suit him to do so; he
is committed to the institutionalizing of guilt:

> [Caín] esperó semanas y meses en la cueva ahumada. Pero Nuestro
> Señor Brausen dejó pasar los siglos; la entrevista se hizo imposible porque los
> caminos de Brausen son insondables o porque deseó instalar el crimen en la raza
> que inventó, o porque quiso instalar para siempre la certidumbre de que el más
> fuerte triunfará durante siglos enfrentando al débil y apacible. (61)

The arresting quality of this whole passage (59-62) derives firstly from the
development of the metaphor beyond its merely illuminating power and into a
specific, if highly allusive node in the text, somewhat heterogeneous to the plot;
and secondly, it derives from the fact that it is uncharacteristic in Onetti to have
such a religious metaphor. More characteristic is that the Cain/Abel reference both
follows the Bible and also does not: the metaphor conforms to the other text and
it does not, it is familiar and it is not. These dualities suggest, once again, the
teasing and elusiveness of *La muerte y la niña*. Not surprisingly, therefore, reading

grips and slips in negotiating the novella, and that interplay is a sign of the Real of its textuality.

CHAPTER 10

AMBIVALENCE AND DESIRE IN

CUANDO ENTONCES

– ... Andá al botiquín y prepara medicinas.

Serna asintió con cabezadas obedientes y se alejó hacia lo que llamaban botiquín. Tuve una pequeña emoción porque se trataba de otro escritorio, recostado contra la tela amarilla que ocultaba la pared, alejado de la confusión de muebles que llenaban la habitación en la que, luego de codearse con mil peripecias, fracasos y dudosos triunfos, reinaba, acaso para su siempre, madame Safó.

El botiquín escritorio me puso momentáneamente nostálgico y suprimió años. Porque, nunca poseído, había sido mío en un pasado cada día más remoto. Lo codicié con apenas un poco menos de la urgencia con que se deseaba a una mujer. La primera vez lo vi en casa de un amigo, luego en un negocio de subastas; yo tenía veinte años y muy poco dinero.

Aunque estropeado por repetidas manos de barniz, aquel era mi escritorio.

Tenía su cortina corrediza y curvada y numerosos cajoncitos, semiocultos ahora por dos filas de botellas y una línea adelantada de vasos de tamaños diversos.

Aquella primera vez que vi un escritorio hermano gemelo de éste me sentí invitado, a la vez que percibía una cierta provocación. Y me imaginé, muy vagamente, sentado frente al mueble y escribiendo en un atardecer o en una mañana lluviosa, con el chorro luminoso de la lámpara que me aislaba en el cuarto y caía rígido sobre mis páginas. Yo solo en el edificio; el piso empolvado.

Nunca supe qué estaba escribiendo; posiblemente la novela total, capaz de sustituir a todas las obras maestras que se habían escrito en el mundo y que yo admiraba. Cada cajoncito tenía un letrero de papel porque yo era un novelista esclavo del orden y la disciplina. Un cajoncito estaba reservado para coleccionar adjetivos poco gastados.   También disponía de refugios provisorios para adverbios, sustantivos y fetos de frases tan nuevas como brillantes que esperaban, pacientes o nerviosas, ser elegidas para triunfar en la página blanca. (59-60)

I begin with this long quote in the hope that it will disconcert as much here as it does in Onetti's novella. For a piece of furniture that is not mentioned again, this amount of attention is odd, and it is that very oddness that I want to consider. The "escritorio/botiquín" then is to act as the point of entry for my analysis: it is a way of opening up the novella, even if only a few of its secret drawers.

By unravelling some of the detail in this passage I will pinpoint the purpose of its weight and extension. The first striking aspect of the "escritorio/botiquín" is its ambivalent identity. It is not just a desk, and it is not just a medicine cabinet. In fact, it is not apparently used as either, since it seems to be a drinks cabinet. The reference to it as a "botiquín" is itself ambivalent, since madame Safó is obviously making a sly joke about alcohol as medicine. So its identity is multiple, and this is compounded when the narrator, Lamas, calls it "his", though it seems that he has never owned it: it is his and yet it is not his. And subsequently, it is unclear whether this is precisely the piece of furniture that he once knew or whether it is another. He begins by seeming to make a precise recognition, but then it becomes a twin of the desk in the past. It is the same desk and it is not. In all this, the "escritorio/botiquín"'s identity slips in and out of focus.

A second element that seems significant in the passage is the role played by time. On first recognition, it is emotion that underpins Lamas' reaction: he is nostalgic and the past suddenly returns to him. And the memory that he has of the desk is centred on emotion: he felt a desire for the desk almost as intense as the desire he might have felt for a woman, though interestingly he could never possess the desk. Here is a nexus of past time and unfulfilled desire. But the past is not exactly reproduced, because, although the memory is important, the desk has been damaged by time which has added coats of varnish. The real desk and desire seem to be only a memory, even if one that can be reactivated vividly.

Thirdly, the "escritorio/botiquín" is mysterious. Its curtain and drawers suggest that things are hidden away inside it, and indeed the drawers are themselves half-hidden by bottles and glasses. Hence, all seems not to be visible on the surface.

Fourthly, the twin functions of the "escritorio/botiquín" – writing and dispensing alcohol – not only gesture in the direction of Onetti's biography, but also create a conjuncture that seems to stimulate the imagination and thence fiction.

Finally, and functionally, the whole passage constitutes a digression in the scene involving Lamas, madame Safó and don Luis, and, in that, seems rather at variance with the imagined, highly controlled writing described by Lamas in the final paragraph.

Now all these features are (not surprisingly) deeply characteristic of *Cuando entonces* as a whole. The novella is full of ambivalent identities; it revolves around the nostalgia for past desire (the desire for desire) which constitutes the impetus underlying the whole novella; it is mysterious in many aspects – not just details but vital information is delayed or elided, slyly omitted or fragmented; it is full of story-telling (not untypically of Onetti), much of which takes place under the influence of alcohol in bars; and it is replete with digressions and apparently tangential material so that its narrative thread is somewhat tenuous. One could argue therefore that, at the level of construction, the "escritorio/botiquín" encapsulates much of what is going on beneath the surface of *Cuando entonces*.

Perhaps the most striking in this series of compositional features is that of ambivalent identities. It is a feature which is registered at the very start of the first chapter. The novella opens on a borderline, between night and day, and between winter and spring: "Una vez más la historia comenzó para mí, en el día-noche de Santa Rosa... Volvía Santa Rosa y amenazaba bromeando a Lavanda y Buenos Aires. Treinta de setiembre. Siempre cumple y arrastra la primavera" (15). The storm that accompanies Santa Rosa marks the borderline: it is the moment of an unsettling switch of weather. It is an opening towards the spring and renewal, but it is also a repetition, both in the cycle of the seasons and insofar as it inaugurates another story. So there is established here a certain unfixing and unsteadiness: the story begins neither on one side nor the other of the divide. And this unsteadiness is figured by the storm with its violent and unsettling connotations. Moreover, Santa Rosa herself/itself is also heterogeneous – a date in the calendar, a saint, but also a prostitute: "Ahora era en Lavanda y era forzoso esperar la llegada estruendosa de la única puta simpática, que figura, con ofensa, en el santoral de Gregorio XIII" (15-16). The saint/whore/date is friendly and yet also offensive, and the anonymous narrator goes on to insist on her/its unpredictability – she/it is a tease: "Yo no recordaba haber conocido a una mujer de coquetería comparable" (16). The storm never quite seems to come, and as a teasing whore she is also curiously incorporeal: she is a moment of transition, neither one thing nor the other, a promise or an idea rather than a fulfilment. Santa Rosa sets the scene for what is to follow.

Compounding this ambivalence, the novella also contains a diversity of narrators, although they all use the "yo" form. But the "yo" in the different chapters varies, and temporal shifts undermine any consistency even when the "yo" is apparently the same. In chapter one, the narrator is an anonymous "yo". In chapter two, the narrating "yo" is Lamas (the novella's central character). In chapter three, the "yo" is Pastor de la Peña.[1] And in chapter four, the narrating "yo" is again Lamas, but at a time rather later than in chapter two. None of these narrators explicitly alludes either to the narrating or to the material narrated in other chapters: even Lamas in chapter four makes no reference to his previous narration in chapter two.

The diversity (and the discreteness) of the narrators is matched by the diversity of the temporal organization. The temporal dislocations in the novella are not simple to sort out. In chapter one Lamas is "in exile" in Lavanda and he begins to tell the story of himself, Magda and the "comandante" in Buenos Aires.

---

[1] Pastor de la Peña's narration also includes a striking switch of mode. For most of the chapter he gives a direct oral account of events to a specified intradiegetic narratee, "el comisario", but on 86-87 he changes into conventional narration with a description of "el comisario" as if he were addressing an implied third party. On 87 he reverts to direct oral address of "el comisario".

This triangle has broken up and Lamas now tells his story to the anonymous narrator of the chapter. Chapter two jumps back to the very beginning of the triangle's story, when Lamas is just about to meet the other two for the first time. This is the remotest point in the past to which the novella returns. This chapter ends over a year later, after Lamas has lost sight of Magda and the "comandante" and when he is about to go to Lavanda. Chapter three moves back to narrate the moments just prior to Magda's suicide at the end of her affair with the "comandante". Chapter three therefore occupies a time before the last section of chapter two (69-72), when Lamas is on his own in Buenos Aires and before he has gone to Lavanda. Chapter four jumps forward to a moment some time after chapter one when Lamas has returned to Buenos Aires.

None of the chapters is explicitly placed with any precision, certainly not against any scale of exact dates, and even their relative positions are not immediately obvious. This temporal vagueness is reflected in the novella's title, the "entonces" being an imprecise temporal indicator, and, although it does suggest that past time is important, it is merely a locus of nostalgia. Moreover, the jumps between the chapters mean that temporal progress cannot be smooth, and that the story (if it can be called that) lays barely any emphasis on forward progress. That is compounded by the quantity of digressive material and by the absence of any move towards a culminating moment or denouement. In fact, the ending of the novella is only suggested by the use of displacement into events which seem to represent a shadowy repeat of what may already have happened to Magda and the "comandante". In a sense, therefore, it is less a question in *Cuando entonces* of a narrative structure than of a loose constellation of moments with an affective relation.

Complementing the diversity of narrators and temporal shifts are the numerous digressions and delays, which tend to fill out the narrative elements and create a general stagnation. In chapter one, the digressions and delays seem to be a function of Lamas' drunkenness. He is full of hints and allusions which he takes no particular trouble to elucidate. Indeed, the purpose of chapter one seems to be to open an affective space: on the analogy with the "escritorio/botiquín", Lamas opens a few drawers and pulls back the curtain a little, but reveals very little that is concrete. This teasing technique even includes references to his own delaying tactics: " – Tal vez estos ataques de delación me llegan cuando se produce cierta conjunción de astros" (22-23); and: " – Me escapé de Magda. Traición canalla" (24). In chapter two, the conversation between Lamas and don Luis covers eighteen pages (51-69). Don Luis clearly has a purpose in summoning Lamas to talk, but it takes over twelve pages before he starts to get to the point: "¿qué sabe usted del comandante?" (64) – hardly a difficult question. And it takes another three pages and the introduction of another character before the strange problems caused by the comandante in the night-club begin to be explained. To cap all this, Lamas actually knows nothing about the "comandante", and rather than throwing any light on the absent centre of the conversation, he simply speculates provocatively: " – En cuanto a sospechar, sospecho. Drogas, tráfico de armas, espionaje bien pagado" (69). In so doing he only confuses the matter further. At the end of eighteen pages very little information has been forthcoming: many drawers are left half-hidden.

That is precisely the point. Delaying the point is the point. There is no centring or final stability in *Cuando entonces*. There is no real interest in revealing anything about the "comandante". The novella is a web of hints and possibilities and of gaps in knowledge. In fact, the novella's digressions seem to work in inverse proportion to the amount of secure knowledge conveyed.

In terms of narrative form, the ending is as tantalizing and mysterious as all the digressions and delays. Rather than a culmination of the triangular relations of Lamas, Magda and the "comandante", there appears to be a displacement and hence a lack of termination. All is left open and ambivalent. What happens at the end of chapter four is the reporting of the death of Petrona García on the Avenida

Santa Fe in Buenos Aires, and then the arrival on the teleprinter of the report of an aircraft crash which has killed all passengers:

> <EL PRESIDENTE> CUMPLIA UN VUELO DE BUENOS AIRES A NUEVA YORK STOP EL ACCIDENTE SE PRODUJO EN LA ETAPA RIO DE JANEIRO - PORT SPAIN (TRINIDAD) A 877 MILLAS DE RIO DE JANEIRO STOP LLEVABA 41 PASAJEROS Y 9 TRIPULANTES STOP TODOS MURIERON STOP LOS RESTOS DEL AVION FUERON LOCALIZADOS A 1.200 METROS SOBRE EL NIVEL DEL MONTE TAMANACO STOP (98)

The relevance of the suicide and the crash to chapters one to three is that they seem to coincide with what may have happened some time before to Magda and the "comandante". In chapter three, Magda is reported to have committed suicide in her apartment on the Avenida Santa Fe, and she has revealed that the "comandante" has just left her to fly north with the president. At the end of the chapter, Lamas reacts badly to the disappearance of Magda and over a period of months laments her absence, appearing not to know that this is caused by her death. In her narrative in chapter three, Magda appears to describe the end of her affair with the "comandante" as though it had just happened – their two years of love are over (82). The "comandante" is being promoted to a new job that requires that he abandon Magda (84), and he appears to be flying off with the president on the day that Magda speaks (84-85). Hence there seems to be an immediate stimulus for Magda to take her own life. But, by the time of the events in chapter four, Lamas has lost Magda, completed his "exile" in Lavanda and returned to Buenos Aires to work on another newspaper. And the routine of working on the newspaper is hinted at (96), to suggest that yet more time has passed. In addition, chapter four ostentatiously underlines the passing of time through the ageing of the peripheral character el Lampiño, who is now married with three children (99), where in chapter two, just before Lamas meets Magda and the "comandante", he is a fresh-faced eighteen year old.

If some time has passed since Magda and the "comandante" disappeared (as Lamas puts it, 69), one is left at the end of chapter four with a disconcerting repetition via displacement: the news of the suicide and the air crash. It is doubly tantalizing since there is room for confusion over names. Magda is only a professional name, and so the death of Petrona García may hint at the real underlying identity of the character. Also, in the report on the teleprinter, the reference to the president, "<EL PRESIDENTE>", in inverted commas is odd and may suggest that this is not a person but perhaps the name of an aircraft. In which case it is not clear that someone called "el presidente" actually died in the crash, though it would seem probable that an aircraft with this name would be used by a president. Hence, there is considerable ambivalence about the ending of the novella, based on the fact that the events mentioned at the end of chapter four appear to follow on so directly from the narrative elements set up in chapters one to three, while there is a considerable period of time between them. The identity of the events which might close the narrative is deeply undecidable. Chapter four may gesture at narrative closure but it is not achieved definitively.

The general principle of instability and ambivalence is continued in the area of character construction. Just as with the "escritorio/botiquín", there is a play of names and functions attributed to almost all characters that precludes fixity. It is as if the characters had no solid centre. This is particularly daring in respect of the permutations with characters' names, since, in realist fiction, the name is conventionally the fundamental element holding character to some sort of stability. The ambivalence of characterization is evident with don Luis, madame Safó and the "comandante", but also with very minor characters like the barman in the *No name*, who is variously called Simons, el Sim and Sims.

Don Luis is virtually (and paradoxically) characterized via permutation, almost as if he were a name and variations. There are doubts about his name from the very start of his appearance in chapter two where Lamas says: "Ahora se hacía llamar Serna y, a veces, en algún diminuto delirio de grandeza, afirmaba que su nombre verdadero era Luis de la Serna" (51). There exists the strong possibility that neither of these is his real name. But out of this ambivalent beginning multiple variations arise. He is called (not necessarily only once): Serna (56), don

Luis (62), Luisito (59), and don Luisito (63). In addition, madame Safó calls him "m'hijo" (65) and "muchacho" (66), and Lamas calls him "barman" (61), "el sirviente" (63), "un semental" (62) and (ironically) "el innombrable" (66), despite the plethora of names provided for him!

Madame Safó is only a little less diverse than don Luis. Initially she is called "la mujer" (57). Then, in the absence of an introduction to Lamas and in view of her apparent similarity to a woman from his youth, she is named madame Safó (58). Having recalled this name for her from his past, Lamas immediately casts doubt on its applicability because of the ravages of time on the woman and the resulting difficulty of identification (58 and 66). Madame Safó is clearly the professional name of a madame in a brothel in any case, and cannot be taken as her real one. Lamas subsequently runs through various other names for her: "vieja remendada" (63), "la señora" (63), "señora abuela" (65), "anciana" (66), "madame" (66) and "madame señora" (67). As with don Luis, these permutations are part of Lamas' reaction, a defensive aggression in an uncertain situation, but there is no independent information and so both characters take shape in the novel via heterogeneity.

Much the same can be said of the "comandante", who is identified with his military role throughout. Or rather with his military roles. In chapter one, he is the "capitán" and in the rest of the book "el comandante". There is no explanation for this switch of rank, indeed there is no allusion to the switch at all. The switch is consolidated by madame Safó's casting doubt on the authenticity of his military position altogether. She says that: "se hace o se hacía llamar comandante" (63), and she suggests that he might have hired his uniform. With no further corroboration, she casts him as simply play-acting.

It is not just the name of the "capitán/comandante" and his military standing that are in doubt. There is a racial complexity in him that is never quite clarified. His dark complexion creates doubts in Lamas' mind, but he decides that he is neither "negro ni mestizo. Morocho" (18). But later he does refer to him as "negro" only then to deny it and claim that he has some Indian blood (21). Later he even calls him "el cobrizo" (24) and "el príncipe indio" (25). These racial oscillations are compounded by the "capitán/comandante"'s physical dualism, for Magda reveals that, although he has a dark face, his body is very white: "Luego vine a saber que estaba curtida por el sol permanente de su país y que su cuerpo era blanco, anémico como el de una muchacha inglesa" (22). Here the racial complexity grows to include yet another point of reference – Englishness. And significantly, it is not just a difference of colour but a pronounced polarization between the body and the face, which seems to preclude any stabilization around a simple centre. Who or what this character is remains entirely open and oscillating.

Interestingly, the two main characters, Lamas and Magda, are a little less heterogeneous than these three, and moreover they are constructed around an apparently stabilizing device. With Magda there is some play on names. From the start it is not clear that Magda is her real name (18), although no other is known. But there are permutations on it: María de Magdala (18) and María Magdalena (20). There are other variations used to describe her: when she is in the Eldorado she is a woman, but in the *No name* she is a "muchacha" (27), a change underlined by the different clothes that she wears in both places (26). And it is pointed out that she has other forms and styles in her repertoire, giving the impression that she is potentially a series of images. This impression is underlined by Pastor de la Peña in chapter three. In his one and only meeting with her he cannot decide whether Magda is refined or common. At first he thinks that she is common but well-dressed (78), but later he is less sure, thinking that she may be the black sheep from a good family (83). This instability in her identity is compounded by the doubts over her suicide, when it may be that the ending of chapter four reveals a truth about her – that she is called Petrona García – , but without giving really solid grounds for this. Through all this ambivalence, there is, however, an important element of continuity: her love for the "comandante" and the constancy of her desire for him.

Lamas, as the extradiegetic narrator in chapters two and four and as the intradiegetic narrator for parts of chapter one, is a less mobile character than any of the others (though he complements them by being the one to move physically throughout to enable the various conjunctures of character). His lesser ambivalence may be explained because he presents himself, so that only in chapter one is he the focus of another's attention. He is constructed around two main axes: masculinity and love/desire.

Lamas' initial characterization in chapter one links him to a pronounced masculinity. He is associated with heavy drinking, horses, gambling and prostitutes (20, 23, 28). Moreover he takes a patriarchal view of Magda and other women. When the "comandante" is absent, he wants to assume responsibility for paying for Magda (25) and so continue her position as a kept woman.[2] When Magda tells Lamas that while having sex with him she made him a cuckold by thinking of the absent "comandante", Lamas' wounded masculinity prompts him to murderous feelings (49). These features, unlike so many with the other characters, are consistently used and relatively conventional. The other stable aspect of Lamas' character is his love for Magda, though it would be more appropriate to call it desire since it is unfulfilled and constantly frustrated (rather like his past desire to possess the desk [60]). Even after their very brief intimacy (which only lasts while the "comandante" is away and because Magda confesses that she cannot do without a man [46-47]), Lamas is thoroughly preoccupied by her, walking past her flat, hoping for a renewal of their relations and for her return to the *No name* (71-72).

---

[2] One of the masculist cliches of *Cuando entonces* is that Magda lacks agency. This is typified by the headings of chapters one to three which all describe her in the passive. Not inconsistently therefore, among her few actions in the novella are agreeing to sleep with Lamas and committing suicide.

Love and desire are the elements which link the fragments of the novella together. But in each case (Lamas' and Magda's), it is a frustrated emotion. For Lamas, there is no sign of reciprocity from Magda: it is not that she dislikes him, simply that she has no real desire for him. There is therefore an asymmetry in the relations of the central triangle: Lamas loves Magda who loves the "comandante". This lack of relation of desire between Lamas and Magda leads to the creation of some tension, and to the absence of any consummation. It is a source of constant destabilizing.

It is important to append a supplement here, for Lamas loves Magda who loves the "comandante" who loves Magda. There is reciprocity in the latter relation – at least Magda insists on it, though the reader is never close enough to the "comandante" for independent corroboration. However, even this reciprocity of emotion is disrupted since the "comandante"'s official responsibilities break the relation and the diplomatic police force him to abandon Magda and return to the respectability of living with his wife (84). (It might be worth pointing out that Magda's dreams of fulfilment with the "comandante" also take the form of respectable domestic banality (82).) So even here, if love is a stable point of reference formally in *Cuando entonces*, it is still not ultimately a stabilizing element at the level of content. Even in the case of Magda, love is superseded by desire and frustration for a lost object, and that uncertainty leads to her suicide.

Viewing the novella through a Lacanian perspective, the implied narrative seems to be the enchaining effect whereby love is linked to desire. The Imaginary realm (where there is an ideal(ized) harmony between mother and child, between self and other, where love coincides with its object) is disrupted: for Lamas, it is disrupted by the absence of reciprocity in Magda; for Magda, it is disrupted by the police (representative of the Law, the Symbolic). The result is the state of desire in which Lamas and Magda cannot achieve satisfaction – the subject is left in isolation in the Symbolic (able only to find Imaginary fulfilment). And in that respect, it is significant that Lamas is a journalist and so defined by words, since the Symbolic is identified with the Law of language. As so often in Onetti, dealing with and living on in the Symbolic is the fundamental problem, and Magda for one cannot do it. To be in the Symbolic is to be set adrift in the unstable world of signifiers, and that is precisely what one finds in *Cuando entonces*: the heterogeneity and ambivalence throughout the novella enact the conditions of the shift from love to desire. Its permutating signifiers are concordant with the signified shift from Imaginary to Symbolic.

I want to end by invoking another piece of furniture only implied in the novella – the roulette table. Roulette is introduced as another object of Lamas' desire: he wants to go to Lavanda to have easy access to roulette, although his attraction to Lavanda is also linked to the desire to avoid the memory of Magda in Buenos Aires. Hence, roulette is linked to both positive and negative desire. But the roulette table is of interest because it suggests an attraction to chance. Roulette, like so much in *Cuando entonces*, is almost synonymous with openness and unpredictability. It is beyond the control of human agency, rather like the motif of desire. In the roulette table one finds a sort of metaphor of the two central relationships in the novella, both of which fail with no reason really being advanced to explain them – *Cuando entonces* does not develop a discourse of explanations and rationalization. In a sense therefore, the roulette table (in its representation of the elements of unpredictability and of human dependence) functions in the novella rather like the "escritorio/botiquín" by hinting at the underlying parameters of the characters' actions, even though neither is particularly foregrounded to do so. By contrast, it is not chance that leads me to finish with this piece of furniture – it cannot be so after the decision to start with the "escritorio/botiquín". Just as that was a means of entry into the novella, so the roulette table is a means of exit via symmetry, a symmetry that need not imply completion, merely chance.

CHAPTER 11

"ONCE MORE...": THE LIMITS OF REPETITION

I want to begin this final chapter by looking briefly at two short stories published late in Onetti's career, "Matías" (1970) and "Presencia" (1986). My readings of them are partial and have a particular purpose: to prepare the way for a certain sort of reflection on all of Onetti's short fiction.

"Matías" takes up (in reverse form) the situation that affects Kirsten in "Esbjerg". He is "exiled" from his home town Pujato (near Santa María) and sent away as the telegraph operator on a cargo boat. The story puts much stress on his being in Northern Europe: Hamburg, Finland and Russia. So, while Kirsten is in the southern hemisphere and longs for rural Denmark, Matías is in the northern hemisphere and longs for rural South America. In both cases, the key question is "can there be a return journey?". For Matías, this question has a strong focus of desire: his "girlfriend" María.

"Matías" also echoes "Esbjerg" in the heavy mediation of its narration. In "Esbjerg", Kirsten's dilemma is recounted by her husband, Montes, who has tried to help her, to another character, who becomes the story's narrator. Similarly in "Matías", the character who has tried to help Matías, Jorge Michel, recounts the other's story and one of his listeners becomes the narrator of the story for the reader. Each time a male helper passes on the story to another who then presents it to the reader.

These are two striking repetitions of structure, but there are variations involved too. The most significant of these is the availability to Matías of a direct telephone link to the place of desire. This replaces the letters and photographs from Denmark in "Esbjerg". There may be no return journey to Pujato yet for Matías, but he can theoretically talk to his "girlfriend". Since Matías is worried that a telegram will not reach María, the narrator suggests that he telephone her from a public communications office in Hamburg. As if to underline the theoretical ease of transnational communication, the telephone company tells the narrator and Matías that they will be the first to use a new link. But two elements work against direct contact with María. Firstly, Matías asks the narrator to make the call, suggesting already his remoteness from Pujato. And secondly, when the narrator talks to María she insults him and hangs up. The question is: does Matías know Maria at all, or has he been telling stories, elaborating nostalgic fictions, as also seems possible with Kirsten? If this is so, it might explain why he asks the narrator to make the call, since he would know that he cannot talk to her himself. After all, it is not his idea to telephone her but the narrator's. However, the question is undecidable. Whether or not he knows María, the point is that there is no communication between them, which is especially ironic as Matías is a specialist in communications. The other place, Pujato, is remote and, perhaps, as constituted in his nostalgic desire, beyond the subject's power to reach it. In a sense, the telephone variation introduced in this story only brings out more clearly the repetition of what was already laid out in "Esbjerg", where Kirsten is locked into the unattainability of Denmark with no possibility of access, but unlimited scope for fantasy.

"Presencia" focuses on a not entirely dissimilar situation of the loss of a loved woman and the fictions built up around her. In this story, Jorge Malabia appears in exile in Madrid and out of direct contact with Santa María and his newspaper *El Liberal*, which he has had to sell. Above all, he is out of touch with María José. To make up for her loss and the lack of information about her, Jorge contrives to have fictions invented about her which might seem to turn her absence into presence. These are fictions which he does not invent himself. A penniless and shoddy private detective, Tubor, is engaged and, in complicity with Jorge, he invents reports about his observation of María José in Madrid. The two never openly discuss the mendacity involved, but both know that this is what is going on. In the end, it is these fictions that Jorge is paying Tubor for, since he knows that María José is in prison in Santa María.

Tubor's first report is an innocent account of María José's supposed daily routine in Madrid. This seems to stimulate Jorge's memory of observing her in the past in Santa María (13-14). With Tubor's first fiction, therefore, Jorge can recall normality. The contentment thus created lasts twenty days. Tubor's second report invents an affair between María José and another man and this stimulates Jorge to recall his own past sexual relation with her and to project it on to the fiction (17-18). Hence, absence stimulates fictional presences which in turn play on memory. These are familiar mechanisms in the operation of desire in Onetti.

However, as is also familiar elsewhere in Onetti, fiction cannot last. Tubor departs and his function as provider of independent "information" is taken up by an exile newspaper, *Presencia*. The newspaper brings the truth of María José's release from prison and her subsequent "disappearance". This report is taken as true in the story and is accepted as such by Jorge. The interesting thing here is how María José's "disappearance" recalls the political dimension of Onetti's second novel, *Para esta noche*, where a General Cot is also a source of repression: "María José Lemos, estudiante, detenida en la isla de Latorre desde el golpe militar, fue apresada por efectivos de la Guardia Nacional el 5 de abril, fecha en la cual abandonaba el penal y recuperaba la libertad. Desde entonces se encuentra *desaparecida*, sin que ninguna autoridad militar ni policial se responsabilice de su paradero" (21, my italics). With her "disappearance" María José is doubly lost, not only out of touch but now also without a specific location and presumably in danger of her life. Hence, the shape of "Presencia" repeats a fundamental narrative paradigm in Onetti: the movement from loss through desire/fiction and back to loss. Desire is almost synonymous with narrative impetus in this model: it sustains the narrative, postponing an ending until the loss of the object becomes too insistent and fiction ceases.

In important ways, "Matías" and "Presencia" both work on a play of places, a here and there, which underpin a relation of presence and absence. The absence of a person or of communication seems to condition fiction, which is impelled by males' desire focused on female characters. This is a structure which Onetti returns to again and again. This is where I would locate Onetti's strength, precisely in the insistent mapping of the movement of desire and of the energies and fissures within subjectivity. The effort is to trace the subject's longing for fulfilment and identifications which always risks confronting lack and obstacles. The unending struggle of desire against the Law, and the breaches in subjectivity that this reveals are the perennial matter of Onetti's writing, together with the question of how to put that into fictional form given that the movement of desire is already closely bound up with fiction.

This insistence in Onetti creates a sort of identity, but one which also gives rise to a pressing question in relation to repetition itself. How is it that a particular crisis in male characters' identity (especially as articulated through their relations with female characters), and in their positioning in the world (especially in relation to age) is so repeatable? One potential answer to this seems to be contained in the articles that Onetti wrote in *Marcha* during 1939-41. In these articles, he insists on the need for Uruguayan writers to be professional, to "durar frente a un tema, al fragmento de vida que hemos elegido como materia de nuestro trabajo, hasta extraer, de él o de nosotros, la esencia única y exacta" (*Réquiem* 21). Later he expresses admiration for Céline for having just one theme: himself (*Réquiem* 156). However, to take the lead from these statements in order to explain the repetitions in Onetti as professionalism or personal obsession seems to me to be inadequate, indeed to be mystificatory. Moreover, it would seek to place a lot of weight on statements written very early in his career. If one does take Onetti's lead here, I would argue that one would confirm the Imaginary function of the early articles in setting up images and models for the writer's own identification. And it is just such confirmation of Imaginary identifications that my readings in this book have sought to undo.

To understand repetition in Onetti, it is first of all important to insist on the obvious, in other words that there is no pure or exact repetition. Even if Onetti had rewritten the same text word for word over fifty years, each rewriting would constitute a difference through its place in the series of texts. In the more complex repetitions of Onetti's actual writing, there is clearly all the more need to insist on the alterity that always insists in repetition. But if there is always an alterity in repetition which modifies, there is also always an absence, a "not-said", which motivates. And this motivation might be located in the mechanism of the discourse's own desire, which will repeat itself until or unless there is recognition. One might conjecture with Jane Gallop that "repetition... is the effect not so much of the frustration of desire but of the lack of recognition of desire" (Gallop 104). Where Gallop is putting her stress (in the whole passage from which this statement is taken) on the lack of recognition of the subject's desire in the Other, I would reread this for my own purposes as the lack of recognition by the discourse itself of what it wants to be and to be *seen* to be. In other words, repetition in Onetti is a function of the relative absence of reflexivity. Hence, I propose to read repetition as a symptom, the effect of a certain structure of thinking, which is precisely ideology.[1] Repetition in Onetti is ideologically driven: the insistence on the crisis of the monadic individual is the recto corresponding to the verso of silence concerning the social and the historical. These dimensions are apparently smothered by an elaborate and insistent discourse about "private" experience which

---

[1] See Zizek, especially chapter one on the symptom and ideology in relation to the structure of thinking.

does not seem to recognize the need to negotiate in and also to resist the social and Symbolic.

Díaz Grey, perhaps the most recurrent character in Onetti, makes a useful case study of this repetition/ideology. Much is invested in Díaz Grey in relation to textual presentation, that is in narrating and focalizing. In Onetti's work as a whole, he is quite often located as the fulcrum of the discourse: he is frequently an unquestioned source of knowledge and critique (for example, in *La muerte y la niña* or *Para una tumba sin nombre*). From the mid 1950s, Díaz Grey occupies a position *within* Santa María that does not preclude knowledge of other worlds or other selves or the desire for them, but this duality in him is not examined, even though it is his double, insider-outsider status which fundamentally lends him authority. He is inside Santa María but has the reflexivity to see beyond/outside the town's values and pretences. But there is no dialectic in the character: he knows (from his own past) the desire for another place or another self, but he lives on passively in Santa María. Quite how Díaz Grey lives these two things can only be described as resignation, as acceptance of the tension between desire for another place or another self and Santa María. But that acceptance rests on a polarization (same/other) which recurs throughout Onetti and which is Imaginary, since desire and Santa María are not mutually exclusive: as is shown time and again in Onetti, the two intertwine and mutually condition each other. To make that point succinctly, it is only necessary to see that desire arises in and out of the demands made on the subject by Santa María (the Symbolic), and that Santa María's own efforts at self-identification are posited on the Imaginary exclusion of others (for example, in "Historia"). But it is precisely this interpenetration that the discourse's repetitions do not focus on, even in Díaz Grey. On the contrary, the exclusive terms of knowledge that it constructs are the paramountcy of desire for another place/self and the inevitability of outright failure in the effort to fulfil that desire, in other words, the return to Santa María or death. This is the manichean exclusivity of knowledge in Onetti.

Hence, repetition in Onetti builds and refines on a restricted nexus of concerns which fosters self-referentiality and closure. Repetition becomes a means of limiting or even eliminating new stimuli, which might create the rupture of innovation and reconceptualization. Repetition thus appears to reduce tension and to provide pleasure and quiescence, as Freud classically argued in *Beyond the Pleasure Principle*. And that same structure of pleasure and quiescence is also implicit in the reading position offered by Onetti's writing: there is a certain comfortable position from which to read and reread his work. In the end, this fundamental problem underpins Onetti's fiction: the more he makes representations and explores the apparently private processes of desire, the more he produces repetitions which place a limitation on the range of desire. Repetition works against what desire aims for.

To see more precisely what repetition constitutively excludes, it is necessary to pay more attention to the social and historical. The social is not absent in Onetti, it could not be since, at the very least, there are characters who have relations. But the social is not focused on explicitly, and its presence is mostly perceptible as negation or repression. To uncover the area of the social is one reason why I have repeatedly looked at gender in Onetti, since that is the most overtly social practice in his work. But gender does not draw attention to itself as part of a critique: in Onetti, sexual relations and gender identities reproduce strongly patriarchal patterns, and in doing that the writing does contain at least one implicit element of social referentiality. The structures of sexuality and gender in Onetti are traditional and oppressive (particularly of the female characters). And yet that oppressiveness is hardly the object of attention, rather, insofar as there is a reaction to the social, there is a barely defined rejection of its constrictions (usually on adult male characters), and a repeated acknowledgement that it is inescapable, which is often expressed as defeat. But the nature of society – how it is what it is and the nature of its class structure – is not considered, even if the rejection of society's demands on the subject might imply a need to understand how they work and why. In the light of this, the processes of socialization of the individual are not seen. So there is a repeated attention to the "already socialized" adult male who may have an identificatory nostalgia for a presocialized image of the self or project his desire for such an image on to a girl; but that precisely polarizes into pre- and post-socialization. "Bienvenido" is a clear example of that binarism, where the distance between Bob and Roberto is a ten year silence in the story. What is known of Roberto and all the other adult males is that they have *already* "fallen" into the social and Symbolic world which obliterates the younger self. Unfulfilled desire is definitive and viewed as highly problematic.

What is therefore absent of the social is the world of work, of family structures, class and nation: precisely the agents of socialization, the agencies demanding compromise. What stands for that area is Santa María, or, before its appearance in the short fiction, Buenos Aires or an unnamed urban environment. Santa María is cast as a trap of repressive demands that is virtually unavoidable this side of insanity or death. But the town is generally articulated as a location of the Symbolic and the Law, as a public sphere, through the views of those who are at odds with it as virtual monads: rarely in the short fiction is it viewed and analyzed by its own "establishment", so that even the "nosotros" voice (for example, in "Historia" and "Infierno") is often ironic and slightly marginal in the town. Santa María can therefore be set up as an easy target for outright rejection. Hence, the nature of Santa María, its operation and class structure are not analyzed or laid out overtly, on the contrary, the town (or its equivalent) tends to be cast as part of an Imaginary binary, the negative pole to the projected fulfilment of desire outside or elsewhere. That binarism is paradoxically also fostered by Santa María's dominant, petit bourgeois ideology, in its efforts at exclusion of the unknown: the other, the outsider is not tolerated or cannot survive in the town as "El álbum", "Historia", "Infierno" and "Novia" clearly show.

Ultimately, however, the choice and treatment of Santa María as the location of the Symbolic and the Law are quite revealing. For Santa María itself is a symbolic construct within Onetti, without the freight that reference to Buenos Aires brings.   The adoption and persistence of Santa María are a sign of abstraction, of attenuated referentiality; the town comes to be part of the social and historical silence in Onetti.   And yet this abstraction of location might be read against itself as a reference to the River Plate's social and cultural history as the place of the immigrant.   In that sense, "Esbjerg" could be taken as Onetti's paradigmatic story, except that in it the immigrant is trapped in Buenos Aires and not in Santa María.   If one pursued this train of thought, immigrant rootlessness would link with the statements which Onetti made in *Marcha* in 1939-41.   In those articles, which in part constitute a literary manifesto, Onetti bemoaned the dearth of Uruguayan cultural roots, the paucity of national literary models to follow.[2] The reaction – to look abroad (outside the River Plate area) for models of writing – is a literary equivalent of the fictional characters' orientation to the exterior.   In this way, the social and historical silence in Onetti could be seen as part of a perception of blankness and cultural isolation.   Like the immigrant in "Esbjerg", and like Periquito el Aguador in the articles, key characters simply want to get outside Santa María and do not interest themselves in the nature of the given.   The private subsumes all else, and any linkage with and location within a relatively new society and culture are not explored.   The private crisis is loss, and adaptation to, compromise with, or contestation of the given are not considered or explored. This privatization helps to explain the polarizing of the same/other in Onetti.   It also accounts for the floating, timeless nature of the crises described: without a strong link to the public, social sphere, the painstaking and ambiguous exploration of the breaches and dilemmas in the subject become rarefied and hermetically abstracted.   Onetti's strength becomes also his limitation.

It is just this sort of writing which may well have appealed to certain sorts of dominant academic reading.   To some extent, it may have been due to the

---

[2] See chapter one of Millington 1985 for a full discussion of the relation between the early articles and Onetti's fictional output.

historical and social silence in Onetti that he has been valued and celebrated by the academic community. The sort of reading space that his writing makes available coincides with traditionally dominant forms of reading, particularly a sort of New Critical practice which aestheticizes texts and adds to the powerful tendency to draw boundaries between public and private life. In other words, much of the critical reception of Onetti has willingly been interpellated by the texts, which have permitted critical desire to mirror itself in them and to operate in apparently closed circuits of mutual confirmation with them. The underlying question now and throughout this analysis is how to resist not only the text's desire for a certain sort of reader (one who would confirm textual identity), but also the reader's own desire for a certain sort of confirming text. The point is to try and break the circuit of mutual, Imaginary confirmations and find a more reflexive position in Symbolic practices. If nothing else, this analysis has tried to highlight the ways in which neither the texts' nor the reader's desire is innocent of conditioning contexts nor of implications in terms of the production of meaning. The insistence on the operation of transference within reading and the foregrounding of the issues of negotiation and rereading has sought to indicate something of reading's possibilities and limits. In the end, perhaps only with a movement back and forth between conjecture and revision is reading actually viable and responsible; perhaps only with that movement can there be a chance to *engage* with the Symbolic rather than an exclusive entrapment in the Imaginary.

BIBLIOGRAPHY

Location of the Works of Juan Carlos Onetti Consulted for this Study:

1   *Obras completas*. Mexico: Aguilar, 1970.
"Un sueño realizado" (first published: 1941)
"Mascarada" (1943)
"Bienvenido Bob" (1944)
"Esbjerg en la costa" (1946)
"La casa en la arena" (1949)
"El álbum" (1953)
"Historia del Caballero de la Rosa y de la virgen encinta que vino de Liliput" (1956)
"El infierno tan temido" (1957)
"La cara de la desgracia" (1960)
"Jacob y el otro" (1961)
"Tan triste como ella" (1963)
"Justo el treintaiuno" (1964)
"La novia robada" (1968)

2   *La muerte y la niña*. Buenos Aires: Corregidor, 1973.

3   "Las mellizas." *Crisis* 1:2 (1973): 32-34.

4   *Cuentos completos*. Buenos Aires: Corregidor, 1974.
"Avenida de Mayo-Diagonal-Avenida de Mayo" (1933)
"El obstáculo" (1935)
"El posible Baldi" (1936)
"Convalecencia" (1940)
"Excursión" (1943)
"La larga historia" (1944)
"Nueve de Julio" (1945)
"Regreso al sur" (1946)
"Matías el telegrafista" (1970)

5   *Réquiem por Faulkner y otros artículos*. Montevideo: Arca/Calicanto, 1975.

6   "El perro tendrá su día." *Tan triste como ella y otros cuentos.* Barcelona:
      Lumen, 1976. 325-36.
7   *Presencia y otros cuentos.* Madrid: Almarabu, 1986.
      "Presencia" (1978)
      "El cerdito" (1982)
      "Los amigos" (1979)
      "Mañana será otro día" (1986)
      "Jabón" (1979)
      "El mercado" (1982)
      "El gato" (1980)
      "Luna llena" (1983)
8   "El árbol." *Cuadernos de Marcha* 13 (1986a): 89-90.
9   *Cuentos secretos. Periquito el aguador y otras máscaras.* Eds Omar Prego
      and María A. Petit. Montevideo: Biblioteca de Marcha, 1986b.
      "El fin trágico de Alfredo Plumet" (1939)
      "Un cuento policial. Crimen perfecto" (1940)
10   *Cuando entonces.* Madrid: Mondadori, 1987.
11   *Goodbyes and Other Stories.* Trans Daniel Balderston. Austin: University
      of Texas, 1990.

Theoretical Works Referred to:

Benjamin, Walter. "The Storyteller." *Illuminations.* Trans Harry Zohn. London:
      Jonathan Cape, 1970. 83-109.
Benvenuto, Bice and Kennedy, Roger. *The Works of Jacques Lacan. An
      Introduction.* London: Free Association Books, 1986.
Chase, Cynthia. "'Transference' as Trope and Persuasion." *Discourse in
      Psychoanalysis and Literature.* Ed S. Rimmon-Kenan. London and New
      York: Methuen, 1987. 211-32.
Connell, R.W. *Gender and Power.* Cambridge: Polity Press, 1987.
de Lauretis, Teresa. *Alice Doesn't. Feminism, Semiotics, Cinema.* London:
      MacMillan, 1984.
Felman, Shoshana. *Jacques Lacan and the Adventure of Insight. Psychoanalysis
      in Contemporary Culture.* Cambridge, Mass. and London: Harvard UP,
      1987.
—   "Turning the Screw of Interpretation." *Yale French Studies* 55-56 (1977):
      94-207.
Flynn, Elizabeth A. and Schweickart, Patrocinio P., eds. *Readers, Texts and
      Contexts.* Baltimore and London: Johns Hopkins University Press, 1986.
Freud, Sigmund. *Introductory Lectures on Psychoanalysis. The Standard Edition
      of the Complete Psychological Works.* Vol 16. London: Hogarth Press,
      1957a.

— "Mourning and Melancholia." *The Standard Edition of the Complete Psychological Works*. Vol 14. London: Hogarth Press, 1957b. 237-58.
— "On Narcissism: An Introduction." *The Standard Edition of the Complete Psychological Works*. Vol 14. London: Hogarth Press, 1957c. 67-102.
— *Three Essays on the Theory of Sexuality. The Standard Edition of the Complete Psychological Works*. Vol 7. London: Hogarth Press, 1957d. 123-245.
Gallop, Jane. *Reading Lacan*. Ithaca: Cornell UP, 1985.
Genette, Gérard. "Le discours du récit." *Figures III*. Paris: Seuil, 1972. 67-273.
Lacan, Jacques. *Ecrits. A Selection*. Trans. Alan Sheridan. London: Tavistock Publications, 1977.
— *The Four Fundamental Concepts of Psychoanalysis*. Ed. Jacques-Alain Miller. Trans. Alan Sheridan. Harmondsworth: Penguin, 1979.
— *Feminine Sexuality. Jacques Lacan and the Ecole Freudienne*. Ed. Juliet Mitchell and Jacqueline Rose. Trans. Jacqueline Rose. London: MacMillan, 1982.
Messner, Michael. "The Meaning of Success. The Athletic Experience and the Development of Male Identity." *The Making of Masculinities. The New Men's Studies*. Ed. Harry Brod. Boston: Allen and Unwin, 1987: 193-209.
Nichols, Bill. *Ideology and the Image*. Bloomington: Indiana University Press, 1981.
Ragland-Sullivan, Ellie. *Jacques Lacan and the Philosophy of Psychoanalysis*. London and Canberra: Croom Helm, 1986.
Rose, Jacqueline. "Introduction - II." J. Lacan, *Feminine Sexuality. Jacques Lacan and the Ecole Freudienne*. Ed. Juliet Mitchell and Jacqueline Rose. Trans. Jacqueline Rose. London: MacMillan, 1982. 27-57.
Segal, Hanna. *Introduction to the Work of Melanie Klein*. London: Hogarth Press, 1973.
Sherrod, Drury "The Bonds of Men: Problems and Possibilities in Close Male Relationships." *The Making of Masculinities. The New Men's Studies*. Ed. Harry Brod. Boston: Allen and Unwin, 1987. 213-39.
Zizek, Slavoj. *The Sublime Object of Ideology*. London: Verso, 1989.

Selected Critical Works on Onetti:

Adams, M. Ian. *Three Authors of Alienation. Bombal, Onetti, Carpentier*. Austin and London: University of Texas Press, 1975. 37-80.
Brower, Gary. "'La casa en la arena' de Onetti: técnica y estructura." *Homenaje a Juan Carlos Onetti. Variaciones interpretativas en torno a su obra*. Ed. Helmy F. Giacomán. New York: Anaya Las Américas, 1974. 215-23.
Crisafio, Raúl. "*La muerte y la niña*: Entre el mito y la historia." *Juan Carlos Onetti*. Ed. Hugo Verani. Madrid: Taurus, 1987. 357-70.

Dellepiane, Angela B. "El humor negro y lo grotesco en Juan Carlos Onetti." *Cuadernos hispanoamericanos* 292-94 (1974): 239-56.

Deredita, John. "El doble en dos cuentos de Onetti." *El cuento hispanoamericano ante la crítica.* Ed. Enrique Pupo-Walker. Madrid: Editorial Castalia, 1973. 150-64.

Diez, Luis A. "'Avenida de Mayo' y 'El posible Baldi': Dos variaciones onettianas sobre el tema *The Man of the Crowd* de Edgar Allan Poe." *Latin American Fiction Today. A Symposium.* Ed. Rose S. Minc. Takoma Park, Maryland: *Hispamérica* and Montclair State College, 1979. 89-98.

— "*La muerte y la niña*: Brausen y el otro." *Cuadernos hispanoamericanos* 292-94 (1974): 610-26.

Fernández, María Luisa. "Los puntos de vista narrativos en 'Jacob y el otro' de Juan Carlos Onetti." *Letras* 15-16 (1986): 64-75.

Geyman, Matthew. "Tangled Trails: In the Footsteps of Juan Carlos Onetti: Meditations on His Short Story 'Jacob y el otro.'" *Papers in Romance* 3:1 (1981): 35-45.

Hiriart, Rosario. "Apuntes sobre los cuentos de Juan Carlos Onetti." *Cuadernos hispanoamericanos* 292-94 (1974): 297-310.

Klahn, Norma. "La problemática del género 'novela corta' en Onetti." *Texto Crítico* 6:18-19 (1980): 204-14.

Luchting, Wolfgang A. "'La cara de la desgracia': Otra lectura." *Texto Crítico* 11:33 (1985): 122-32.

Ludmer, Josefina. "*La novia* (carta) *robada* (a Faulkner)." *Onetti. Los procesos de construcción del relato.* Buenos Aires: Editorial Sudamericana, 1977). 189-212.

Mattalía, Sonia. *La figura en el tapiz. Teoría y práctica narrativa en Juan Carlos Onetti.* London: Tamesis Books, 1990.

Mercier, Lucien. "Juan Carlos Onetti en busca del infierno." *Homenaje a Juan Carlos Onetti. Variaciones interpretativas en torno a su obra.* Ed. Helmy F. Giacomán. New York: Anaya Las Américas, 1974. 225-34.

Millington, Mark I. "Ambivalence and Desire in Onetti's *Cuando entonces.*" *Antípodas* III (1991): 113-23.

— "Masculinity and the Fight for Ignorance: Onetti's 'Jacob y el otro.'" *Bulletin of Hispanic Studies* LXIX (1992): 357-68.

— "Negotiating the Text: Onetti's 'La cara de la desgracia.'" *Dispositio* XV:40 (1990): 119-30.

— "No Woman's Land: The Representation of Woman in Onetti." *Modern Language Notes* 102:2 (1987): 358-77.

— "Objects and Objections: Onetti's 'Tan triste como ella.'" *Neophilologus* LXXV:2 (1991): 207-21.

— *Reading Onetti. Language, Narrative and the Subject.* Liverpool: Francis Cairns Publications, 1985.

— "Una lectura del deseo: 'La cara de la desgracia' de Juan Carlos Onetti." *Coloquio internacional, Escritura y sexualidad en la literatura hispanoamericana.* Madrid: Editorial Fundamentos, 1990. 285-95.

Murray, Jack. "Plot and Space in Juan Carlos Onetti's 'Tan triste como ella.'" *Symposium* XXXVII:1 (1983): 68-83.

Ocampo, Aurora M. "La mujer en 'El infierno tan temido.'" *Texto Crítico* 6:18-19 (1980): 223-34.

Ortega, Julio. "La temporalidad en cuatro relatos de Juan Carlos Onetti." *Cuadernos hispanoamericanos* 292-94 (1974). 339-56.

Pereda, Rosa María. "Juan Carlos Onetti y su cuento 'único': 'La novia robada.'" *Cuadernos hispanoamericanos* 292-94 (1974): 311-19.

Prego, Omar and Petit, María A. "Mujer sin cara." *Texto crítico* 6:18-19 (1980): 252-64.

Puccini, Dario. "Vida y muerte como representación en 'Un sueño realizado' de Onetti." *Hispamérica: Revista de Literatura* 13:38 (1984): 19-26.

Rodríguez Santibáñez, Marta. "'La cara de la desgracia' o el sentido de la ambigüedad." *Cuadernos hispanoamericanos* 292-94 (1974): 320-33

Ruffinelli, Jorge. "Análisis de 'Un sueño realizado.'" *El realismo mágico en el cuento hispanoamericano.* Ed. Angel Flores. Tlahuapan, Mexico: Premia, 1985. 167-77.

Saad, Gabriel. "'Jacob y el otro' o las señales de la victoria." *En torno a Juan Carlos Onetti.* Ed. Lídice Gómez Mango. Montevideo: Fundación de Cultura Universitaria, 1970. 91-105.

— "Técnica de la narración en un cuento de Onetti." *Juan Carlos Onetti.* Ed. Hugo Verani. Madrid: Taurus, 1987. 279-88.

Terry, Arthur. "Onetti and the Meaning of Fiction: Notes on *La muerte y la niña.*" *Contemporary Latin American Fiction.* Ed. Salvador Bacarisse. Edinburgh: Scottish University Press, 1980. 54-72

Turton, Peter. "Las permutaciones de la desgracia o 'Esbjerg en la costa' de Juan Carlos Onetti." *Revista Canadiense de Estudios Hispánicos* 8:1 (1983): 75-87.

Verani, Hugo J. *Onetti: el ritual de la impostura.* Caracas: Monte Avila, 1981.

INDEX

Adams, M.I., 116, 117, 131

Benjamin, W., 5
Benvenuto, B and Kennedy, R., 3
Brower, G., 36

Chase, C., 134
Connell, R.W., 43

de Lauretis, T., 110
Derrida, J., 1
Diez, L.A., 14

Felman, S., 9, 93, 96, 113
Faulkner, W., 143
Flynn, E.A., 113
Freud, S., 82, 85, 88, 169
    Beyond the Pleasure Principle, 203

Gallop, J., 1, 8, 94, 96, 127, 201
Genette, G., 95, 142
Geyman, M., 109, 111

Klahn, N., 2
Klein, M., 102-03

Lacan, J., 3, 6-7, 12, 88, 90, 108, 120, 125, 126, 132
    Imaginary, 3-6, 9-10, 12-14, 16, 30, 35, 46, 47, 49, 51, 56, 61, 63, 64-65, 79, 86, 89, 91, 93, 94, 106-07, 117-18, 120-23, 125, 127, 129-30, 132, 133, 154, 177, 194-95, 201-202, 204, 206
    Real, 6, 8-9, 107, 132-34, 181
    Symbolic, 3-7, 9-10, 25, 35, 41, 49, 52, 53, 89, 91, 92, 94, 106-07, 109, 120, 123, 126, 127, 130, 132, 133, 154, 194-95, 202, 204, 206
    transference, 8-9, 85, 134-35, 206
Ludmer, J., 141, 144

Marcha, 200, 205
Messner, M., 107
Millington, M.I., 8, 47, 48, 85, 118, 205
    Reading Onetti, 1
Murray, J., 116, 118

Nichols, B., 95

Onetti, J.C.,
    "Avenida de Mayo-Diagonal-Avenida de mayo", 11, 12, 13, 16, 17

"Bienvenido Bob", 12, 16, 17,
    26-30, 31, 35, 45, 204
"Convalecencia", 8, 12, 15-16,
    17, 18, 31
Cuando entonces, 1, 155, 156,
    161, 172, 183-95
"El álbum", 44-53, 54, 58, 62,
    63-65, 68, 76, 79, 169,
    204
El astillero, 51, 105, 106, 118,
    142, 174, 176
"El fin trágico de Alfredo
    Plumet", 11
"El infierno tan temido", 8,
    53-65, 76, 106, 204
"El obstáculo", 12, 15, 18
"El posible Baldi", 12, 13-14,
    16, 17
El pozo, 1, 8, 53
"Esbjerg en la costa", 8, 12,
    14, 17, 18, 30-36, 150,
    197-98, 205
"Excursión", 12, 14-15, 17, 18
"Historia del caballero de la
    rosa...", 53, 67-80, 168,
    202, 204
"Jacob y el otro", 68, 97-113,
    123
Juntacadáveres, 51, 73, 76,
    118
"La cara de la desgracia", 8,
    52, 82-96, 106, 123,
    168
"La casa en la arena", 11, 15,
    31, 36-41, 118
"La larga historia", 15, 31
La muerte y la niña, 1, 123,
    142, 155-81, 202
"La novia robada", 8, 53, 59,
    77, 137-54, 155, 162,
    204
La vida breve, 53, 86
Los adioses, 1, 53, 68, 79, 106

"Mascarada", 16-17

"Matías el telegrafista", 197-
    97, 200
"Nueve de julio", 12, 16, 17,
Para esta noche, 86, 118, 199
Para una tumba sin nombre,
    1, 32, 46, 47, 51, 53,
    59, 61, 62, 86, 118,
    168, 169, 170, 202
"Presencia", 197-200
"Regreso al sur", 12, 17
Réquiem por Faulkner y otros
    artículos, 200
"Tan triste como ella", 8, 47,
    59, 105, 115-35
Tierra de nadie, 53, 86
"Un cuento policial. Crimen
    perfecto", 11
"Un sueño realizado", 17-18,
    19-26, 32, 34, 35, 57

Petit, M.A., 11, 179
Prego, O., 11, 179
Puccini, D., 25

Ragland-Sullivan, E., 3, 106, 108,
    109, 132
Rose, J., 3, 9
Ruffinelli, J., 25

Saad, G., 107
Schweickart, P., 113
Segal, H., 103
Sherrod, D., 102

Terry, A., 174

Zizek, S., 201